Changes for this edition

The following amendments and additions have been made for edition 43

NEW SECTIONS

2.2.4
POLYPHARMACY

2.3.4
PROFESSIONAL INDEMNITY

2.8.1
REVALIDATION

3.3.1
GENERAL PRESCRIPTION REQUIREMENTS
Falsified Medicines Directive (which came into force on 9th February 2019)

3.3.1
GENERAL PRESCRIPTION REQUIREMENTS
Prescriptions from the Crown Dependencies (Jersey, Guernsey and Isle of Man)

3.6.1
CONTROLLED DRUGS BACKGROUND
Added a section on Gosport report

3.6.7
PRESCRIPTION REQUIREMENTS FOR SCHEDULE 2 AND 3 CONTROLLED DRUGS
Added guidance on the rescheduling of gabapentin and pregabalin

3.6.15
CANNABIS-BASED PRODUCTS FOR MEDICINAL USE IN HUMANS

APPENDIX 11
GPHC GUIDANCE TO ENSURE A SAFE AND EFFECTIVE PHARMACY TEAM

REMOVED SECTIONS

2.8.1 (EDITION 42)
CONTINUING PROFESSIONAL DEVELOPMENT (CPD) REPLACED WITH INFORMATION ON REVALIDATION

3.2.5 (EDITION 42)
COUGH AND COLD MEDICINES FOR CHILDREN

3.7.3 (EDITION 42)
COSMETIC CONTACT LENSES (ZERO POWERED)

UPDATED SECTIONS

Updated references and further reading signposting in all sections

2.2.2
PHARMACEUTICAL CARE, SCOTLAND
At time of writing, the Chronic Medication service had a name change to the Medicines Care and Review Service

2.3.1
PROFESSIONALISM
Added more examples of pharmacy professionalism

2.3.3
SOCIAL MEDIA
Included reference to the use of Whatsapp instead of bleeping colleagues

2.4
PROFESSIONAL EMPOWERMENT
Moved section on Professional Empowerment from 2.7 to 2.4, to follow on from Professionalism and Professional Judgement

2.9
RESEARCH INVOLVEMENT
Changes to examples of how the GPhC standards apply to research

3.2.2
ORAL EMERGENCY CONTRACEPTIVES AS PHARMACY MEDICINES
Included further guidance on religious and moral beliefs impacting on the supply of EHC

3.2.3
PARACETAMOL AND ASPIRIN
Updates to Table 1 (OTC legal restrictions)

3.2.5
RECLASSIFIED MEDICINES
Updated further reading box to include signposting to RPS guidance on the following:

- Anti-malarials as Pharmacy medicines
- Mometasone 0.05% nasal spray
- Oral lidocaine-containing products for teething in children

3.3.1
GENERAL PRESCRIPTION REQUIREMENTS
Added signposting to information on EPS and CDs in the 'Electronic Prescriptions' box in this section

3.3.1
GENERAL PRESCRIPTION REQUIREMENTS
Repeatable prescriptions: added reference to use in hospitals and homecare settings, and updated guidance on prisons

3.3.6
MILITARY PRESCRIPTIONS
Updated in line with current practice

3.3.8
ADMINISTRATION
Updated to current guidance as published in RPS *Professional guidance on the administration of medicines in healthcare settings* 2019 and RPS *Professional guidance on the safe and secure handling of medicines* 2018 www.rpharms.com

3.3.12
SUPPLYING ISOTRETINOIN AND PREGNANCY PREVENTION
Updated this section to include information on all oral retinoids. Title changed to 'SUPPLYING ORAL RETINOIDS AND PREGNANCY PREVENTION'

3.3.15
SUMMARY OF PRESCRIBER TYPES AND PRESCRIBING RESTRICTIONS

Updated table 4: Different types of prescriber and restrictions on what can be prescribed – to include information on the following prescribers:

• Physiotherapist and Podiatrist independent prescriber – added signposting to Health and Care Professionals Council (HCPC) and NHS England have issued a joint statement (www.hcpc-uk.org/registrants/updates/2019/ reclassification-of-gabapentin-and-pregabalin/) on the reclassification of gabapentin and pregabalin giving details of which prescribers can issue prescriptions for CDs

• Paramedic independent prescriber

3.3.16
CHECKING REGISTRATION OF HEALTHCARE PROFESSIONALS AND ADDITIONAL INFORMATION ON CONDITIONS OF SUPPLY

Updated table 5 to include information on advanced paramedics prescribing medicines

3.4
WHOLESALE DEALING

Added section 3.4.6 on Falsified Medicines Directive (FMD)

3.6.2
CONTROLLED DRUGS CLASSIFICATION

Added reference to new the section on cannabis based products for medicinal use in humans (3.6.15) and the rescheduling of gabapentin and pregabalin to Schedule 3 CD

3.6.7
PRESCRIPTION REQUIREMENTS FOR SCHEDULE 2 AND 3 CONTROLLED DRUGS

• Replaced Formulation with Form in line with the Misuse of Drugs Regulations 2001

• Updated guidance on the Total Quantity to provide clarification on expressing it as the total number of dosage units or the total quantity of the drug. Included reference to Home Office advice on expressing the quantity of different strength tablets of the same CD on the prescription

• Added signposting information on CD electronic prescriptions

• Added further guidance on the using the approved

Home Office wording for instalment prescribing of CDs during periods when pharmacy is closed

• Updated printing errors in table 13 CONTROLLED DRUGS PRIVATE PRESCRIPTION FORMS on the type of form used in England and Wales

3.7.8
EMERGENCY CONNECTION TO EX-DIRECTORY TELEPHONE NUMBERS

Updated in line with advice from BT

3.7.11
COLLECTION AND PURCHASE OF MEDICINES BY CHILDREN

Updated to consider additional factors on whether supply of dispensed medicines is appropriate or not

3.7.17
DRUGS AND DRIVING

Included signposting to information on new safety laws being introduced in Scotland during October 2019

3.7.20
NEW PSYCHOACTIVE SUBSTANCES

Removed detailed information on what NPS are – signposted to the RPS website for information in the quick reference guide and factsheet

6
PROFESSIONAL STANDARDS

Added to the list – professional standards and framework currently under development

7
RPS CODE OF CODUCT

Updated RPS Code of Conduct reproduced

GPHC APPENDICES

Updated in line with any changes GPhC has made to the contents of their standards and guidance and included the following changes:

• Title change of Appendix 7 'GPhC guidance on the provision of pharmacy services affected by religious and moral beliefs' to 'GPhC in practice: Guidance on religion, personal values and beliefs'

• Significant changes to Appendix 10 'GPhC guidance for registered pharmacies providing pharmacy services at a distance, including on the internet' as revised by GPhC in April 2019

Core concepts and skills

2

This section on core concepts will equip you with knowledge and skills to help you practise confidently and professionally as a pharmacist.

2.1

Patient or person-centred healthcare

The concept of patient or person-centred healthcare is important to all health and social care professionals, and is integrated into healthcare policy throughout Great Britain.

Common themes are:

- Treating patients as people and as equal partners in decisions about their care

- Putting people at the centre of all decisions

- Respect for patient preferences

- Compassion, dignity and empathy

- Support for self-care, enablement, autonomy and independence

- Patient choice, control and influence

- Good communication.

Examples of person-centred healthcare in practice include:

- People being called by the name they prefer rather than by the name on official documentation (e.g. prefer being called Mike instead of Michael)

- Being asked to do something and not being told

- Being able to make informed choices

- Being able to speak openly about their experiences of taking or not taking medicines (including any complaints or concerns they have with their medicines/services received). Their views about what medicines mean to them, and how medicines impact on their daily life (e.g. when to wake up, when to sleep)

- Involving people in decisions about their medicines and self care (including listening to patients (or relatives) when they raise concerns about their medicines/treatment)

- Identify problematic polypharmacy and having a shared decision making process on managing this

- Explain your role(s) clearly and explicitly to patients

FURTHER READING

Royal Pharmaceutical Society
Your care, your medicines. Pharmacy at the heart of patient-centred care.
www.rpharms.com

Health Foundation
Person-centred care made simple. What everyone should know about person-centred care.
www.health.org.uk

National Voices
Person-centred care in 2017 – Evidence from service users.
www.nationalvoices.org.uk/publications/our-publications/person-centred-care-2017

NHS England
Developing patient-centred care.
www.england.nhs.uk/integrated-care-pioneers/resources/patient-care

NHS Scotland Quality Improvement Hub
Person-centred care.
www.qihub.scot.nhs.uk/default.aspx

Public Health Wales
1000 Lives Improvement.
www.1000livesplus.wales.nhs.uk

2.2

Medicines optimisation and pharmaceutical care

The contact you have with people receiving healthcare allows the profession to champion a person-centred approach. This enables better outcomes through medicines optimisation (England), pharmaceutical care (Scotland) and pharmaceutical care and prudent pharmacy (Wales).

2.2.1
MEDICINES OPTIMISATION
ENGLAND

- Medicines optimisation is about ensuring that patients get the best possible outcomes from their medicines. The first step is to ensure that the right patients get the right choice of medicine, at the right time. But the focus needs to be on the individual patient, their beliefs and their experiences. The goal is to help patients to:

  - improve their outcomes

  - take their medicines correctly

  - improve adherence

  - avoid taking unnecessary medicines

  - reduce wastage of medicines

  - improve medicines and patient safety.

Ultimately, medicines optimisation can help encourage patients to take ownership of their treatment.

It is a patient-focused approach to getting the best from investment in and use of medicines. It requires a holistic approach, an enhanced level of patient-centred professionalism, and partnership between clinical professionals and a patient.

ELEMENTS OF MEDICINES OPTIMISATION

To empower patients and the public to make the most of medicines healthcare professionals need to understand the concept of medicines optimisation. Diagram 1 outlines the seven elements of medicines optimisation which comprise of the four principles as well as measurement and monitoring, improved patient outcomes, and ensuring a patient-centred approach. These describe medicines optimisation in practice and the outcomes it is intended to impact.

DIAGRAM 1:
SUMMARY OF THE FOUR PRINCIPLES
OF MEDICINE OPTIMISATION

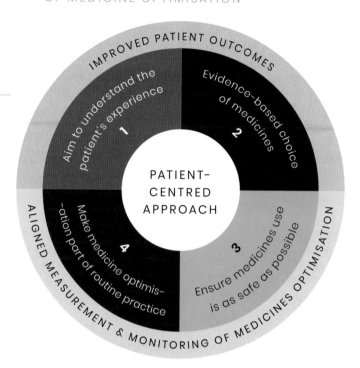

PRINCIPLE 1:
AIM TO UNDERSTAND THE PATIENT'S EXPERIENCE

To ensure the best possible outcomes from medicines, there is an ongoing, open dialogue with the patient and/or their carer about the patient's choice and experience of using medicines to manage their condition; recognising that the patient's experience may change over time even if the medicines do not.

PRINCIPLE 2:
EVIDENCE-BASED CHOICE OF MEDICINES

Ensure that the most appropriate choice of clinically and cost-effective medicines (informed by the best available evidence base) are made which can best meet the needs of the patient.

PRINCIPLE 3:
ENSURE MEDICINES USE IS AS SAFE AS POSSIBLE

The safe use of medicines is the responsibility of all professionals, healthcare organisations and patients, and should be discussed with patients and/or their carers. Safety covers all aspects of medicines usage, including unwanted effects, interactions, safe processes and systems, and effective communication between professionals.

PRINCIPLE 4:
MAKE MEDICINES OPTIMISATION
PART OF ROUTINE PRACTICE

Health professionals routinely discuss with each other and with patients and/or their carers how to get the best outcomes from medicines throughout the patient's care.

Further detail on medicines optimisation and the above principles is available on the RPS website in guidance titled Helping patients make the most of their medicines: Good practice guidance for healthcare professionals in England www.rpharms.com

FURTHER READING

Royal Pharmaceutical Society
Medicines optimisation hub.
www.rpharms.com

National Institute for Health and Care Excellence
Medicines optimisation: the safe and effective use of medicines to enable the best possible outcomes. NICE guideline. 2015.
www.nice.org.uk

NHS England
Medicines optimisation hub.
www.england.nhs.uk

2.2.2
PHARMACEUTICAL CARE
SCOTLAND

Pharmaceutical care evolved from clinical pharmacy practice in the hospital setting and was defined in 1990 as: 'the responsible provision of drug therapy for the purpose of achieving definite outcomes that improve the patient's quality of life.'

Pharmaceutical care is a person-centred philosophy and practice that aims to optimise the benefits of drug therapy and minimise the risk of drug therapy to patients by providing the framework for pharmacists to apply their knowledge and skills. The pharmacist will assess the pharmaceutical needs of patients and take responsibility for meeting those needs in collaboration with other health and social care professionals.

Key components are:

- The patient assessment to identify unmet pharmaceutical care needs and issues

- The development of a pharmaceutical care plan to document the needs identified

- To agree patient outcomes, the actions required or taken and the follow-up required.

In Scotland pharmaceutical care has become the cornerstone of national policy and practice in all settings. Pharmaceutical care is embedded within undergraduate and postgraduate education, the community pharmacy contractual framework and clinical pharmacy services within hospital and primary care, including pharmacist prescribing.

In practice, the assessment will identify any pharmaceutical care issues with concordance and sets out to establish within the available information:

- If the drug therapy and dose is appropriate for the condition in this patient

- If any additional therapy (drug and non-pharmacological) is required

- If the drug therapy and dose is safe

- If the person is suffering from any avoidable side effects

- If the drug therapy, dose and non-pharmacological therapy are effective and achieving a defined desired outcome.

It is a holistic philosophy and practice that will also identify and address the following needs:

- Public health, educational, medicines management, non-pharmacological management and changes in clinical need.

Achieving excellence in pharmaceutical care: a strategy for Scotland (published in Aug 2017) aims to transform the role of pharmacy across all areas of pharmacy practice, increase capacity, and offer the best person-centred care. The vision is for pharmacy as an integral and enhanced part of a modern NHS in Scotland. See full document for further details www.gov.scot/publications/achieving-excellence-pharmaceutical-care-strategy-scotland/

FURTHER READING

Clinical Resource and Audit Group National Health Service in Scotland
Clinical Pharmacy in the Hospital Pharmaceutical Service: a Framework for Practice. 1996.

Clinical Resource and Audit Group. Scottish Office.
Clinical Pharmacy Practice in Primary Care; a framework for the provision of community-based NHS pharmaceutical services. 1999.

Hepler CD, Strand LM
Opportunities and responsibilities in pharmaceutical care.
American Journal of Hospital Pharmacy.
March 1990, Volume 47, p533-543.
www.ncbi.nlm.nih.gov/pubmed/2316538

NHS Scotland Community Pharmacy
Medicines Care and Review Service
(At the time of writing the MEP, the Chronic Medication Services is changing its name to the Medicines Care and Review Service).
www.communitypharmacy.scot.nhs.uk

Scottish Government
Achieving excellence in pharmaceutical care: a strategy for Scotland, Aug 2017.
www.gov.scot

2.2.3
PHARMACEUTICAL CARE AND PRUDENT PHARMACY
WALES

Your Care, Your Medicines: Pharmacy at the heart of patient centred care presents a vision for pharmacy in Wales.

It is the result of work led by the Welsh Pharmaceutical Committee, the committee responsible for advising the Welsh Government on pharmacy issues. It has been supported by the RPS with contributions from leaders from all sectors of the profession. It is an ambition that takes into account the current policy drivers for healthcare in Wales that will contribute to:

- The delivery of prudent healthcare

- A change in culture to encourage greater co-production with patients and collaborative working between health professionals

- A rebalancing of services between health care sectors to deliver an increased primary care-based focus

- Creating seamless patient care and closing the gaps between services

- Empowering people to take greater responsibility for their own health and wellbeing.

The model of pharmacy engagement presented in Your Care, Your Medicines (Diagram 2) demonstrates patient interactions with the pharmacy team at various points of their healthcare journey.

The ambition is for patients in Wales to be put at the centre of their care, to benefit from the full integration of the pharmacy team into the NHS and to ensure every intervention involving medicines is supported, communicated and coordinated across the health and social care system.

The key ambitions in the document are:

AMBITION 1
Patients will routinely access health promotion advice and self-care support from the pharmacy team. This will include healthy lifestyle information, medicines advice and opportunistic interventions at the point of medicines supply.

Advances in technology will be exploited to maximise benefits for patients in accessing pharmacy support.

AMBITION 2
The people of Wales will benefit from early detection and treatment of health conditions when engaging with the pharmacy team. Patients will expect the symptoms of minor ailments and non-life threatening emergencies to be treated by the pharmacy team and to be referred to other health services when symptoms require further and more specialised investigation and treatment.

AMBITION 3
Patients with chronic conditions will have regular reviews with a pharmacist who will provide medication advice and coaching in a setting that is most suitable for the patient. A pharmaceutical care plan will be initiated, discussed and jointly managed between the patient and the pharmacist and made available to other health professionals involved in the patient's care.

AMBITION 4

When patients require planned hospital care or any intensive health care they will feel confident that a holistic approach is taken to the management of their conditions and that all decisions on medication changes will be led by expert advice from the pharmacy team.

AMBITION 5

Patients with supported living needs, whether living independently in their own homes or in a care home setting, must benefit from access to the pharmacy team to help manage their medicines effectively and to maintain their health and wellbeing.

AMBITION 6

Patients with palliative care and end of life care needs will be treated with dignity and respect and empowered to shape their clinical pathway with support from the pharmacy team.

FURTHER READING

Royal Pharmaceutical Society
Your care, your medicines:
Pharmacy at the heart of patient-centred care
www.rpharms.com

Further information on the prudent agenda can be found at www.prudenthealthcare.org.uk

2.2.4
POLYPHARMACY

The RPS has published guidance on polypharmacy for pharmacists and all healthcare organisations involved with medicines. It provides a summary of the scale and complexity of the issue of polypharmacy. It outlines how healthcare professionals, patients and carers can find solutions when polypharmacy causes problems for patients and points to useful resources that can help. It recommends that all healthcare organisations have systems in place to ensure people taking multiple medicines (especially those taking 10 or more) can be identified and highlighted as requiring a comprehensive medication review with a pharmacist.

The benefits of such reviews include:

- A reduction in problematic polypharmacy
- Improved health
- Patients more likely to take their medicines
- Fewer wasted medicines

The guidance titled 'Polypharmacy: Getting our medicines right' can be viewed on the RPS website at www.rpharms.com

DIAGRAM 2: MODEL OF
PHARMACY ENGAGEMENT

PALLIATIVE CARE & END OF LIFE
RESIDENTIAL CARE & HOME SUPPORT
INTENSIVE INTERVENTION & MANAGEMENT
MEDICINES MANAGEMENT FOR CHRONIC CONDITIONS
PRE-SCREENING & UNSCHEDULED CARE
SUPPORT FOR COMMON AILMENTS
SUPPORT FOR HEALTH & WELLBEING

2.3

Professionalism and professional judgement

Pharmacy is a profession and pharmacists are professionals who exercise professionalism and professional judgement on a day-to-day basis.

The concepts of a 'profession', a 'professional' and 'professionalism' are not rigidly defined. However, these are concepts that are important for any pharmacist, including those who work in non-patient facing roles.

A profession can be described as:

- An occupation that is recognised by the public as a profession

- An occupation for which there is a recognised representative professional body

- An occupation that benefits from professional standards and codes of conduct

- An occupation that is regulated to ensure the maintenance of standards and codes of conduct

A professional can be described as:

- A member of a profession

- A member of a professional body

- An individual who:

  - Behaves and acts professionally

  - Exercises professionalism and professional judgement

  - Has professional values, attitudes and behaviours

2.3.1
PROFESSIONALISM

Pharmacy professionalism can be defined as a set of values, behaviours and relationships that underpin the trust the public has in pharmacists.

Examples of these are:

- Altruism

- Appropriate accountability

- Compassion

- Duty

- Excellence and continuous improvement

- Honour and integrity

- Professional judgement

- Respect for other patients, colleagues and other healthcare professionals (including listening to and acting on feedback when needed)

- Working in partnership with patients, doctors and the wider healthcare team in the patient's/ public's best interest

- Work within competence

- Ensure patient is placed at the centre of all decision making

- Being honest about scope of practice

- Knowing when to seek support

  Many of these values, attitudes and behaviours are also reflected in the mandatory GPhC Standards for pharmacy professionals (see Appendix 1)

  Pharmacists who are working in industry should also adhere to the Association of the British Pharmaceutical Industry (ABPI) Code of Practice for the Pharmaceutical Industry (www.abpi.org.uk)

DECLARING CONFLICTS OF INTEREST

It is important to declare conflicts of interest appropriately whether they are actual or potential.

An actual conflict of interest is when one or more interests materially conflict.

A potential conflict of interest is where there is a possibility of a conflict between one or more interests in the future.

Some examples of conflicts of interest include:

- Having another job or receiving consultancy fees (i.e. having an outside employment) which impacts upon another role

- Receiving or being offered gifts from patients or suppliers to the NHS or your employer

- Receiving or being offered hospitality such as travel, accommodation, meals or refreshments e.g. in relation to attending a meeting, conference or training event

- Receiving or being offered sponsorship for events, research grants or posts

- Owning shares in a company whose value could be influenced by your role

- Having an indirect interest or non-financial interest e.g. If a spouse, close relative, business partner or close friend has an interest

- Receiving any other payments or 'transfers of value'.

Declarations will most commonly be made to:

- Your employer through a line manager, governance or conflict lead

- Someone commissioning your services

- A chairperson at the meetings which you attend

A declaration of an interest does not necessarily prevent an individual from carrying out a role, but it ensures that there can be no perception that they are seeking to influence decisions improperly.

2.3.2
PROFESSIONAL JUDGEMENT

Professional judgement can be described as the use of accumulated knowledge and experience, as well as critical reasoning, to make an informed professional decision – often to help solve a problem presented by, or in relation to, a patient; or policies and procedures affecting patients. It takes into account the law, ethical considerations, relevant standards and all other relevant factors related to the surrounding circumstances. Furthermore, it will resonate with the core values, attitudes and behavioural indicators of professionalism.

HOW DO I EXERCISE PROFESSIONAL JUDGEMENT?

Many pharmacists exercise their professional judgement instinctively but it may be helpful to break the process down into smaller steps:

DIAGRAM 3:
EXERCISING PROFESSIONAL JUDGEMENT

1. IDENTIFY THE ETHICAL DILEMNA OR PROFESSIONAL ISSUE
↓
2. GATHER RELEVANT INFORMATION
↓
3. IDENTIFY THE POSSIBLE OPTIONS
↓
4. WEIGH UP THE BENEFITS AND RISKS OF EACH OPTION
↓
5. CHOOSE AN OPTION
↓
6. RECORD

1

Identify the ethical dilemma or professional issue you are faced with, e.g. deciding whether to supply a medicine or not.

2

Gather all the relevant information and research the problem – i.e. obtain the following:

- Facts

- Knowledge

- Laws

- Standards

- Good practice guidance

- Advice from support services, head office, line managers or colleagues.

3

Identify all the possible options.

4

Weigh up all the benefits and risks, advantages and disadvantages of each of the possible options you have identified.

5

Choose an option. It is important you can justify the decision you have made because often when faced with an ethical dilemma or professional issue pharmacists are weighing up conflicting obligations which could be genuine patient interest, legal obligations, professional standards, public interest, contractual Terms of Service and company policies.

6

It is important to make a record of the decision-making process and your reasons leading to a particular course of action where appropriate. This may be a record in the patient's medication record (PMR), medical record, the back of the prescription register or an intervention record book. This is important as evidence of the thought processes leading to a decision.

It is entirely possible for two different pharmacists, faced with the same facts and circumstances, to choose two different courses of action. This is the nature of a finely balanced ethical dilemma. Both options could be justifiable and legitimate choices for a significant proportion of pharmacists if faced with the same dilemma.

It is important to point out that professional judgement is not a blanket defence or a blanket reason to take the most convenient choice. It must be exercised properly, logically and for valid reasons. If there are mechanisms to achieve the required goal it would be risky to choose an illegal alternative. For example, lending medication would be very difficult to justify if an emergency supply could have been used.

The process of making a professional judgement is underpinned by knowledge. The following chapters of the MEP provide information on the core knowledge required by pharmacists in their day-to-day practice.

FURTHER READING

Royal Pharmaceutical Society
Joint statement on conflicts of interest.
www.rpharms.com

Association of the British Pharmaceutical Industry
Disclosure of payments to individual healthcare professionals. 2015.
www.abpi.org.uk

Elvey R, Lewis P, et al
Patient-centred professionalism among newly registered pharmacists. 2011.
www.pharmacyresearchuk.org select the 'Our research' and 'Download a report' tabs.

General Pharmaceutical Council
Demonstrating professionalism online. 2016.
www.pharmacyregulation.org

General Pharmaceutical Council
Joint statement on professional duty of candour.
www.pharmacyregulation.org

NHS England
Managing conflicts of interest in the NHS.
www.england.nhs.uk/ourwork/coi

Schafheutle E, Hassell K, et al
Professionalism in pharmacy education. 2010.
www.pharmacyresearchuk.org select the 'Our research' and 'Download a report' tabs.

Wingfield J, Pitchford K, editors
Dale and Appelbe's Pharmacy and Medicines Law. 11th edition. 2017. London; Pharmaceutical Press.
www.pharmpress.com/

2.3.3
SOCIAL MEDIA

Pharmacists and aspiring pharmacists who use social media and social networking* should do so responsibly and with the same high standards which they would apply in real world interactions.

It is important to maintain proper professional boundaries in relationships and interactions with patients and at all times to respect the confidentiality of others, including patients and colleagues.

Be aware of the potential audience of your online activity, that this may be publicly accessible, circulated and shared beyond your control. This activity could impact upon your professional image and the reputation of the profession as a whole.

Organisations may use social media, such as Whatsapp, to communicate with healthcare professionals in other departments (i.e between wards), instead of bleeping them. It is important pharmacists understand and follow their company or NHS Trust policies on this practice.

Social media includes blogging, web forums including professional web forums, Twitter, Facebook, online, Whatsapp messaging and virtual networks (this list is not exhaustive).

FURTHER READING

Royal Pharmaceutical Society
Social media guidance – toolkit.
www.rpharms.com

British Medical Association
Social Media Use: Practical and ethical guidance for doctors and medical students.
www.bma.org.uk

General Pharmaceutical Council
Demonstrating professionalism online. 2016.
www.pharmacyregulation.org

General Pharmaceutical Council
Guidance for registered pharmacies providing pharmacy services at a distance, including on the internet. 2015.
www.pharmacyregulation.org
(see MEP Appendix 10)

General Pharmaceutical Council
Guidance on patient confidentiality. 2018.
www.pharmacyregulation.org (see MEP Appendix 3)

Health and Care Professionals Council
Guidance on the use of social media.
www.hcpc-uk.org

NHS Digital
Social media security: user guide.
https://digital.nhs.uk

NHS Education for Scotland
Core clinical assessment skills courses (two-day training course).
www.nes.scot.nhs.uk

Royal College of General Practitioners
Social Media Highway Code.
www.rcgp.org.uk

2.3.4
PROFESSIONAL INDEMNITY

It is a requirement if you are registered with the GPhC that you have professional indemnity insurance in place before you start working in your role.

The GPhC has advised *"that the professional indemnity arrangement you have in place provides appropriate cover. This means that the cover needs to be appropriate to the nature and extent of the risks involved in your practice."* Further information and useful FAQs can be viewed on the GPhC website at www.pharmacyregulation.org/professional-indemnity-requirements.

Please contact the RPS Professional Support team if you wanted to discuss further.

2.4
Professional empowerment

Professional empowerment is about enabling professionalism.

At an individual level for pharmacists and future pharmacists, it is about the development of knowledge; development of skills, experience and confidence; and the cultivation of professional values and behaviours which collectively imbue the pharmacist with authority, empowering and enabling professionalism.

At a wider level it is about creating an environment around an individual which enables all of the above.

Professional training starts at university and is enhanced with pre-registration training by learning, pre-registration tutors and training programmes. In professional practice it is self-cultivated through continuing professional development (CPD), continuing education, and supported by the RPS through our Foundation and Faculty professional development programmes.

The GPhC standards for registered pharmacies require that staff are empowered and competent to safeguard the health, safety and wellbeing of patients and the public (see Appendix 2 for further information).

The RPS contributes to creating empowerment through guidance, standards, news and alerts; through webinars and our mentoring programme; through our Leadership Development Framework; through influencing policy and embedding and nurturing the right culture (see section 2.7).

In 2011 we published Reducing workplace pressure through professional empowerment a resource which discusses various ways to reduce workplace pressure, including:

- Mechanisms for raising concerns

- Promoting management skills

- Ensuring pharmacists take breaks

- Professionalism and commercial pressures

- Job satisfaction

Employers play a key role by providing structured training resources and events; conferences; opportunity and time for CPD; support from the superintendent or office of the superintendent; company alerts and updates; developing and implementing the right organisation culture which enables professional empowerment.

Other pharmacy organisations, stakeholders and training providers are also integral to enabling professionalism through training, and enabling the right environment for professionalism to flourish, including through *getting the culture right*.

FURTHER READING

Royal Pharmaceutical Society
Leadership development framework and accompanying handbook.
www.rpharms.com

Royal Pharmaceutical Society
Reducing workplace pressure through professional empowerment. 2011.
www.rpharms.com

Royal Pharmaceutical Society
Working as a locum in community pharmacy – quick reference guide.
www.rpharms.com

General Pharmaceutical Council
Guidance to support the standards for registered pharmacies.
www.pharmacyregulation.org

2.5
Clinical check

2.5.1	PATIENT CHARACTERISTICS
2.5.2	MEDICATION REGIMEN FACTORS
2.5.3	ADMINISTRATION AND MONITORING
2.5.4	RECORD KEEPING

One of the key skills of a pharmacist is to perform a clinical assessment or clinical check for medicines to be supplied or administered. Clinical checks involve identifying potential pharmacotherapeutic problems by collating and evaluating all relevant information, including patient characteristics, disease states, medication regimen and, where possible, laboratory results.

Importantly, it is not a mere dose and interaction check, or a simple tick box exercise but rather a complex activity which often requires interaction with patients and healthcare professionals. A clinical check is underpinned by knowledge of human pathophysiology as well as medicines (pharmacokinetics, pharmacology, pharmaceutics, pharmacognosy) coupled with clinical experience and the rational application of professional judgement. It is a key part of clinical pharmacy contributing to patient safety and public health.

By using a structured, logical approach to a clinical check, you can balance the risks and benefits of a prescribed medicine regimen and, in doing so, improve the medicine's safety and effectiveness.

OBTAINING INFORMATION

The sources for obtaining information, and the level of detail available, will vary depending on the pharmacy setting. It may not always be practicable to obtain all the information needed and sometimes, decisions will need to be made on limited information. You should consider the level of risk when deciding if further information is required from one or more additional sources.

In primary care, you may be able to obtain information from:

- The prescription

- The patient, patient's representative or carer

- The patient's GP or other healthcare professionals involved in the patient's care

- The patient's medication record

- Other patient medical records where available (e.g. in Scotland – access to the Emergency Care Summary; access to the Summary Care Record where available; in a prison – access to medical records).

In secondary care, additional sources of information available would include other healthcare professionals involved in the patient's care (e.g. dieticians, microbiologists and physiotherapists), medical and nursing care notes, additional ward charts and laboratory results.

The areas that you need to consider when undertaking a clinical check include:

- Patient characteristics

- Medication regimen

- How treatment will be administered and monitored

2.5.1
PATIENT CHARACTERISTICS

Factors relating to patient characteristics that should be considered during a clinical check include:

PATIENT TYPE

Establish whether the patient falls into a group where treatment is contraindicated or cautioned. Specific groups of patients to be aware of include:

- Children

- Women who are pregnant or breastfeeding

- The elderly

- Certain ethnic groups – a patient's ethnic origin can affect the choice of medicine or dose (e.g. the initial and maximum dose of rosuvastatin is lower for patients of Asian origin)

- For some medicines, the gender of the patient should be considered. For example, finasteride is contraindicated for women

CO-MORBIDITIES

Patient co-morbidities, such as renal or hepatic impairment or heart failure, can exclude the use of a particular treatment or necessitate dose adjustments.

PATIENT INTOLERANCES AND PREFERENCES

Other patient factors that can affect the choice of treatment include known medication adverse events (e.g. allergies), dietary intolerances (e.g. to lactose containing products), patient preferences (e.g. vegan patients may refuse products of porcine origin), religious beliefs, and patients' knowledge and understanding of medicines and why they are being taken (patient beliefs about medicines).

2.5.2
MEDICATION REGIMEN FACTORS

Aspects of the prescribed medication regimen that should be considered during a clinical check include:

INDICATION

Ascertain the indication for treatment to check whether the medicine prescribed is appropriate for the indication and compatible with recommended guidelines.

CHANGES IN REGULAR TREATMENT

Where there are changes in regular therapy (e.g. strength or dose), you should confirm that these are intentional.

DOSE, FREQUENCY AND STRENGTH

You should check that the dose, frequency and strength of the prescribed medicine are appropriate – having considered the patient's age, renal and hepatic function, weight (and surface area where appropriate), comorbidities, concomitant drug treatments and lifestyle pattern.

THE DOSING OF THE FORMULATION

Check that, for the formulation prescribed, the dose and frequency are appropriate.

DRUG COMPATIBILITY

Regular and new therapies should be evaluated for any clinically significant interactions, duplications and antagonistic activity.

MONITORING REQUIREMENTS

For medicines that require monitoring, you should check for the latest test results and ascertain whether any dose adjustments are required.

2.5.3
ADMINISTRATION AND MONITORING

Aspects relating to the administration and monitoring of a medicine that should be considered during a clinical check include:

THE ROUTE OF ADMINISTRATION

Check whether the prescribed route of administration is suitable for the patient and whether a preparation is available for that route. Also, check for compatibility issues that may arise from administering via that route (e.g. due to co-administration of food or other medicines). For example, phenytoin can interact with enteral feeds so administration via an enteral feeding tube would need to be managed accordingly.

AIDS TO ADMINISTRATION

Check whether any aids are required to support administration. For example, spacer devices, eye drop devices, Braille or large type or pictogram labels, additional information sheets or verbal information and multi-compartment compliance aids (MCAs).

2.5.4
RECORD KEEPING

Record keeping is important for continuity of care, evidence of the benefit of pharmacy input and improving patient care. You should make a record of significant clinical checks, and interventions made. This should include details of discussions and agreed decisions with other healthcare professionals. Depending upon the circumstances it may be appropriate to make this record in the patient's medication record (PMR), an interventions record book, handover record book or prescription register.

FURTHER READING

Royal Pharmaceutical Society
Clinical checks – quick reference guide.
www.rpharms.com

Royal Pharmaceutical Society
Professional guidance on the administration of medicines in healthcare settings. 2019.
www.rpharms.com

Royal Pharmaceutical Society
Quick reference guides (various titles re pharmacy practice and clinical aspects of pharmacy).
www.rpharms.com

Royal Pharmaceutical Society
Improving patient outcomes through MCA. 2013.
www.rpharms.com

Royal Pharmaceutical Society
Polypharmacy: Getting our medicines right
www.rpharms.com

Avery AJ, Barber N, et al (archived)
Investigating the prevalence and causes of prescribing errors in general practice: The PRACtICe Study. 2012.
www.gmc-uk.org/about/what-we-do-and-why/data-and-research/research-and-insight-archive/investigating-the-prevalence-and-causes-of-prescribing-errors-in-general-practice

Avery AJ, Rodgers S, et al
Pharmacist-led information technology enabled intervention for reducing medication errors: Multicentre cluster randomised controlled trial and cost effectiveness analysis (PINCER Trial).
The Lancet; Vol 379, Issue 9823, April 07 2012.
www.thelancet.com/journals/lancet/article/PIIS0140-6736(11)61817-5/fulltext

British National Formulary
www.medicinescomplete.com
or www.evidence.nhs.uk

British National Formulary for Children
www.medicinescomplete.com
or www.evidence.nhs.uk

Clinical Pharmacist
www.pharmaceutical-journal.com/publications/clinical-pharmacist

Dornan T, Ashcroft D, et al
An in depth investigation into causes of prescribing errors by foundation trainees in relation to their medical education. EQUIP Study. 2009.
www.gmc-uk.org (search EQUIP study)

General Pharmaceutical Council (GPhC)
Guidance on consent. 2018.
www.pharmacyregulation.org
(see MEP Appendix 4)

Gray AH, Wright J, et al
Clinical Pharmacy Pocket Companion (2nd edition). 2015. London; Pharmaceutical Press.
www.pharmpress.com

Stephens M
Hospital Pharmacy (2nd edition). 2011.
London; Pharmaceutical Press.
www.pharmpress.com

2.6

The pharmacist consultation in practice

2.6.1   MEDICINE RECONCILIATION

2.6.2   HELPING PATIENTS TO
        UNDERSTAND THEIR MEDICINE

A pharmacist consultation is any discussion between a pharmacist and a patient and is an essential part of providing patient-centred care in practice. Patients should be encouraged to engage in the consultation to ensure that it is a two-way discussion where they can share their views and be involved in decision-making around their treatment.

The Consultation Skills Assessment (also known as the Medication Related Consultation Framework) is one of the Foundation Pharmacy Framework tools and can be used to assess and demonstrate your consultation behaviours and skills. Further information can be found in the Foundation programme area on the RPS website: www.rpharms.com/professionaldevelopment/foundation-programme

2.6.1
MEDICINES RECONCILIATION

Medicines reconciliation is the process of identifying an accurate list of a patient's current medicines (including over-the-counter and complementary medicines) and carrying out a comparison of these with the current list in use, recognising any discrepancies, and documenting any changes. It also takes into account the current health of the patient and any active or long-standing issues. The result is a complete list of medicines that is then accurately communicated. The pharmacist who is carrying out medicines reconciliation should ensure that

any discrepancies are resolved by highlighting these and working with relevant members of the multidisciplinary team. The pharmacist should also keep the patient informed.

Medicines reconciliation should take place whenever patients are transferred from one care setting to another, when they are admitted to hospital, transferred between wards and on discharge. The way that the process is carried out will vary between care settings.
Further information on medicines reconciliation in different settings can be found in NICE Guideline Medicines optimisation: the safe and effective use of medicines to enable the best possible outcomes: www.nice.org.uk/guidance/ng5

Accurate medicines reconciliation prevents medication errors and provides a foundation for assessing the appropriateness of a patient's current medicines and directing future treatment choices to ensure that the patient receive the best care. The process also allows other pharmaceutical issues such as poor adherence or non-adherence to be identified.

SOURCES OF INFORMATION

Sources of information that may be used when carrying out medicines reconciliation include:

1   Patient or patient's representative

2   Patient's medicines

3   Repeat prescriptions

4   GP referral letters

5   The patient's GP surgery

6   Hospital discharge summaries or outpatient appointment notes

7   Community pharmacy patient medication records

8   Care home records

9   Drug treatment centre records

10 Other healthcare professionals and specialist clinics

11 Patient medical records where available (e.g. in prisons or the Emergency Care Summary (Scotland), Summary Care Record (England), or Welsh GP Record (see also section 2.5)

GENERAL TIPS FOR OBTAINING A MEDICATION HISTORY FROM A PATIENT

- Explain to the patient why the history is being taken

- Use a balance of open-ended questions (e.g. what, how, why, when) with closed questions (i.e. those requiring yes/no answers)

- Avoid jargon – keep it simple

- Clarify vague responses with further questioning or by using other sources of information

- Keep the patient at ease

KEY POINTS

ARE THE SOURCES YOU USE UP-TO-DATE?

Aim to use the most complete, reliable and up-to-date source(s) of information.

CROSS-CHECK ADHERENCE

Medication histories should be cross-checked against different sources and confirmed with the patient or patient's representative. The medicines they are actually taking, and how they are taking them, may differ from written documentation (e.g. the prescribing record held by the patient's GP).

NON-DAILY MEDICINES

Remember to ask patients whether they take any medicines 'when required' (e.g. reliever inhalers) ,or on certain days of the week. Also remember to ask about the sorts of formulations that might be forgotten (e.g. nasal sprays, eye or ear drops, ointments, depot injections, patches, etc.). Patients may also need prompting to remember medicines such as oral contraceptives and hormone replacement therapy.

HISTORICAL MEDICINES

The medication history should not be restricted to current therapies but should include any recently stopped or changed medicines.

SELF-SELECTED MEDICINES

Include any medicinal product that the patient is taking – whether prescribed or not – and do not restrict the medication history to medicines obtained on prescription. Over-the-counter (OTC) medicines, herbal products, vitamins, dietary supplements, recreational drugs (e.g. alcohol and tobacco) and remedies purchased over the internet should also be included.

WHAT INFORMATION SHOULD I OBTAIN WHEN TAKING A MEDICATION HISTORY?

For each medicine, the following should be determined:

- Generic name of the drug

- Brand name of the drug, where appropriate (for example, where bioavailability variations between brands can have clinical consequences, such as lithium therapy)

- Dose – both the prescribed dose and the actual dose the patient is taking (*NB: This may best be described to the patient as a quantity of tablets rather than as milligrams of active ingredient*)

- Strength of the medicine taken

- Formulation used (e.g. phenytoin – 100mg as a liquid does not deliver the same dose as a 100mg tablet)

- Route of administration (this could be an unlicensed route – e.g. ciprofloxacin eye drops for the ear)

- Frequency of administration – this should include the time of administration for certain medicines (e.g. levodopa)

- Length of therapy, if appropriate (e.g. for antibiotics)

- Administration device and brand for injectables (e.g. insulin)

- Day or date of administration for medicines taken on specific days of the week or month

FURTHER READING

Royal Pharmaceutical Society
Medication history – quick reference guide. 2011.
www.rpharms.com

East and South East England Specialist Pharmacy Services
Medicines reconciliation: Best practice resource and toolkit. 2015.
www.sps.nhs.uk

Healthcare Improvement Scotland
Medicines reconciliation care bundle. 2015.
https://ihub.scot/

National Institute for Health and Care Excellence (NICE)
Medicines optimisation. Quality standard. 2016.
www.nice.org.uk

National Institute for Health and Care Excellence (NICE)
Medicines optimisation: the safe and effective use of medicines to enable the best possible outcomes. NICE guideline. 2015.
www.nice.org.uk

Stephens M.
Hospital Pharmacy (2nd edition). 2011.
London; Pharmaceutical Press.
www.pharmpress.com

Illustrative examples of opportunities include:

- Point of sale for over-the-counter medicines
- Any medication reviews
- Diagnostic testing and screening
- Patient group directions
- Minor ailment schemes
- Whilst taking medication history
- During a hospital stay
- Point of discharge
- Outpatient clinics
- When a change has been made to a current medicine
- Point of a supply of a regular prescription

2.6.2
HELPING PATIENTS TO UNDERSTAND THEIR MEDICINES

An important key role of pharmacists is ensuring that patients understand their medicines, the role that they play in maintaining their wellbeing and to empower patients to use these safely and effectively to get the most from their treatment. Providing information for patients on their medicines involves being able to build a rapport with the patient, having good communication skills, empathy, being able to put the patient at ease and being able to confer an understanding and belief that the health of the patient is important to the pharmacist. Involving and engaging the patient in this process is essential in ensuring that the pharmacist-patient relationship is concordant.

OPPORTUNITIES FOR HELPING PATIENTS UNDERSTAND THEIR MEDICINES

Consultations should not be limited to when a supply of newly prescribed medicines is made, and almost any interaction with the patient can be used as an opportunity to help them understand their medicines. A simple question asking, "How are you getting on with your medicines?" can often be a successful engaging starting point.

ADVICE FOR SUCCESSFUL PATIENT CONSULTATIONS

- Try to understand the level of existing knowledge, understanding and concerns the patient has regarding their medicines. Consider any misunderstandings which could be a barrier to adherence. Explore what the patient has already been told about their medicines, whether there are any concerns and what the patient's expectations are

- Ensure you are familiar with the medicines you will be providing counselling on and any additional information that is relevant to those medicines. If in doubt, take time to review and re-familiarise yourself with the medicine. For example – look out for interactions with other medicines, food, or supplements, or medicines with common or significant side effects, complex administration regimens, special storage requirements, or narrow therapeutic index. Check standard references (e.g. BNF or national guidelines for additional patient and carer advice)

- Aim for a structured approach and tailor the language and level of detail used to the patient. The format that is appropriate will depend upon both patient characteristics and the medicines that are taken. As an illustration, the patient may be knowledgeable about their medicines and condition, for example as a result of caring for a family member with the same condition

- Where appropriate use different methods of communication to support your discussions such as pictograms and medication cards

- Respect patient privacy and ensure that confidentiality is protected

- Ensure that the process is two-way and interactive, not simply a list of facts about medicines. There should be opportunities for questions and discussion.

- As a minimum, you should consider discussing the following points:

  - What is the medicine and why has it been prescribed? How does it impact upon the medical condition and how does it alleviate the symptoms? e.g. This is a blood pressure medicine which should lower your blood pressure to normal levels which will help prevent further complications

  - How and when to take the medicine

  - How much to take and what to expect, e.g. antibiotics need to be taken regularly and the course completed even after symptoms subside

  - What to do if the patient misses a dose

  - What are the likely side effects and how to manage them

  - If applicable, any lifestyle or dietary changes that need to be made or that can affect the treatment

  - Additional information relating to storage requirements, expiry dates, disposal and monitoring requirements can also be included where appropriate

  - Check patient understanding by asking them to describe back to you the key information you have provided.

FURTHER READING

Royal Pharmaceutical Society
Counselling patients on medicines – quick reference guide.
www.rpharms.com

Royal Pharmaceutical Society
Medication review – quick reference guide.
www.rpharms.com

Royal Pharmaceutical Society
Medicines adherence – quick reference guide.
www.rpharms.com

Royal Pharmaceutical Society
Polypharmacy: Getting our medicines right
www.rpharms.com

CPPE and NHS Health Education England
Consultation skills for pharmacy practice: practice standards for England.
www.consultationskillsforpharmacy.com
(endorsed by the RPS)

Health Education and Improvement Wales
Various training resources available.
www.wcppe.org.uk

National Institute for Health and Care Excellence
Medicines adherence: Involving patients in decisions about prescribed medicines and supporting adherence. Clinical guideline. 2009.
www.nice.org.uk

NHS Education for Scotland
Patient-centred consultation skills training (one-day training course).
www.nes.scot.nhs.uk

2.7
Getting the culture right

2.7.1   A JUST CULTURE

"In the end, culture will trump rules, standards and control strategies every single time."
Professor Donald Berwick
A promise to learn – a commitment to act (2013)

We know that it is important for the profession to get the culture right. There have been infamous examples across industries and organisations of the problems caused by the wrong culture, including within the banking industry, the media and within healthcare. The wrong type of culture contributed to the unacceptable failings at Mid-Staffordshire NHS Foundation Trust hospital between 2005 and 2008, those at Orchid View care home and also the abuse at Winterbourne View private hospital.

The types of culture which collectively help us to achieve patient-centred, safe and effective care together with professional empowerment are interlinked and include a culture that is based upon the principles and values of fairness, quality, safety, transparency, learning and reporting.

Underpinning getting the culture right is a 'just culture'. This is a culture based upon fairness and is achieved when attitudes, behaviours and practices are fair.

2.7.1
A JUST CULTURE

PROBLEMS WITH A
PUNITIVE CULTURE

PUNITIVE CULTURE: PUNISHMENT
↓
STIFLES REPORTING AND LEARNING
↓
REDUCTION IN PATIENT SAFETY AND QUALITY OF CARE

A **punitive culture** is based upon assigning blame and punishment. It contributes to creating a culture of fear. People and organisations see what happens to others and if what they see is perceived to be draconian or unjust, this leads to fear, stifling reporting and stifling the raising of concerns. We lose the opportunity to learn, and patient safety is affected. A single instance of perceived punitive action can have a wide effect on how large groups of people choose to act.

WHY A NO-BLAME
CULTURE IS INADEQUATE

NO-BLAME CULTURE: BLANKET IMMUNITY
↓
LACK OF ACCOUNTABILITY
↓
NOT ACCEPTABLE TO SOCIETY. UNFAIR

A **no-blame culture** may not be better than a punitive culture. It can breed complacency or nonchalance which can also impact upon patient safety. At its worst it can appear unacceptable to society overall due to the immunity from accountability which can also be abused. For example, there is a perception that at times diplomatic immunity can be unfair and abused

THE 'RIGHT CULTURE'
OR A JUST CULTURE

JUST CULTURE
↓
OPEN CULTURE REPORTING CULTURE LEARNING CULTURE
↓
SAFETY & QUALITY CULTURE: BALANCED ACCOUNTABILITY AND LEARNING
↓
FAIR WORKING ENVIRONMENT, IMPROVED PATIENT EXPERIENCE, IMPROVED PATIENT SAFETY & QUALITY OF CARE

Instead, the **'right culture'** is needed which is a culture based upon the principles of fairness, quality, transparency, reporting, learning and safety. A just culture promotes an open culture (transparency and discussion), a reporting culture (raising concerns), and a learning culture (learning from mistakes). These cultures support each other to create a safety culture – balancing accountability and learning and leading to improved patient safety. It also creates a just and open working environment which is rewarding to work in, fosters professional empowerment, and enhances the quality of service to patients and the patient experience.

WHY IS IT NEEDED?

When applied to the provision of healthcare and pharmacy services, a just culture means removing fears, increasing sharing and reporting of concerns, being able to learn from mistakes or incidents, being able to share lessons learnt (throughout the profession where appropriate) and using this shared learning to reduce the likelihood of similar mistakes and incidents happening again. This is a vital component contributing to better patient safety.When a mistake or incident occurs, we all want assurances that actions are being taken so that it will never happen again and that there will be fair accountability. It is not possible to stop errors occurring, however, a just culture will contribute to a system that improves continuously which should in time result in fewer errors.

HOW DO WE COLLECTIVELY ACHIEVE A JUST CULTURE?

> **COMMITMENT TO THE RIGHT CULTURE**
>
> ↓
>
> **RECOGNISING WHERE IT EXISTS**
>
> ↓
>
> **GETTING THE INFRASTRUCTURE RIGHT**
>
> ↓
>
> **LIVING THE RIGHT CULTURE**

The journey to achieving the right culture requires the embedding of just culture principles into attitudes, behaviours and practices, and the design of legislation, regulation, standards, policies and systems.

It requires commitment by all stakeholders to apply and 'live' the culture routinely, through all activities and all interfaces and for this to be habitual. It is a continuous and evolving movement and may take years to achieve, but one to which the RPS and others are committed. Policies and procedures for a just and safe culture are simply words on paper if they are not 'lived' in actions and interactions. We all have responsibilities for living the culture and embedding the habit. Individuals and organisations can do this through strong leadership and educating people about a just and safe culture appreciating when it is in action through reflection, through benchmarking and through commitment of time.

In October 2012, on behalf of the profession, the RPS was instrumental in designing and creating The Speaking Up Charter together with NHS Employers and other stakeholders. This charter incorporates

just culture ideals and has been supported by major healthcare organisations. (www.nhsemployers.org/retention-and-staff-experience/raising-concerns-whistleblowing)

A JUST CULTURE AND PATIENT SAFETY INCIDENTS

Patient safety can be improved by the reporting of concerns and learning from these reports. The reporting of concerns will only take place if individuals feel they will not be victimised and that it is 'safe' to report these concerns. To provide assurance and confidence, everybody needs to know where they stand.

The airline industry has been embedding just culture principles into its practices for decades to improve safety. Adapting from what the airline industry has learnt, together with consideration of similar workstreams within the NHS, we believe in the following just culture principles for patient safety incidents:

1 Patient safety is paramount

2 Deliberate harm and unacceptable risk impacting on patient safety must not be tolerated

3 Patient safety is maintained by healthcare professionals being candid and raising concerns and learning fromincidents to improve systems, standards, policies, legislation and people

4 To ensure that concerns will be raised and learning from incidents occurs, individual accountability must always be fair and proportionate, and viewed in the context of root cause, system deficiencies, mitigating circumstances and the entirety of contributing factors (i.e. the whole picture)

The NHS has developed an incident decision tree (see Diagram 4) based upon the work of Professor James Reason, an expert on patient safety. This decision-making tool embodies just culture principles and uses a series of tests to decide on the appropriate course of action following an incident.

STANDARDS FOR REPORTING, SHARING, LEARNING, TAKING ACTION AND REVIEW OF INCIDENTS

In collaboration with the Pharmacy Forum of Northern Ireland and the Association of Pharmacy Technicians UK, the RPS has published standards for the reporting, sharing, learning, taking action and review of incidents. The standards are supplemented by an explanation of how pharmacy services protect patients, the link with patient safety, practical aspects and barriers to reporting, sharing, learning, taking action and review. The standards are available from the RPS website www.rpharms.com

GPhC guidance on responding to complaints and concerns (reproduced in Appendix 8) may also be useful and includes guidance for the review of errors and minimising the risk of making a dispensing error.

NATIONAL REPORTING AND LEARNING SYSTEM (NRLS)

From June 2012 the key functions for patient safety developed by the National Patient Safety Agency (NPSA) were transferred to the NHS Commissioning Board Special Health Authority. The NPSA website continues to offer key information, guidance, tools and alerts. Healthcare organisations in England and Wales should report patient safety incidents to the NRLS (www.nrls.npsa.nhs.uk/report-a-patient-safety-incident). The NRLS does not seek to collect identifiable information relating to staff and patients involved in an incident and so reporting is anonymous for the reporter, staff and patients.

In Scotland each NHS Board operates its own reporting system.

NEAR MISS ERRORS

Regular review of near miss errors and action taken can prevent similar mistakes from happening in the future. The RPS has produced tools and guidance to help support clinical governance in pharmacy, and to promote an open culture of recording of near miss errors so that all pharmacy staff can reflect and learn from them. The Near Miss Error

Log and Near Miss Error Improvement Tool, along with supporting guidance are available on the RPS website (www.rpharms.com/resources).

FURTHER READING

Royal Pharmaceutical Society (RPS)
Leadership development framework and accompanying handbook.
www.rpharms.com

Royal Pharmaceutical Society (RPS)
Raising concerns, whistleblowing – quick reference guide.
www.rpharms.com

Royal Pharmaceutical Society (RPS)
Whistleblowing policies and procedures – quick reference guide.
www.rpharms.com

General Pharmaceutical Council (GPhC)
In practice: Guidance on raising concerns. 2017.
www.pharmacyregulation.org
(see MEP Appendix 5)

Leonard M, Frankel A.
How can leaders influence a safety culture?
The Health Foundation. 2012.
www.health.org.uk

National Patient Safety Agency
Seven steps to patient safety: A guide for NHS staff. 2014.
www.nrls.npsa.nhs.uk

NHS Improvement
A just culture guide.
https://improvement.nhs.uk/

NHS Improvement
Freedom to speak up: raising concerns (whistleblowing) policy for the NHS.
https://improvement.nhs.uk/

PharmacyQS.com
10 Improvement challenges: improve culture.
www.pharmacyqs.com

DIAGRAM 4: A JUST CULTURE GUIDE
Supporting consistent, constructive and
fair evaluation of the actions of staff involved
in patient safety incidents

WAS THERE ANY INTENTION
TO CAUSE HARM?

NO   YES

Recommendation
Follow organisational guidance for
appropriate management action. This could
involve: contact relevant regulatory bodies,
suspension of staff, and referral to police and
disciplinary processes. Wider investigation
is still needed to understand how and why
patients were not protected from the actions
of the individual.

ARE THERE
INDICATIONS
OF SUBSTANCE
ABUSE?

ARE THERE
INDICATIONS
OF PHYSICAL ILL
HEALTH?

ARE THERE
INDICATIONS
OF MENTAL ILL
HEALTH?

NO   YES   NO   YES   NO   YES

Recommendation
Follow organisational substance abuse at work
guidance. Wider investigation is still needed
to understand if substance abuse could have
been recognised and addressed earlier.

Recommendation
Follow organisational guidance for health issues affecting
work, which is likely to include occupational health referral.
Wider investigation is still needed to understand if health
issues could have been recognised and addressed earlier.

ARE THERE AGREED PROTOCOLS/ ACCEPTED PRACTICE IN PLACE
THAT APPLY TO THE ACTION/OMISSION IN QUESTION?

WERE THE PROTOCOLS/ACCEPTED PRACTICE
WORKABLE AND IN ROUTINE USE?

DID THE INDIVIDUAL KNOWINGLY DEPART
FROM THESE PROTOCOLS?

Recommendation
Action singling out the individual
is unlikely to be appropriate;
the patient safety incident
investigation should indicate
the wider actions needed to
improve safety for future patients.
These actions may include,
but not be limited to, the individual.

IF YES TO ALL   IF NO TO ANY

ARE THERE INDICATIONS THAT OTHER INDIVIDUALS FROM THE SAME
PEER GROUP, WITH COMPARABLE EXPERIENCE AND QUALIFICATIONS,
WOULD BEHAVE IN THE SAME WAY IN SIMILAR CIRCUMSTANCE?

WAS THE INDIVIDUAL MISSED OUT WHEN RELEVANT TRAINING WAS
PROVIDED TO THEIR PEER GROUP?

DID MORE SENIOR MEMBERS OF THE TEAM FAIL TO PROVIDE
SUPERVISION THAT NORMALLY SHOULD BE PROVIDED?

IF YES TO ANY

IF NO TO ALL

Recommendation
Action directed at the individual may not be appropriate; follow organisational
guidance, which is likely to include senior HR advice on what degree
of mitigation applies. The patient safety incident investigation should indicate
the wider actions needed to improve safety for future patients.

WERE THERE ANY
SIGNIFICANT MITIGATING
CIRCUMSTANCES?

YES

Recommendation
Follow organisational guidance for appropriate management action.
This could involve individual training, performance management,
competency assessments, changes to role or increased supervision,
and may require relevant regulatory bodies to be contacted, staff suspension
and disciplinary processes. The patient safety incident investigation should
indicate the wider actions needed to improve safety for future patients.

NO

BASED ON THE NHS IMPROVEMENT
JUST CULTURE GUIDE
HTTPS://IMPROVEMENT.NHS.UK/RESOURCES/
JUST-CULTURE-GUIDE/

2.8
Professional development

We support all members with their revalidation and provide a range of resources, programmes and services including guidance, one to one advice and support through the RPS Professional Support service and support for members with their professional development using the RPS professional development tools, portfolios and frameworks that underpin the Foundation and Faculty programmes. www.rpharms.com/development/revalidation

2.8.1
REVALIDATION

The GPhC has introduced requirements for the revalidation of pharmacy professionals.

From 2019, you'll need to submit the following six records each year:

- Four CPD records (at least two planned)

- A peer discussion

- A reflective account

Further details, including templates and case studies are available on the GPhC website www.pharmacyregulation.org/revalidation-pharmacy-professionals

The RPS can support you with revalidation www.rpharms.com/development/revalidation

2.8.2
RPS FACULTY

The RPS Faculty is the pharmacy professional recognition programme for RPS members which provides you with a way of identifying what you need to know at different levels of practice, across all sectors. It allows you to advance as a specialist or generalist and recognise your development thereby demonstrating to colleagues, healthcare professionals, patients and the public your advanced or specialised level of practice through the award and use of post nominals. The Faculty is for RPS members who have completed their early/foundation years of practice (www.rpharms.com/development/education-development).

2.8.3
RPS FOUNDATION PROGRAMME

Foundation Practice is the knowledge, skills and behaviours that collectively form the building blocks for all pharmacists across all sectors. We know that pharmacy practitioners who are well supported and understand what is required are better equipped to adapt and deliver pharmaceutical care.

The Foundation Pharmacy Framework provides a structure for you to realise your competence, demonstrate your experience, facilitate advancement or develop special interests.

The Foundation Programme is for individuals who have recently qualified, those who are returning to work after career breaks, and for those who may be changing their scope of practice, practice environment, or simply working steadily (www.rpharms.com/development/education-development).

2.8.4
DEVELOPING LEADERSHIP

We have published a Leadership Development Framework for pharmacists and pharmaceutical scientists.

The framework is based on the concept of engaging, collective leadership for all, whether in a leadership role or not. It promotes leadership behaviours (the 'how-to-do' of leadership) across all sectors of the profession and encourages a collective responsibility for the success of an organisation and its services. Engaging leadership can come from anyone in an organisation, as appropriate, and at different times, and is an essential element of good practice and professional development (www.rpharms.com/resources/frameworks/leadership-development-framework).

2.9
Research involvement

Pharmacists are becoming increasingly involved in research activities. For some pharmacists, particularly those working in industry and academia, research will be a major part of their role; other pharmacists will be involved to a lesser extent e.g. in research support activities such as recruiting patients to clinical trials. All pharmacists, regardless of their sector or level of practice, will have had experience of using research to inform practice (see Diagram 5).

It is important that pharmacists have a good understanding of the ethical implications and requirements for research and how these impact on their working practices and outcomes of the study. This applies whether they are leading the research themselves or being asked to participate in research led by others – research is often a multidisciplinary team activity.

Ethical principles must be considered at all stages of the research process (see Diagram 6) – regardless of whether research ethics and governance approval is required in its own right (e.g. through the Health Research Authority Research Ethics Committees). Further information can be found in the RPS Research and Evaluation Hub. (www.rpharms.com/development/research-and-evaluation)

DIAGRAM 5: PHARMACISTS: INVOLVEMENT IN RESEARCH

USING RESEARCH EVIDENCE TO INFORM PRACTICE

SUPPORTING RESEARCH LED BY OTHERS

COLLABORATING IN RESEARCH AS A PARTNER

LEADING RESEARCH

DIAGRAM 6: STEPS OF THE RESEARCH PROCESS

IDENTIFY TOPIC, BROADLY DEFINE AIM & QUESTIONS

EVALUATE ACTIVITY AND OUTCOMES

CRITICALLY REVIEW EVIDENCE

DISSEMINATION OF FINDINGS (PRESENT, PUBLISH)

CLARIFY RESEARCH QUESTIONS AND AIM

INTERPRETATION OF FINDINGS

SELECT RESEARCH DESIGN AND METHOD

DATA COLLECTION AND ANALYSIS

DEVELOP RESEARCH PROTOCOL/PROPOSAL

ETHICS & RESEARCH GOVERNANCE APPROVALS

The GPhC's Standards for pharmacy professionals
(see Appendix 1) apply to all stages of research just
as they do to any other areas of pharmacy practice.

**Examples of how they apply to research
are provided below:**

GPhC STANDARD PHARMACY PROFESSIONAL MUST:	APPLICATION TO RESEARCH:
1 **PROVIDE PERSON-CENTRED CARE**	• Ensure participants are fully informed about the research and their consent to participate is freely given • Ensure the research is relevant to the patient/service user population • Check the research has the necessary approvals (Ethics, NHS R&D) • Consider the harm and benefit of the research to patients, carers and/or the public and protect their health, safety and wellbeing
2 **WORK IN PARTNERSHIP WITH OTHERS**	• Consider other individuals that could be involved in the study. These could be people who may share similar research ideas or have common goals. This could include other healthcare professionals, carers or the public in general • Ensure collegiality and work in a collaborative manner
3 **COMMUNICATE EFFECTIVELY**	• Where possible, encourage patients, their carers and the public to get involved in the design of the research and its dissemination • Help to disseminate the results once the study has been published to share knowledge, evidence and inform best practice
4 **MAINTAIN, DEVELOP AND USE THEIR PROFESSIONAL KNOWLEDGE AND SKILLS**	• The reasons for doing the research should be fully understood • Strict adherence to research protocol to ensure intervention or data collection from different sites are delivered consistently • Ensure all pharmacy staff are competent (or seek training) in all areas of the research in which they are involved to inform best practice

GPhC STANDARD PHARMACY PROFESSIONAL MUST:	APPLICATION TO RESEARCH:
5 **USE PROFESSIONAL JUDGEMENT**	Consider: • Who is proposing the research? • Are there any areas for potential conflict of interest? • Do you need to make any adjustments to achieve the desired outcome?
6 **BEHAVE IN A PROFESSIONAL MANNER**	• Consider other individuals that could be involved in the study. These could be people who may share similar research ideas or have common goals. This could include other healthcare professionals, carers or the public in general • Ensure collegiality and work in a collaborative manner
7. **RESPECT AND MAINTAIN THE PERSON'S CONFIDENTIALITY AND PRIVACY**	• Respect and protect participant confidentiality, respect individuals' decisions if they choose not to participate in the study • Maintain privacy and confidentiality, respect all other colleagues involved in the research
8. **SPEAK UP WHEN THEY HAVE CONCERNS OR WHEN THINGS GO WRONG**	• Express any concerns you might have at any stage of the research process, from design all the way through to dissemination of a study. Examples may include situations of misconduct such as fabrication, falsification or plagiarism
9 **DEMONSTRATE LEADERSHIP**	• Take responsibility for the level of participation within the research, i.e. the length of time and activities involved • Ensure your organisation has the appropriate resources to participate in the research • Lead by example: every pharmacy professional should be involved in research, leading studies, sharing ideas and collaborating with others

OTHER CONSIDERATIONS

- Is the purpose of your research clear and relevant?

- Are you clear about your role in the study?

- Does your employer agree to the organisation participating in research activities and do you have the appropriate resources (staff and facilities) to accommodate the research?

- Do you have the relevant skills or do you require training e.g. Good Clinical Practice training?

- What training will your support staff need?

- Has the study been granted ethical approval through an NHS research ethics committee or another appropriate department/ organisation? If not, was there an independent assessment that informed the decision?

- Do you understand the implications of any research contracts or finance agreements relating to the study?

- Has there been appropriate patient and public involvement in the design of the study?

- Has participant consent been addressed and confidentiality assured?

- Will all participants be informed of the results?

- What records are required?

- Where and how is data being stored?

- Is data transfer to a third party secure and appropriate?

FURTHER READING

Royal Pharmaceutical Society
Research and evaluation guide.
www.rpharms.com

Health and Care Research Wales
www.healthandcareresearch.gov.wales

Health Research Authority (England)
www.hra.nhs.uk

National Institute for Health Research (England)
www.nihr.ac.uk

NHS Research Scotland
www.nhsresearchscotland.org.uk

Underpinning knowledge – legislation and professional issues

An awareness of pharmacy legislation, professional standards and good practice helps pharmacists exercise their professional judgement.

The Human Medicines Regulations 2012 consolidated most of the legislation regulating the authorisation, sale and supply of medicinal products for human use, made under the Medicines Act 1968. It is important to understand that the Medicines Act 1968 has not been replaced fully and that certain parts are still active. Further information on the Human Medicines Regulations 2012 and the consolidation can be found in Chapter 2 of Dale and Appelbe's Pharmacy and Medicines Law (11th Edition) and the MHRA website: www.gov.uk/government/organisations/medicines-and-healthcare-products-regulatory-agency (search for 'HumanMedicines Regulations 2012').

The Veterinary Medicines Regulations 2013 covers the prescribing and supply for animals. Further information on the Veterinary Medicines Regulations can be found in Chapter 16 of Dale and Appelbe's Pharmacy and Medicines Law (11th Edition) and the Veterinary Medicines Directorate (VMD) website at www.gov.uk/government/organisations/veterinary-medicines-directorate (search for 'Veterinary Medicines Regulations').

The Programme Board for Rebalancing Medicines Legislation and Pharmacy Regulation reviews relevant pharmacy legislation and regulation to ensure it provides safety for users of pharmacy services. It facilitates a systematic approach to quality in pharmacy, allowing innovation and development of pharmacy practice, whilst reducing the burden of unnecessary and inflexible regulations. The Programme will build on and propose amendments to legislation as required, to deliver a modern approach to regulation which maintains patient and public safety, whilst supporting professional and quality systems development, including learning from dispensing errors made in registered pharmacies.

Further information and updates on the Rebalancing Medicines Legislation and Pharmacy Regulation Programme Board can be found on the UK government website at www.gov.uk/government/groups/pharmacy-regulation-programme-board

The MEP is not intended to be a complete repository of pharmacy legislation and aims instead to provide a practical resource, professional guide and digest to the most relevant aspects of pharmacy legislation.

3.1
Classification of medicines

3.1.1   GENERAL SALE LIST (GSL) MEDICINES

3.1.2   PHARMACY (P) MEDICINES

3.1.3   PRESCRIPTION-ONLY MEDICINES (POM)

Pharmacists deal with three classes of medicinal products for humans under the Human Medicines Regulations 2012 and several classes of veterinary medicinal products under the Veterinary Medicines Regulations. An understanding of these and associated professional issues is important to pharmacists as medicines should not be considered normal items of commerce, and the final decision on sale or supply is one determined by the professional judgement of the pharmacist.

Pharmacists are empowered to refuse to sell or supply ANY medicines, if the sale or supply is contrary to the pharmacist's clinical judgement.

3.1.1
GENERAL SALE LIST (GSL) MEDICINES

General Sale List medicines (GSL medicines) are those that can be sold in registered pharmacies but also in other retail outlets that can 'close so as to exclude the public'. They are classified as GSL mostly because of an EU or UK marketing authorisation (product licence), if they hold a traditional herbal registration or if they have a certificate of registration as a general sale medicine homeopathic product. The term (PO) medicine is sometimes used by manufacturers to describe a product that is licensed as a GSL medicine but for which the manufacturer wishes to restrict sales or supplies through pharmacies only (e.g. 30-sachet packs of Fybogel).

Within a pharmacy, GSL medicines can only be sold when a pharmacist has assumed the role of responsible pharmacist; however, the pharmacist may be physically absent for a limited period of time while remaining responsible, thus permitting sales of general sale medicines during this absence (see Chapter 4).

3.1.2
PHARMACY (P) MEDICINES

A pharmacy medicine is a medicinal product that can be sold from a registered pharmacy premises by a pharmacist or a person acting under the supervision of a pharmacist.

Together with GSL medicines, P medicines are collectively known as over-the-counter (OTC) or non-prescription medicines. The sale of some of these medicines is associated with additional legal and professional considerations; the most common issues are explained in section 3.2.

SELF-SELECTION OF P MEDICINES

The GPhC at its 13 September 2012 meeting made it clear that the self-selection of P medicines is prohibited until they are able to enforce standards for registered pharmacies and that a further additional regulatory pre-condition around self selection is that guidance on compliance in this area would need to have been developed and communicated in advance of any change.

In addition to the regulatory standards outlined above, our interim statement of professional standard for the supply of OTC medicines also references self-selection and states that 'Pharmacy medicines must not be accessible to the public by self selection'. For a full copy of the interim statement see our website at www.rpharms.com/resources.

3.1.3
PRESCRIPTION-ONLY MEDICINES (POM)

A prescription-only medicine (POM) is a medicine that is generally subject to the restriction of requiring a prescription written by an appropriate practitioner.

An appropriate practitioner includes the following:

- doctor
- dentist
- supplementary prescriber
- nurse independent prescriber
- pharmacist independent prescriber
- EEA and Swiss doctors and dentists (but not for all Controlled Drugs)
- EEA and Swiss prescribing pharmacist and prescribing nurse where they exist
- Community practitioner nurses (for a limited selection of POMs)
- optometrist independent prescribers (not for Controlled Drugs, or parenteral medicines)
- podiatrist
- physiotherapist
- therapeutic radiographer independent prescribers (for certain medicines see section 3.3.15)

There are exemptions to requiring a prescription in some circumstances (see section 3.3.10). Further details about the legal and professional issues associated with POMs are discussed in section 3.3. Some medicines can be classified under more than one category and this can depend upon formulation, strength, quantity, indication or marketing authorisation.

FURTHER READING

Wingfield J, Pitchford K, editors
Dale and Appelbe's Pharmacy and Medicines Law.
11th edition. 2017. London; Pharmaceutical Press.
www.pharmpress.com/

3.2
Professional and legal issues: pharmacy medicines

3.2.1
PSEUDOEPHEDRINE AND EPHEDRINE

Pseudoephedrine and ephedrine are widely-used decongestant pharmacy medicines.

- It is unlawful to supply a product or combination of products that contain more than 720mg of pseudoephedrine OR 180mg of ephedrine at any one time, without a prescription (Regulation 237 of *Human Medicines Regulations 2012*)

- It is unlawful to sell or supply any pseudoephedrine product at the same time as an ephedrine product without a prescription (Regulation 237 of *Human Medicines Regulations 2012*).

However, due to their potential for misuse in the illicit production of methylamphetamine (crystal meth) – a class A Controlled Drug – there are legal restrictions on the quantities that can be sold or supplied without prescription. A class A drug is associated with the most severe penalties for possession and dealing.

SIGNS OF POSSIBLE MISUSE

The following signs in combination can be useful for identifying when a request is more likely to be suspicious:

- **Lack of symptoms**
  Not suffering from cough, cold or flu symptoms, or unable to describe these in the patient if buying for someone else

- **Rehearsed Answers**
  Gives answers that appear to be rehearsed or scripted

- **Impatient Or Aggressive**
  In a rush or hurrying to complete the transaction

- **Opportunistic**
  Waiting for busy periods in the shop or until less experienced staff are available

- **Specific Products**
  Wants certain brands that contain only pseudoephedrine or ephedrine

- **Paraphernalia**
  Wishes also to purchase other items which can be used to manufacture methylamphetamine (e.g. lithium batteries, chemicals such as acetone)

- **Quantities**
  Requests large quantities

- **Frequency**
  Makes frequent requests

Sales or supplies of pseudoephedrine or ephedrine should either be made personally by the pharmacist or by pharmacy staff who have been trained and are competent to deal with pseudoephedrine and ephedrine issues, and who know when it is necessary to refer to the pharmacist.

Even when a request is made for a lawful quantity, the sale or supply can be refused where there are reasonable grounds for suspecting misuse. A person purchasing pseudoephedrine and ephedrine for illicit purposes may not be a 'user' of methylamphetamine and, therefore, may not conform to stereotypes. They may be of any gender and of any age or background.

Suspicions can be reported to your local GPhC inspector, local Controlled Drugs liaison police officer or accountable officer.

FURTHER READING

Royal Pharmaceutical Society
Pseudoephedrine and ephedrine –
quick reference guide.
www.rpharms.com

3.2.2
ORAL EMERGENCY CONTRACEPTIVES AS PHARMACY MEDICINES

Levonorgestrel 1500 microgram tablet and ulipristal acetate 30mg tablet are licensed as pharmacy medicines for emergency hormonal contraception (EHC). Levonorgestrel is licensed for women aged 16 years or over for emergency contraception within 72 hours of unprotected sexual intercourse or failure of a contraceptive method. Ulipristal acetate is licensed for emergency contraception within 120 hours (five days) of unprotected sexual intercourse or failure of a contraceptive method. The pharmacist should be involved in assessing suitability and approving sales.

ADVANCE SUPPLY OF ORAL EHC

Pharmacists can provide an advance supply of oral emergency contraception (i.e. prior to unprotected sexual intercourse or in case of failure of a contraceptive method) to a patient requesting it at a pharmacy. The patient should be assessed to ensure that they are competent, they intend to use the medicine appropriately and it is clinically appropriate.

RELIGIOUS OR MORAL BELIEFS

The GPhC have published regulatory guidance on the provision of pharmacy services affected by religious or moral beliefs (see appendix 7).

If your religious or moral beliefs impact on your willingness to supply oral emergency contraception, inform your employer, your locum agency and colleagues you will be working with, as soon as possible.

The GPhC practice guidance on religion, personal values and moral beliefs describes the factors to consider if a patient requests a supply of oral emergency contraception and the questions you should ask yourself so you can ensure patient-centred care. Referral is an option but may not always be possible. The GPhC have outlined factors to consider when deciding whether a referral is appropriate.

Employers and pharmacy professionals need to work together to consider a broad range of situations.

VULNERABLE ADULTS AND CHILDREN

Be aware that, in some circumstances, requests for EHC could be linked to abuse (non-consensual intercourse) of children or vulnerable adults. The Department of Health has published a document called Responding to domestic abuse: A handbook for health professionals, which provides practical advice on dealing with domestic abuse, keeping records, confidentiality and sharing information.

The Department for Education has published a guidance document called Working together to safeguard children, which includes sections for health professionals and on referral.

The supply of ulipristal acetate to patients under the age of 16 years is not contraindicated by the manufacturer. However, pharmacists may wish to consider the following additional factors:

- Children under the age of 13 are legally too young to consent to any sexual activity. Instances should be treated seriously with a presumption that the case should be reported to social services, unless there are exceptional circumstances backed by documented reasons for not sharing information

- Sexual activity with children under the age of 16 is also an offence but may be consensual. The law is not intended to prosecute mutually agreed sexual activity between young people of a similar age, unless it involves abuse or exploitation.

- Pharmacists can provide contraception or sexual health advice to a child under the age of 16 and the general duty of patient confidentiality applies, so where there is a decision to share information, consent should be sought whenever possible prior to disclosing patient information. This duty is not absolute and information may be shared if you judge on a case-by-case basis that sharing is in the child's best interest (e.g. to prevent harm to the child or where the child's welfare overrides the need to keep information confidential). Remember that it is possible to seek advice from experts without disclosing identifiable details of a child and breaking patient confidentiality – and that where there is a decision to share information, this should be proportionate.

OTHER MECHANISMS FOR SUPPLY

There are various mechanisms for the supply of EHC and it may be appropriate to refer to other service providers rather than make a sale, in some circumstances (e.g. where a sale would be outside of the terms of the marketing authorisation). Other providers include family planning clinics, general practice clinics and providers of PGDs for EHC and genitourinary medicine (GUM) clinics.

The quick reference guide Oral Emergency Contraceptives as Pharmacy Medicines can be used to obtain relevant information to determine whether supply is appropriate or not. The guidance also includes advice that can be given to a patient after a supply has been made. It is available on the RPS website at: www.rpharms.com/resources

FURTHER READING

Department for Education
Working together to safeguard children. 2018.
www.gov.uk

Department of Health
Responding to domestic abuse: a resource for health professionals. 2017.
www.gov.uk/government/publications/domestic-abuse-a-resource-for-health-professionals

Faculty of Sexual and Reproductive Healthcare
Various online resources available.
www.fsrh.org

Family Planning Association
Law on sex factsheet. 2015.
www.fpa.org.uk

General Pharmaceutical Council
Guidance on consent. 2018.
www.pharmacyregulation.org
(see MEP Appendix 4)

General Pharmaceutical Council
Guidance on patient confidentiality. 2018.
www.pharmacyregulation.org
(see MEP Appendix 3)

National Institute for Health and Care Excellence
*Contraceptive services for under 25s.
Public health guideline.* 2014.
www.nice.org.uk

National Institute for Health and Care Excellence
Domestic violence and abuse: multi-agency working. Public health guideline. 2014.
www.nice.org.uk

National Society for the Prevention of Cruelty to Children
Various online resources available.
www.nspcc.org.uk The society also has a helpline (Tel: 0808 800 5000).

Scottish Government
National Guidance. Underage sexual activity: meeting the needs of children and young people and identifying child protection concerns. 2010.
www.gov.scot

Scottish Government
National Guidance for Child Protection in Scotland: Guidance for Health Professionals in Scotland
www.gov.scot/publications/national-guidance-child-protection-scotland-guidance-health-professionals-scotland/

3.2.3
PARACETAMOL AND ASPIRIN

Paracetamol and aspirin are medicinal products that are available in a range of formulations, strengths and packaged quantities. They have marketing authorisations as POM, P and GSL medicines – depending upon pack size and formulation. Table 1 illustrates the quantities of paracetamol and aspirin that can be sold legally.

TABLE 1: PARACETAMOL AND ASPIRIN –
OTC LEGAL RESTRICTIONS

	LEGAL RESTRICTION	ADDITIONAL NOTE
PARACETAMOL	Not more than 100 non effervescent* tablets or capsules can be sold to a person at any one time. Since most OTC pack sizes are for 16 or 32 dose units, this means that, in practice, 96 is the maximum number that can be sold.	There are no legal limits on the quantity of over-the-counter effervescent* tablets, powders, granules or liquids that can be sold to a person at any one time. Use professional judgement to decide the appropriate quantity to supply and what limits to impose.
ASPIRIN	Not more than 100 non-effervescent* tablets or capsules can be sold to a person at any one time. Since most OTC pack sizes are for 16 or 32 dose units, this means that, in practice, 96 is the maximum number that can be sold.	There are no legal limits on the quantities of over-the-counter effervescent* tablets or powders that can be sold to a person at any one time. Use professional judgement to decide the appropriate quantity to supply and what limits to impose.

*NB: The definition of effervescent for the purposes of the restrictions above is provided by medicines legislation. Soluble or dispersible formulations as defined by the British Pharmacopoeia may not meet the definition of effervescent in medicines legislation. Where in doubt, quantities of soluble or dispersible formulations sold should be restricted as non-effervescent preparations.

3.2.4
CODEINE AND DIHYDROCODEINE

There are tighter controls and warnings on packaging of OTC solid dose medicines (e.g. tablets and capsules) containing codeine or dihydrocodeine. These were introduced to minimise the risk of overuse and addiction to these medicines. The changes include:

- **Indications**
  Indications for solid dose OTC codeine and dihydrocodeine products are now restricted to the short-term treatment of acute, moderate pain that is not relieved by paracetamol, ibuprofen or aspirin alone. All other previous indications, including cold, flu, cough, sore throats and minor pain have been removed

- **Pack sizes**
  Any pack containing more than 32 dose units (including effervescent formulations) is a POM.

- **Patient information leaflet and labels**
  The warning 'Can cause addiction. For three days use only' must be positioned in a prominent clear position on the front of the pack. In addition, both the PIL and packaging must state the indication and that the medicine can cause addiction or headache if used continuously for more than three days. The PIL must also contain information about the warning signs of addiction.

We support these tighter controls and recommend that only one pack of OTC medication containing codeine or dihydrocodeine should be sold, as sale of more than one pack would undermine the reduction in pack size and POM restriction on packs containing more than 32 dose units.

3.2.5
RECLASSIFIED MEDICINES

More medicines are being reclassified from POM to P, providing pharmacists with a larger range of medicines to select from to treat patients. It is important that pharmacists and pharmacy support staff involved in the sale of medicines are appropriately trained to support patients with the medicines that they need.

FURTHER READING

Guidance for the following reclassified medicines are available from the RPS website www.rpharms.com:

- Amorolfine nail lacquer
- Anti-malarials as Pharmacy medicines
- Chloramphenicol eye drops and eye ointment
- Emergency contraceptives
- Mometasone 0.05% nasal spray
- Proton pump inhibitors
- Oral lidocaine-containing products for teething in children
- Orlistat
- Sildenafil
- Sumatriptan
- Tamsulosin
- Tranexamic acid

3.3
Professional and legal issues: prescription-only medicines

3.3.1
GENERAL PRESCRIPTION REQUIREMENTS

The sale, supply and administration of prescription-only medicines (POMs) are restricted by the Human Medicines Regulations 2012. A pharmacist is able to sell or supply a POM under the authority of a prescription from an appropriate practitioner (for example, a doctor, dentist, supplementary prescriber, independent prescriber or community practitioner nurse, etc), or via an exemption (see section 3.3.9 and 3.3.10). A full list of different types of appropriate practitioner, prescribing restrictions and checking registration can be found in sections 3.3.15 and 3.3.16. Information on requirements for prescriptions issued by prescribers registered in an EEA country or Switzerland can be found in section 3.3.5.

NB: The additional prescription requirements for Controlled Drugs are discussed in section 3.6.7.

Several pieces of information must be present for a prescription to be legal (Regulation 217 and 218 Human Medicines Regulations 2012). These are specified in Diagram 7.

DIAGRAM 7: PRESCRIPTION REQUIREMENTS

Pharmacy Stamp	Age 7 AGE D.o.B.	Title, Forename, Surname & Address: 5 PATIENT NAME 6 PATIENT ADDRESS
Please don't stamp over age box		
Number of days' treatment NB Ensure dose is stated		NHS Number:
Endorsements		

Signature of Prescriber 1 SIGNATURE OF PRESCRIBER	Date 3 DATE
For dispenser No. of Prescns. on form 4 PARTICULARS OF PRESCRIBER 2 ADDRESS OF PRESCRIBER	

NHS

1 **Signature**
Prescriptions need to be signed in ink by an appropriate practitioner (see sections 3.1.3 and 3.3.15) in his or her own name. An 'advanced electronic signature' can be used to authorise an electronic prescription (see Advanced Electronic Signature)

2 **Address**
Prescriptions must include the address of the appropriate practitioner

3 **Date**
A prescription is valid for up to six months from the appropriate date (for prescriptions for Schedules 2, 3 or 4 Controlled Drugs, see section 3.6.7). For an NHS prescription, the appropriate date is the later of either the date on which the prescription was signed or a date indicated by the appropriate practitioner as the date before which it should not be dispensed. For private prescriptions, the appropriate date will always be the date on which it was signed

4 **Particulars**
Prescriptions require particulars that indicate the type of appropriate practitioner

5 **Name of the patient**

6 **Address of the patient**

7 **AGE OF THE PATIENT**
If under 12 years

NOTE

- **Indelible**
Prescriptions need to be written in indelible ink, for example they may be computer generated or typed.

- **Private prescriptions**
Diagram 7 shows the image of an NHS prescription; however, the same requirements apply to private prescriptions.

- **Carbon copies**
It is permissible to issue carbon copies of NHS prescriptions as long as they are signed in ink.

See section 3.3.5 for EEA and Swiss prescription requirements.

ADVANCED ELECTRONIC SIGNATURE

An advanced electronic signature is a signature that is linked uniquely to the signatory, capable of identifying the signatory and created using means over which the signatory can maintain sole control (Regulation 219(5) Human Medicines Regulations 2012). The RPS is unable to confirm whether or not individual systems are able to issue advanced electronic signatures. Suitable assurances should be obtained from the system manufacturer and business indemnity providers.

ELECTRONIC PRESCRIPTIONS

Detailed information on existing electronic prescription systems is available from the following websites:

NHS Digital
Electronic Prescription Service (EPS)
www.digital.nhs.uk/

Pharmaceutical Services Negotiating Committee (PSNC)
Electronic Prescription Service (EPS)
www.psnc.org.uk

NHS Education for Scotland
Electronic Transfer of Prescriptions (ETP)
Implementation Pack to Support eAMS
www.nes.scot.nhs.uk

NHS England
Electronic Repeat Dispensing Guidance. 2015.
www.england.nhs.uk

EPS AND CDS

At the time of writing, the national roll out of CDs in EPS was underway. Further information on this can be viewed on the NHS Digital website https://digital.nhs.uk/services/electronic-prescription-service/controlled-drugs#summary

The PSNC has published information on EPS and CDs including a FAQ factsheet on dispensing and supplying CDs via EPS http://psnc.org.uk/dispensing-supply/eps/dispensing-in-eps-release-2/eps-legality-and-scope/eps-and-controlled-drugs/

DISPENSING A PRESCRIPTION IN WELSH LANGUAGE

Medicines legislation describes the requirements which need to be on a legally valid prescription. Language is not specified. There is currently no law or act that specifies that prescriptions in Wales have to be bilingual.

If the pharmacist is not a Welsh speaker and can't understand the prescription, the RPS advice is to put patient safety first.

The pharmacist is responsible for finding the best way to help the patient. If the pharmacist is presented with a prescription they do not fully understand, this might be through translation services or informal networks. Some local health boards use LanguageLine.

In the interests of patient safety, the RPS Welsh Pharmacy Board recommends that medicines should be labelled in english to ensure that if a patient is seen by a non-welsh speaker these important instructions are understood.

FURTHER READING

Royal Pharmaceutical Society
Use of the Welsh language in pharmacy – quick reference guide.
www.rpharms.com

PRESCRIPTIONS FROM THE CROWN DEPENDENCIES (JERSEY, GUERNSEY AND ISLE OF MAN)

Pharmacists may be presented with prescriptions written by prescribers from the Crown Dependencies (Jersey, Guernsey and Isle of Man).

You should be satisfied that all prescription requirements (see diagram 7, section 3.3.1) are present for the prescription to be legally valid. Please note: Prescriptions for Schedule 2 and 3 CDs, the prescriber's address must be within the UK (see diagram 12 , section 3.6.7).

A report published by the GMC "*GMC regulation in Crown Dependencies and other overseas territories*" www.gmc-uk.org advises the following: "*Crown Dependencies such as the Channel Islands and Isle of Man are not part of the UK. We have nevertheless established agreements* with those territories to facilitate the revalidation of doctors within their jurisdiction using local system." Therefore, doctors from Crown Dependencies are expected to be registered with GMC.

Details on checking registration of healthcare professionals can be found in section 3.3.16.

Requests for emergency supply from a patient or prescriber should be considered on a case by case basis considering the legal requirements as detailed in section 3.3.10.2 and using your professional judgement in the best interests of the patient.

PRESCRIPTION FORMS

Details of prescription forms which are allowed and not allowed on the NHS in England and Wales is available on PSNC website at https://psnc.org.uk/ (search for 'Is this prescription form valid').

For Scotland contact Community Pharmacy Scotland www.cps.scot/ for information.

REPEATABLE PRESCRIPTIONS

Repeatable prescriptions are private prescriptions which contain a direction that they can be dispensed more than once e.g. "repeat x 5".

They are commonly used in the community, hospital (where a prescriber can issue a private prescription in a private hospital or NHS hospital providing private services) and the homecare setting.

This section relates to repeatable prescriptions where a prescriber has added a direction for a prescription to be repeated. Repeatable prescriptions are commonly found on private prescriptions; FP10, WP10, and GP10 type NHS prescriptions are not used in this way. For information about veterinary prescriptions see section 3.5.

Repeatable prescriptions can be repeated as indicated by the prescriber.

If a number is not stated, they can only be repeated once (dispensed twice) unless the prescription is for an oral contraceptive in which case it can be repeated five times (dispensed six times in total)

- Prescriptions for Schedule 2 and 3 CDs are not repeatable; however, those for Schedule 4 and 5 are repeatable

- The first dispensing must be made within six months of the appropriate date, following which there is no legal time limit for the remaining repeats

- If the prescription is for a Schedule 4 CD, the first dispensing must be made within 28 days of the appropriate date, following which there is no time limit for remaining repeats

While there is no time limit for remaining repeats, pharmacists should use professional judgement, taking into consideration clinical factors, to determine whether further repeat dispensing is appropriate. The patient can choose to have repeats dispensed from different pharmacies and can retain the prescription. To maintain an audit trail mark on the prescription the name and address of the pharmacy from where supply has been made and the date of supply.

Prisons and other residential custodial secure environments in England provide NHS healthcare and pharmacy services to detained people. FP10 forms are not used for routine prescribing as a customised prescription form, generated by the clinical IT system, is used instead, however these are still considered a NHS prescription. FP10s are available in these settings but are only used to access urgent medicines (e.g. out of hours) or are supplied to a released person to access medicines that couldn't be supplied to them on release. Therefore the NHS repeat dispensing scheme using FP10s or EPS cannot be used. Further information about how medicines are handled in secure environments can be found in the RPS Professional Standards Optimising Medicines in Secure Environments www.rpharms.com.

The word 'repeat' is also used in various contexts in relation to prescribing and dispensing:

- **Repeat slips**
These are not prescriptions, themselves, but a list of medications which patients can use to reorder their regular medication.

- **Instalment prescriptions**
These provide for a single prescription for a CD to be dispensed in several instalments (see section 3.6.7).

- **NHS repeat dispensing service**
Where the prescriber authorises a prescription with a specified number of 'batch' issues that may be

dispensed at specified intervals from a pharmacy (England and Wales only).

VALIDITY OF OWINGS ON PRESCRIPTIONS

Medicines must be supplied within a certain period from the appropriate date (i.e. the date on which the prescription was signed by the prescriber or the date indicated as being the start date), therefore any owed medicines should be supplied within this validity period.

Table 2 summarises the validity of owings on NHS and private prescriptions (please note that this table does not cover repeatable prescriptions, NHS repeat dispensing prescriptions in England and Wales or CDs instalment prescriptions).

RECORD KEEPING

Private prescriptions for a POM must be retained for two years from the date of the sale or supply or for repeatable prescriptions from the date of the last sale or supply. Private prescriptions for Schedule 2 and 3 CDs must be submitted to the relevant NHS agency (for further information see section 3.6.7). Records must be made in the POM register (written or electronically), which should be retained for two years from the date of the last entry in the register. The record must include:

- **Supply date**
  The date on which the medicine was sold or supplied

- **Prescription date**
  The date on the prescription

- **Medicine details**
  The name, quantity, formulation and strength of medicine supplied (where not apparent from the name)

- **Prescriber details**
  The name and address of the practitioner

- **Patient details**
  The name and address of the patient.

The record should be made on the day the sale or supply takes place or if that is not practical, on the next day following.

Prescriptions for oral contraceptives are exempt from record keeping; as are prescriptions for Schedule 2 CDs where a separate CD register record has been made (see section 3.6.11).

Appendix 3 of the Records Management Code of Practice for Health and Social Care 2016 guide provides detail on how long records should be retained, either due to their ongoing administrative value or as a result of statutory requirement https://digital.nhs.uk/binaries/content/assets/legacy/pdf/n/b/records-management-cop-hsc-2016.pdf

INCOMPLETE PRESCRIPTIONS

Although details of the medicinal product, such as name strength, form, quantity and dose are not legal requirements for POM prescriptions, they are important to identify which medicine to supply, how much to supply and at what dose. They are also important from a pricing and remuneration perspective.

Information on endorsing incomplete prescriptions is available from:

- **England**
  Pharmaceutical Services Negotiating Committee (PSNC) Alphabetical Guide to Prescription Endorsement for Pharmacy Contractors Quick Reference Guide
  https://psnc.org.uk/

TABLE 2: VALIDITY OF OWINGS ON NHS AND PRIVATE PRESCRIPTIONS

MEDICINE	VALIDITY OF OWINGS
POMS AND CDS SCHEDULE 5	Six months from the appropriate date (see 'Date' in Diagram 7, section 3.3.1)
P AND GSL MEDICINES	Six months from the appropriate date (see 'Date' in Diagram 7, section 3.3.1)*
SCHEDULE 2, 3 AND 4 CDS	28 days after the appropriate date (see 'Date' in Diagram 12, section 3.6.7)

Please note this is a professional requirement.

- **Scotland**

  Community Pharmacy Scotland Endorsing Guidance for electronic and paper prescriptions www.cps.scot/

- **Wales**

  Shared Services Partnership Alphabetical Guide to Prescription Endorsement www.primarycareservices.wales.nhs.uk/ pharmacy-services

PRESCRIPTIONS FOR DISCHARGED PRISONERS
ENGLAND

FP10 prescriptions are not allowed for patients while they are in prison (unless authorised by the Prison Trust). However, those who are about to be discharged from prison without the usual methods for ensuring continuity of supply of their medicines (e.g. those released unexpectedly from court, those who fail to obtain a take-out supply of their medicines or those who fail to obtain a same or next day prescribing appointment with a drug treatment agency) can be given an FP10 or FP10[MDA] prescription to take to their community pharmacy.

These FP10 forms have the name and address of the prison printed on them and the patient is exempt from payment by virtue of having HMP in the address.

For more information, the Department of Health has produced guidance entitled Provision of FP10 and FP10[MDA] prescription forms by HM Prison Service for released prisoners (available under National Archives at https://webarchive.nationalarchives. gov.uk/20081108134040/http://www.dh.gov.uk/ en/Publicationsandstatistics/Publications/ PublicationsPolicyAndGuidance/DH_083474

FALSIFIED MEDICINES DIRECTIVE (FMD)

The EU Falsified Medicines Directive (FMD) legislation aims to create a system that ensures medicines supplied in the UK are safe. It ensures the trade in medicines is controlled to reduce the risk of fake medicines entering the medicines supply chain and reaching patients.

Delegated Regulation to the FMD came into force on 9th February 2019. It includes new security features on individual packs and a new electronic scanning authentication process to be undertaken at the point of dispensing.

FMD will affect every pharmacist in the NHS and private sector who dispenses, handles or supplies POMs.

Further information on this can be viewed on the FMD hub on RPS website www.rpharms.com. The 'Joint statement from the RPS and GPhC on the safety features under coming into force' (8th Feb 2019) can be viewed on the RPS website www.rpharms.com

3.3.2
FAXED PRESCRIPTIONS

A fax of a prescription does not fall within the definition of a legally valid prescription within human medicines legislation because it is not written in indelible ink and has not been signed in ink by an appropriate practitioner.

Supplying medicines against a fax is associated with considerable risks:

1. Uncertainty that the supply has been made in accordance with a legally valid prescription

2. Risks of poor reproduction

3. Risks of non-receipt of the original prescription and therefore inability to demonstrate that a supply had been made in accordance with a prescription

4. Risks that the original prescription is subsequently amended by the prescriber in which case the supply would not have been made in accordance with the prescription

5. Risks the fax is sent to multiple pharmacies and duplicate supplies are made.

6. Risks that the prescription is not genuine

7. Risks that the system of sending and receiving of the fax is not secure

Alternative mechanisms for the supply of medicines in an emergency exist for pharmacists working in registered pharmacies and can achieve a similar outcome in many scenarios with a better risk profile. Where this option can be used, it should be used.

Electronic prescriptions are also recognised in Human Medicines Regulations 2012 and where a system is being developed should be considered as an option.

Pharmacists considering supplying medicines against a fax should make an informed decision and take steps to safeguard patient safety, and where possible mitigate the risks identified above. Where appropriate, you should consider making a record of the decision-making process and your reasons leading to a particular course of action. The supply of Schedule 2 and 3 CDs without possession of a lawful prescription could be prosecuted as a criminal offence.

FURTHER READING

See the news story 'Health and Social Care Secretary bans fax machines in NHS' www.gov.uk/government/news/health-and-social-care-secretary-bans-fax-machines-in-nhs

3.3.3
DENTAL PRESCRIPTIONS

Dentists can legally write prescriptions for any POM. The General Dental Council advises that dentists should restrict their prescribing to areas in which they are competent and generally only prescribe medicines that have uses in dentistry.

When prescribing on an NHS dental prescription, dentists are restricted to the medicines listed in the Dental Prescribers' Formulary (Part 8a of the Drug Tariff for Scotland or Part XVIIa of the Drug Tariff for England and Wales). The dental formulary is also reproduced within the British National Formulary.

3.3.4
FORGED PRESCRIPTIONS

Although it can be difficult to detect a forged prescription, every pharmacist should be alert to the possibility that any prescription could be a forgery.

The following checklist may be useful to help detect fraudulent prescriptions and prompt further investigation:

- Is a large or excessive quantity prescribed and is this appropriate for the medicine and condition being treated?

- Is the prescriber known?

- Is the patient known?

- Has the title 'Dr' been inserted before the signature?

- Is the behaviour of the patient indicative? (e.g. nervous, agitated, aggressive, etc.)

- Is the medicine known to be commonly misused?

Further investigation may be necessary. The following are appropriate actions to take:

1 Scrutinise the signature carefully – possibly checking against a known genuine prescription from the same prescriber

2 Confirm details with the prescriber (e.g. whether or not a prescription has been issued, the original intention of the prescriber and whether or not there has been an alteration)

3 Use contact details for the prescriber that are obtained from a source other than the suspicious prescription (e.g. directory enquiries)

REPORTING CONCERNS
Depending upon the nature of the fraudulent prescription, use your professional judgement to assess whether or not it is a matter that requires referral to the police, NHS Counter Fraud Services (for NHS prescriptions only) or whether the matter can be resolved by discussions with the patient and prescriber.

FURTHER READING

NHS Counter Fraud Authority (England)
www.nhsbsa.nhs.uk/protect.aspx

NHS Scotland Counter Fraud Services
www.cfs.scot.nhs.uk

NHS Wales Counter Fraud Service
www.nwssp.wales.nhs.uk/counter-fraud

3.3.5
PRESCRIPTIONS FROM THE EEA OR SWITZERLAND

Prescriptions and repeatable prescriptions issued by an appropriate practitioner registered in an EEA country or Switzerland are legally recognised in the UK. Emergency supplies for patients of these healthcare professionals registered are also permitted.

LIST OF EEA COUNTRIES

Austria, Belgium, Bulgaria, Croatia, Cyprus, Czech Republic, Denmark, Estonia, Finland, France, Germany, Greece, Hungary, Iceland, Republic of Ireland, Italy, Latvia, Liechtenstein, Lithuania, Luxembourg, Malta, Netherlands, Norway, Poland, Portugal, Romania, Slovakia, Slovenia, Spain, Sweden.

PRESCRIPTION REQUIREMENTS
The following details are required on a prescription:

- **Patient details**
  Patient's full first name(s), surname and date of birth

- **Prescriber Details**
  Prescriber's full first name(s), surname, professional qualifications, direct contact details including email address and telephone or fax number (with international prefix), work address (including the country they work in)

- **Prescribed medicine(s) details**
  Name of the medicine (brand name where appropriate), pharmaceutical form, quantity, strength and dosage details

- **Prescriber signature**

- **Date of issue**
  Valid for up to six months from the appropriate date (prescriptions for Schedule 4 CDs 28 days). For prescriptions from these countries the appropriate date is the date on which the prescription was signed.

Please note:
Even if the prescription requirements have been written in a foreign language the prescription is still legally acceptable. However, the pharmacist needs to have enough information to enable the *safe supply of medicines considering patient care and wellbeing.*

MEDICINES NOT AVAILABLE ON AN EEA PRESCRIPTION
Schedule 1, 2 and 3 CDs and medicinal products without a marketing authorisation valid in the UK, cannot be dispensed in the UK when prescribed on an EEA prescription. Consider referral to an appropriate UK-registered prescriber if such items are requested.

CHECKING THE REGISTRATION STATUS OF EEA OR SWISS PRESCRIBER
A pan-EEA database of prescribers does not exist and, indeed, not all of the other EEA countries have a register of practitioners or online registers in English. Therefore, it may not always be possible to check the registration of an EEA or Swiss prescriber. However, up-to-date contact details for EEA competent authorities to check registration details of the following healthcare professionals can be obtained from:

- **Doctors**
  General Medical Council (GMC)
  www.gmc-uk.org/registration-and-licensing/ join%20the%20register/eea-countries

- **Dentists**
  General Dental Council (GDC)
  www.gdc-uk.org
  (search for 'List of EEA competent authorities')

- **Nurses**
  Nursing and Midwifery Council (NMC)
  www.nmc.org.uk
  (search for 'Trained in the EU or EEA')

INABILITY TO CONFIRM REGISTRATION STATUS
If it is not possible to confirm the registration status of the EEA prescriber after taking all reasonable steps to do so, then it may still be possible to make a safe and legal supply in the interests of patient care. It would be beneficial to keep a record of the details of any interventions and steps taken. This would require checking (and being satisfied) that prescription requirements are fulfilled, questioning the patient and careful use of professional judgement. A due diligence defence exists for EEA prescriptions. However, only a court could decide, ultimately on a

case-by-case basis, whether due diligence has been exercised.

EMERGENCY SUPPLY

Emergency supplies at the request of a patient, or at the request of the EEA or Swiss prescriber, are legally possible. The usual emergency supply process (see section 3.3.10.2) should be used and, where the request originates from an EEA prescriber, then a prescription needs to be received within 72 hours. Remember that Schedule 1, 2 and 3 CDs (including phenobarbital) cannot be supplied to a patient. A Schedule 4 and 5 CD can be supplied as an emergency supply to a patient of an EEA or Swiss prescriber.

REFERRAL

It is important to bear in mind that the legislation outlined above is enabling – it is not obligatory to dispense an EEA or Swiss prescription if presented with one. If a pharmacist is not satisfied that a prescription is clinically appropriate, or legally valid, and an emergency supply is not appropriate, then a valid alternative remains to refer the patient to a prescriber based in the UK.

FURTHER READING

GOV.UK
Guidance on prescriptions issued in the EEA and Switzerland: guidance for pharmacist (this guidance came into place from 12th April 2019 if UK left the EU with no deal). www.gov.uk/guidance/prescriptions-issued-in-the-eea-and-switzerland-guidance-for-pharmacists?utm_source=589bed95-15b7-4039-9122-d430802b7890&utm_medium=email&utm_campaign=govuk-notifications&utm_content=immediate

3.3.6
MILITARY PRESCRIPTIONS

Military primary healthcare medical centres are broadly similar to Dispensing Doctors practices in the NHS, where the doctor in charge delegates the dispensing function to a suitably trained individual. However, only large medical centres have retained their in-house dispensary. The remaining, smaller medical centres have

outsourced the dispensing process to designated community pharmacies under a Ministry of Defence (MOD) contract. Community pharmacies not covered by the contract will not routinely handle military prescriptions.

Military prescriptions are written on a military form FMed 296, see Diagram 8.

Pharmacies with a dispensing contract with the MOD will usually invoice the MOD directly.

DIAGRAM 8: EXAMPLE OF AN FMED 296 PRESCRIPTION

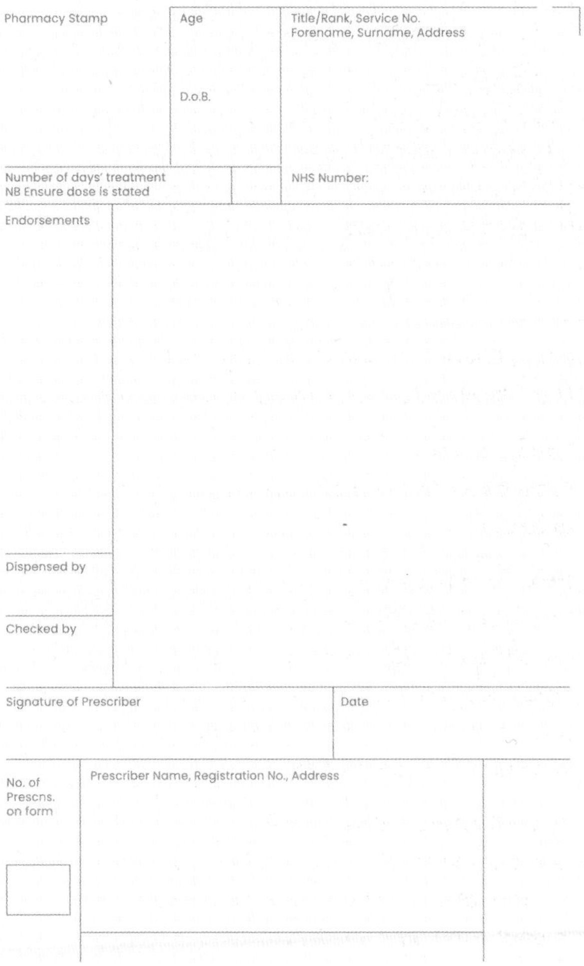

In the unusual event that an FMed 296 is presented to a non-contracted pharmacy, then the prescription should be treated as a private prescription. In these circumstances, non-contracted pharmacies are not to invoice the MOD directly but are to charge the patient the appropriate fee. It is then up to the individual patient to recover any costs incurred from their military unit (please note: this practice should only be used in exceptional circumstances). Similarly, any military personnel that presents an NHS or other private prescription (including using an FMed 296 as a private prescription) should pay the appropriate fee and request a receipt to reclaim any costs, if eligible. This is unless, of course, for an NHS prescription they fall into an NHS exemption category and present an exemption certificate.

All CD prescriptions are written on pink FP10PCD forms (or equivalent in Devolved Administrations, which prescribers obtain from their regional Defence Primary Health Care headquarters supplied by NHS England and NHS Scotland. A CD written on an MOD FMed296 form cannot be legally dispensed by community pharmacies. If there is any doubt to the validity of the FMed 296, normal procedures should be employed (see section 3.3.4). Particular attention should be paid in the following circumstances:

- **Handwritten FMed 296**
The majority of FMed 296 prescriptions will be computer generated. It is highly unusual to see handwritten prescriptions, especially for MOD accountable drugs (these include Schedule 3, 4 and 5 CDs, codeine, sedatives and medicines for erectile dysfunction).

- **British Forces Post Office (BFPO) address stamp**
Prescriptions with a BFPO address stamp have been generated abroad and are normally not seen in the UK. If there is any doubt, pharmacists are advised to check the registration status of the doctor, dentist or independent prescriber (see section 3.3.16).

3.3.7
LABELLING OF DISPENSED MEDICINAL PRODUCTS

It is a legal requirement for the following to appear on dispensed medicinal products:

- Name of the patient

- Name and address of the supplying pharmacy

- Date of dispensing

- Name of the medicine

- Directions for use

- Precautions relating to the use of the medicine.

The RPS recommends the following also appears on the dispensing label:

- 'Keep out of the reach and sight of children'

- 'Use this medicine only on your skin' where applicable.

NB: In secure environments it is strongly recommended that the prisoner number is also included on the label as a definitive patient identifier.

Additional information can be added to the dispensing label if the pharmacist considers it to be necessary.

Outer container
Whilst it is lawful to label the outer container, we advise that the labelling recommendations of the National Patient Safety Agency are followed. These guidelines raise the issue that the outer container may be discarded and, therefore, the labelling information could be lost, so the actual container (e.g. inhaler or tube of cream) should be labelled rather than the outer container.

Optimisation of labelling
Subject to the professional skill and judgement of a pharmacist, if he/she is of the opinion that the directions for use, name or common name of the medicine, or precautions, relating to the use of the medicine, are not appropriate on the prescription, they can substitute these with appropriate particulars of a similar kind when producing the dispensing label without contacting the prescriber.

It would be good practice to make a record to maintain a clinical audit trail underpinning patient care. It is important to understand that the above is enabling and not mandatory. The options to contact the prescriber or refer the patient to the prescriber remain available and should be used where this is appropriate in the opinion of the pharmacist having exercised professional skill and judgement.

Full details can be viewed in 'Optimising Dispensing Labels and Medicines Use – quick reference guide. 2012' on the RPS website at www.rpharms.com

ASSEMBLY AND PRE-PACKING MEDICINES

The assembly or pre-packing of medicines by the pharmacy to be supplied to a separate legal entity (e.g. for a NHS Trust to supply a different NHS Trust or an out of hours medical practice) requires the appropriate licence from the MHRA (i.e. Manufacturer's/importer's licence (MIA)

or Manufacturer 'specials' licence (MS)).
The MHRA can be contacted for further details on the licence and any additional requirements (www.gov.uk/government/organisations/medicines-and-healthcare-products-regulatory-agency).

For activities that include over-labelling for supply, the RPS also advise you contact the MHRA for further details.

LABELLING OF MEDICINES BROKEN DOWN FROM BULK CONTAINERS FOR DISPENSING

Pharmacists are able to break down bulk containers into smaller quantities more appropriate for dispensing against prescriptions which have already been received and are being dispensed or in anticipation of these prescriptions.

For the latter case medicines must be labelled with the:

- Name of the medicine

- Quantity of the medicine in the container

- Quantitative particulars of the medicine (i.e. the ingredients)

- Handling and storage requirements where appropriate

- Expiry date

- Batch reference number (e.g. LOT number or BN).

The medicines which have been broken down from bulk need to be labelled with usual labelling requirements upon dispensing.

If both of the above (Assembly and pre-packing medicines and Labelling of medicines broken down from bulk containers for dispensing) do not apply to you, you should contact the MHRA for further information.

FURTHER READING

Royal Pharmaceutical Society
Professional guidance on the safe and secure handling of medicines.
www.rpharms.com

Medicines and Healthcare products Regulatory Agency
Additional warning statements for inclusion on the label and/or in the leaflet of certain medicines. 2014.
www.gov.uk/government/publications/warning-statements-for-labels-and-leaflets-of-certain-medicines

Medicines and Healthcare products Regulatory Agency
Best practice guidance on the labelling and packaging of medicines. 2014.
www.gov.uk/government/publications/best-practice-in-the-labelling-and-packaging-of-medicines

National Institute for Health and Care Excellence
Patient group directions. Medicines practice guideline. 2013.
www.nice.org.uk

National Patient Safety Agency (archived)
Design for patient safety: a guide to the design of dispensed medicines. 2007.
https://webarchive.nationalarchives.gov.uk

National Patient Safety Agency (archived)
Design for patient safety: a guide to the design of the dispensing environment. 2007.
https://webarchive.nationalarchives.gov.uk

3.3.8
ADMINISTRATION

In healthcare settings organisational policies define who can administer medicines, or the appropriate delegation of the administration of medicines, within that setting.

(Please note: The organisation should have a policy for self administration of medicines. Patients maintain responsibility for the administration of some or all of their medicines, during a stay in the healthcare setting, unless a risk assessment indicates otherwise.)

Registered healthcare professionals who administer medicines, or when appropriate delegate the administration of medicines, are accountable for their actions, non-actions and omissions, and exercise professionalism and professional judgement at all times. They would be expected to meet their own professional and regulatory standards and guidance. Non registered healthcare professionals are appropriately trained, assessed as competent and meet relevant organisational guidance on medicines administration.

Before administration, the person administering the medicine must have an overall understanding of the medicine being administered and seeks advice if necessary from a prescriber or a pharmacy professional.

Parenteral POMs can only be administered to another person in accordance with the directions of an appropriate practitioner or by an appropriate practitioner. There is an exemption allowing administration for saving life in an emergency and a list of parenteral medicines authorised for this purpose can be found in Schedule 19 of The Human Medicines Regulations 2012 (www.legislation.gov.uk)

One example is administering adrenaline injection 1 in 1000 (1mg/ml) for the emergency treatment of anaphylaxis (see section 3.7.15 for further information).

Further exemptions apply to the administration of smallpox vaccine or administration linked to medical exposure (including radioactive medicines).

Specific classes of persons, such as midwives, paramedics and others can also administer POMs under certain conditions. Details are available in Schedule 17 of the Human Medicines Regulations 2012 (as amended). Certain healthcare professionals can also administer medicines in accordance with a Patient Group Direction (see section 3.3.10.1).

Medicines that are not POMs may be administered according to a locally agreed homely remedy protocol (for further information see NICE *Guideline SC1: Managing medicines in care homes* (2014) www.nice.org.uk and the *Regional Medicines Optimisation Committee (Midland and East) Homely Remedies – Position Statement* (2018) www.sps.nhs.uk/articles/rmoc-guidance-homely-remedies/)

COVERT ADMINISTRATION OF MEDICINES

'Covert administration' is the term used when medicines are administered in a disguised format without the knowledge or consent of the person receiving them, for example, in food or in a drink. Medicines are administered covertly only to people

who actively refuse their medication and who are considered to lack mental capacity in accordance with an agreed management plan. Where deemed necessary, covert administration of medicines takes place within the context of existing legal and best practice frameworks. Organisational policies and procedures in place covering covert administration should be followed.

Pharmacists who are asked to sign covert administration documentation should check carefully what they are being asked to sign off as this may indicate they have performed a clinical medication review, and provided advice on how medicines should be administered or what to do if a patient consumes only part of their food or drink.

FURTHER READING

Royal Pharmaceutical Society
Professional guidance on the administration of medicines in healthcare settings. 2019.
www.rpharms.com

Royal Pharmaceutical Society
Professional guidance on the safe and secure handling of medicines.
www.rpharms.com

Mental Welfare Commission for Scotland
Covert Medication. 2017.
www.mwcscot.org.uk/media/140485/covert_medication.pdf

National Institute for Health and Care Excellence
Managing medicines for adults receiving social care in the community. NICE guidance. 2017.
www.nice.org.uk

National Institute for Health and Care Excellence
Medicines management in care homes Social care guideline. 2014.
www.nice.org.uk

National Institute for Health and Care Excellence
Medicines management in care homes Quality Statement 6: Covert administration. 2015.
www.nice.org.uk

National Union of Teachers
Administration of Medicines
www.teachers.org.uk/help-and-advice/

PrescQIPP

Best practice guidance in covert administration of medicines. 2015. www.prescqipp.info/our-resources/bulletins/ bulletin-101-care-homes-covert-administration/

UKMi

What legal and pharmaceutical issues should be considered when administering medicines covertly? 2017. www.sps.nhs.uk/articles/what-legal-and- pharmaceutical-issues-should-be-considered- when-administering-medicines-covertly-2/

3.3.9
PATIENT SPECIFIC DIRECTIONS AND ADMINISTRATION, SALE AND SUPPLY IN HOSPITALS AND OTHER SETTINGS

The Human Medicines Regulations 2012 provides a range of exemptions to the restrictions on the sale, supply and administration of medicines.

A number of these exemptions are collectively described as patient specific directions (PSDs).

Legislation does not specifically define a PSD. However, it is generally accepted to mean a written instruction from a doctor, dentist or other independent prescriber for a medicine to be supplied or administered to a named patient after the prescriber has assessed that patient on an individual basis.

Some organisations may limit who is authorised to supply and/or administer medicines under a PSD within their local medicines policies and governance arrangements. Any trained and competent health professional would be suitable. PSDs relate to a specific named patient but do not need to comply with the requirements specified for a prescription.

In a hospital ward, written PSDs are encountered on inpatient charts as directions to administer. While the law does not stipulate what should be included in a PSD, sufficient information must be available for the person administering the specified medicine to do so safely. In addition a PSD, if sufficiently clear, may also be a direction to make a sale or supply.

Typically the directions within an inpatient chart are copied onto an order form for the pharmacy to prepare discharge ('take home') medicines. The pharmacist in this instance is not prescribing, and the supply is made under the authority of the original written direction to supply. This process should be carried out or counter-checked by a pharmacist. This order form does not replace a discharge letter; however, it can form part of the discharge letter.

For the purpose of administration (rather than supply) it is also possible for the directions of an appropriate practitioner to be verbal or telephoned. This is because not all of the exemptions specify that the authorisation to administer a medicine needs to be in writing. Nevertheless, a written authorisation should be used wherever possible and any applicable standards that require the authorisation to be in writing should be adhered to. For example, in England, the Care Quality Commission fundamental standards, and the standards of any relevant healthcare professionals involved in administration (e.g. nurses) will be applicable.

Some hospitals have formulated policies to permit, in an emergency, the administration of medicines following a telephoned or verbal request from an appropriate practitioner – usually involving two nurses checking one another.

Some hospitals have also formulated policies for the supply and/or administration of POMs (and P or GSL) to ensure that medicines are handled safely, securely and appropriately. Such policies should be carefully considered and agreed by medical, nursing and pharmacy staff to ensure that patients are not put at risk. The policy should be cross-referenced against standards set by any applicable body, including regulatory and professional bodies of relevant healthcare professionals involved in the process. If in doubt, the Department of Health should be consulted for hospitals in England (along with the hospital's legal advisors). Hospitals in Scotland should contact the Scottish Executive, while hospitals in Wales should contact the Department of Health and Social Services.

FURTHER READING

Royal Pharmaceutical Society
*Professional guidance on the administration
of medicines in healthcare settings. 2019.*
www.rpharms.com

Royal Pharmaceutical Society
*Professional guidance on the safe
and secure handling of medicines.*
www.rpharms.com

British Medical Association
*Patient group directions and patient specific
directions in general practice. 2016.*
www.bma.org.uk

Care Quality Commission
Various online resources available.
www.cqc.org.uk

NHS Education for Scotland
Various online resources available.
www.nes.scot.nhs.uk

Specialist Pharmacy Service
*Medicine matters: A guide to mechanisms
for the prescribing, supply and administration
of medicines (in England). 2018.*
www.sps.nhs.uk/

Specialist Pharmacy Service
Various PSD and PGD resources available.
www.sps.nhs.uk/

3.3.10
EXEMPTIONS: SALE AND SUPPLY WITHOUT A PRESCRIPTION

3.3.10.1 PATIENT GROUP DIRECTIONS

3.3.10.2 EMERGENCY SUPPLY

3.3.10.3 PANDEMIC EXEMPTIONS

3.3.10.4 OPTOMETRIST OR PODIATRIST SIGNED PATIENT ORDERS

3.3.10.5 SUPPLY OF SALBUTAMOL INHALERS TO SCHOOLS

3.3.10.6 SUPPLY OF ADRENALINE AUTOINJECTORS TO SCHOOLS

3.3.10.7 SUPPLY OF NALOXONE BY INDIVIDUALS PROVIDING RECOGNISED DRUG TREATMENT SERVICES

There are several exemptions that allow POMs
to be sold or supplied without a prescription.

**Pharmacists are likely to be involved in many
of these mechanisms and need to be aware of:**

* Patient group directions (PGDs)
* Patient specific directions (PSDs) (see section 3.3.9)
* Emergency supplies
* Pandemic exemptions
* Optometrist or podiatrist signed patient orders
* Supply of salbutamol inhalers to schools
* Supply of adrenaline autoinjectors to schools
* Supply of naloxone by individuals providing recognised drug treatment services

3.3.10.1
PATIENT GROUP DIRECTIONS (PGDS)
A PGD is a written direction that allows the supply
and/or administration of a specified medicine
or medicines, by named authorised health
professionals, to a well-defined group of patients
requiring treatment for a specific condition.

It is important that pharmacists involved with PGDs
understand the scope and limitations of PGDs
as well as the wider context into which they fit to
ensure safe, effective services for patients.

The supply and administration of medicines under
a PGD should only be reserved for those limited
situations where this offers an advantage for
patient care, without compromising patient safety.

A PGD should only be developed after careful
consideration of all the potential methods of supply
and/or administration of medicines, including
prescribing, by medical or nonmedical prescribers.

Pharmacists can supply, offer to supply and
administer diamorphine or morphine under a PGD
for the immediate, necessary treatment of sick
or injured persons.

FURTHER READING

Medicines and Healthcare products Regulatory Agency
Patient group directions: who can use them. 2017.
www.gov.uk/government/publications/patient-group-directions-pgds

National Institute for Health and Care Excellence
Patient group directions. Medicines practice guidelines (including a PGD template). 2013.
www.nice.org.uk

NHS Education for Scotland
Patient group directions.
www.nes.scot.nhs.uk

Specialist Pharmacy Service
Various online PGD resources available.
www.sps.nhs.uk/

3.3.10.2
EMERGENCY SUPPLY

In an emergency a pharmacist working in a registered pharmacy can supply POMs to a patient (humans not animals) without a prescription on the request of a 'relevant prescriber' or a patient (conditions apply, see below).

Each request should be considered on a case-by-case basis, using professional judgement in the best interests of the patient.

A 'relevant prescriber' includes:

- A doctor

- A dentist

- A supplementary prescriber

- A nurse independent prescriber

- A pharmacist independent prescriber

- A community practitioner nurse prescriber

- A physiotherapist independent prescriber

- A podiatrist independent prescriber

- A therapeutic radiographer independent prescriber

- An optometrist independent prescriber

- An EEA or Swiss health professional.

- A paramedic independent prescriber

Healthcare professionals from countries outside of the EEA or Switzerland are not recognised as "relevant prescribers" in the United Kingdom.

In Scotland, a national PGD allows participating pharmacies and pharmacists to supply medicines for the urgent provision of current repeat medicines, appliances and ACBS (borderline) items (www.cps.scot/nhs-services/national/unscheduled-care-cpus/). Emergency supply remains an option for patients who are not eligible for treatment under the national PGD.

EMERGENCY SUPPLY AT THE REQUEST OF A PRESCRIBER

The conditions for an emergency supply at the request of a prescriber are:

- **Relevant prescriber**
  The pharmacist is satisfied that the request is from one of the prescribers stated above

- **Emergency**
  The pharmacist is satisfied that a prescription cannot be provided immediately due to an emergency (e.g. patient cannot collect the prescription from the prescriber, the prescriber is unable to drop off prescription at the pharmacy and patient urgently needs the medicine(s), etc.)

- **Prescription within 72 hours**
  The prescriber agrees to provide a written prescription within 72 hours

- **Directions**
  The medicine is supplied in accordance with the direction given by the prescriber

- **Not for CDs, except phenobarbital**
  Schedule 1, 2 or 3 CDs cannot be supplied in an emergency whether requested by UK, EEA or Swiss health professionals. Phenobarbital (also known as phenobarbitone or phenobarbitone sodium) is the exception and can be authorised by UK doctor, dentist, nurse or pharmacist independent prescriber or supplementary prescriber in an emergency for the treatment of epilepsy

- **Record kept**
  An entry must be made into the POM register on the day of the supply (or, if impractical, on the following day). The entry needs to include:

- The date the POM was supplied

- The name (including strength and form where appropriate) and quantity of medicine supplied

- The name and address of the prescriber requesting the emergency supply

- The name and address of the patient for whom the POM was required

- The date on the prescription (this can be added to the entry when the prescription is received by the pharmacy)

- The date on which the prescription is received (this should be added to the entry when the prescription is received in the pharmacy)

- **Labelling**
Usual labelling requirements apply (see section 3.3.7).

EMERGENCY SUPPLY AT THE REQUEST OF A PATIENT
The conditions for an emergency supply at the request of a patient are:

- **Interview**
Regulation 225 Human Medicines Regulations 2012 requires a pharmacist to interview the patient. The RPS recognises that in some circumstances this might not be possible, for example if the patient is a child, or being cared for, etc. In these circumstances the RPS advises pharmacists to use their professional judgement and consider the best interest of the patient

- **Immediate need**
The pharmacist must be satisfied that there is an immediate need for the POM and that it is not practical for the patient to obtain a prescription without undue delay

Legislation does not prevent a pharmacist from making an emergency supply when a doctor's surgery is open. As with any request for an emergency supply, pharmacists must consider the best interests of the patient. Where a pharmacist believes that it would be impracticable in the circumstances for a patient to obtain a prescription without undue delay they may decide that an emergency supply is necessary. Automatically referring patients who are away from home and have forgotten or run out of their medication to the nearest local surgery to register as a temporary

resident may not always be the most appropriate course of action.

- **Previous treatment**
The POM requested must previously have been used as a treatment and prescribed by a UK, EEA or Swiss prescriber listed above.

NB: The time interval from when the medicine was last prescribed to when it is requested as an emergency supply would need to be considered and you should use your professional judgement to decide whether a supply or referral to a prescriber is appropriate

- **Dose**
The pharmacist must be satisfied of knowing the dose that the patient needs to take (e.g. refer to the PMR, electronic health record, prescription repeat slip, labelled medicine box, etc.).

- **Not for CDs, except phenobarbital**
Phenobarbital can be supplied to patients of UK-registered prescribers for the purpose of treating epilepsy. Medicinal products cannot be supplied if they consist of or contain any other Schedule 1, 2 or 3 CDs or the substances listed below: ammonium bromide, calcium bromide, calcium bromidolactobionate, embutramide, fencamfamin hydrochloride, fluanisone, hexobarbitone, hexobarbitone sodium, hydrobromic acid, meclofenoxate hydrochloride, methohexitone sodium, pemoline, piracetam, potassium bromide, prolintane hydrochloride, sodium bromide, strychnine hydrochloride, tacrine hydrochloride, thiopentone sodium

(NB: Requests made by a patient of an EEA or Swiss doctor, dentist, prescribing pharmacist or prescribing nurse cannot be supplied if they are for medicines that do not have a marketing authorisation valid in the UK – see section 3.3.5)

- **Length of treatment**
If the emergency supply is for a CD (i.e. phenobarbital or Schedule 4 or 5 CD), the maximum quantity that can be supplied is for five days' treatment. For any other POM, no more than 30 days can be supplied except in the following circumstances:

  - If the POM is insulin, an ointment, a cream, or an inhaler for asthma (i.e. the packs cannot be broken), the smallest pack available in the pharmacy should be supplied

- If the POM is an oral contraceptive, a full treatment cycle should be supplied

If the POM is an antibiotic in liquid form for oral administration, the smallest quantity that will provide a full course of treatment should be supplied. (NB: Pharmacists should also consider whether it is appropriate to supply less than the maximum quantity allowed in legislation. See RPS AMS Portal for further information www.rpharms.com. Professional judgement should be used to supply a reasonable quantity that is clinically appropriate and lasts until the patient is able to see a prescriber to obtain a further supply)

- **Records kept**

  An entry must be made in the POM register on the day of the supply (or, if impractical, on the following day). The entry needs to include:

  - The date the POM was supplied

  - The name (including strength and form where appropriate) and quantity of medicine supplied

  - The name and address of the patient for whom the POM was supplied

  - Information on the nature of the emergency, such as why the patient needs the POM and why a prescription cannot be obtained, etc.

- **Labelling**

  In addition to standard labelling requirements, the words 'Emergency supply' need to be added to the dispensing label.

OTHER POINTS TO CONSIDER WHEN FACED WITH REQUESTS FOR AN EMERGENCY SUPPLY

Pharmacists should be mindful of patients abusing emergency supplies (for example, where a patient medication record shows that a patient has requested a medicine as an emergency supply on several occasions). It is possible to make an emergency supply even during surgery opening hours; trying to obtain a prescription can sometimes cause undue delay in treatment and, potentially, harm to the patient. If patients are away from home and have run out of their medicines, referring them to the nearest surgery to register as a temporary patient may not always be appropriate. An emergency supply can be made provided the conditions above are met.

REFUSAL TO SUPPLY

If a pharmacist decides not to make an emergency supply after gathering and considering the information discussed in this guidance, the patient should be advised on how to obtain a prescription for the medicine or appropriate medical care. This could involve referral to a doctor, NHS walk-in centre or to an Accident and Emergency department.

A record could be made of why request was refused for audit purposes.

FURTHER READING

Royal Pharmaceutical Society
Electronic health record – ultimate guide (includes Using electronic health records professionally).
www.rpharms.com

Royal Pharmaceutical Society
Emergency supply – quick reference guide.
www.rpharms.com

Royal Pharmaceutical Society
Professional judgement – quick reference guide.
www.rpharms.com

Royal Pharmaceutical Society
Summary care records – England – pharmacy guide.
www.rpharms.com

Amin R.
Emergency supply: law versus ethics.
The Pharmaceutical Journal,
Vol 286, p598, May 01 2011.
www.pharmaceutical-journal.com (URI: 11076311)

3.3.10.3
PANDEMIC EXEMPTIONS

Legislation is in place that relaxes emergency supply requirements in the event of a pandemic or imminent pandemic being declared by the Department of Health. It means that pharmacists would not need to interview the patient who requires a medicine through emergency supply.

Provisions are also in place to allow the supply of medicines against a protocol from designated collection points when a disease is pandemic or imminently pandemic and there is a serious or potentially serious risk to human health. This would require an announcement by the

Department of Health in England, the Scottish Government or the Welsh Government.

These collection points would not need to be registered pharmacy premises and supplies would not need to take place under the supervision of a pharmacist. Further information is available in Regulations 226 and 247 of the *Human Medicines Regulations 2012* (www.legislation.gov.uk)

3.3.10.4
OPTOMETRIST OR PODIATRIST SIGNED PATIENT ORDERS

Optometrists and podiatrists cannot authorise supplies of POMs by writing prescriptions unless they are additionally qualified as independent or supplementary prescribers.

However, pharmacists working in a registered pharmacy can supply certain POMs directly to patients in accordance with a signed patient order from any registered optometrist or podiatrist.

The medicine requested must be one which can be legally sold or supplied by the optometrist or podiatrist rather than one which they can only administer. See MHRA website for list.

Please note: Optometrists who have undertaken additional training and are accredited by the GOC as 'additional supply optometrists' can issue signed patient orders for an extended range of medicines.

The signed patient order is not a prescription; therefore the usual prescription requirements would not be needed. However, you should be satisfied the optometrist or the podiatrist has provided sufficient advice to enable the patient to use the medicine safely and effectively.

If the supply is made, the pharmacist should ensure that the medicine is labelled accordingly as a dispensed medicinal product (see section 3.3.7), a patient information leaflet is supplied to the patient and an appropriate record is made in the POM register.

Any additional information or advice that enables the patient to use the medicine safely and effectively should also be provided if it has not already been provided by the optometrist or podiatrist. Details on how to check the registration of the optometrist or podiatrist can be found in section 3.3.16.

FURTHER READING

Royal Pharmaceutical Society
Medicines that optometrists can order –
quick reference guide.
www.rpharms.com

Royal Pharmaceutical Society
Supply of medicines to podiatrists –
quick reference guide.
www.rpharms.com

College of Optometrists
Use and supply of drugs or medicines
in optometric practice.
https://guidance.college-optometrists.org/home/

Medicines and Healthcare products Regulatory Agency
Rules for the sale, supply and administration
of medicines for specific healthcare
professionals. 2014.
www.gov.uk/government/publications/rules-for-
the-sale-supply-and-administration-of-medicines/
rules-for-the-sale-supply-and-administration-of-
medicines-for-specific-healthcare-professionals

3.3.10.5
SUPPLY OF SALBUTAMOL INHALERS TO SCHOOLS

Since October 2014, schools can hold stocks of salbutamol inhalers. These can then be supplied in an emergency by persons trained to administer them to pupils who are known to require such medication in schools.

WHO CAN PROVIDE A SIGNED ORDER FOR SALBUTAMOL INHALERS FOR A SCHOOL?

A written order signed by the principal or head teacher at the school must be provided to enable a supply to be made to the school.

WHAT INFORMATION SHOULD BE INCLUDED IN THE SIGNED ORDER?

In line with legislation requirements;

"The order must be signed by the principal or head teacher at the school concerned and state

(i) the name of the school for which the medicinal product is required,

(ii) the purpose for which that product is required, and

(iii) the total quantity required"

Ideally, appropriately headed paper should be used; however, this is not a legislative requirement.

HOW MANY INHALERS CAN A SCHOOL OBTAIN?

The number of inhalers that can be obtained by individual schools is not specified in legislation. As part of the consultation process it was acknowledged that the number held for emergency used would be dependent on a variety of factors including; the school size and the number of sites it is comprised of, the number of children known to have asthma, and past experiences of children who had not been able to access their inhaler. It was however agreed, generally that only a small number of inhalers were likely to be needed annually. Schools can purchase salbutamol inhalers from pharmacies provided it is for small quantities, on an occasional basis and not for profit thus in line with MHRA Guidance for pharmacists on the repeal of Section 10(7) of the Medicines Act 1968 (see also section 3.4).

WHAT RECORDS NEED TO BE KEPT IN THE PHARMACY?

The signed order needs to be retained for two years from the date of supply or an entry made into the POM register. Even where the signed order is retained it is good practice to make a record in POM register for audit purposes. In line with normal record keeping requirements an entry in the POM register must include:

* Date the POM was supplied

* Name, quantity and where it is not apparent, formulation and strength of POM supplied

* Name and address, trade, business or profession of the person to whom the medicine was supplied

* The purpose for which it was sold or supplied.

WHAT OTHER INFORMATION COULD I BE ASKED TO PROVIDE?

The pharmacist could be also be asked to:

* Explain how to use a salbutamol inhaler and any associated information

* Advise schools on the selection of the most appropriate spacer device for the different age groups and how to use them correctly

WHAT GUIDANCE IS AVAILABLE FOR SCHOOLS ON THE CHANGES?

The Department of Health has issued guidance outlining the principles of safe use of inhalers to capture the good practice which schools in England should observe (www.gov.uk/government/publications/emergency-asthma-inhalers-for-use-in-schools) and the Welsh Government has issued guidance that schools in Wales should observe (https://gov.wales/use-emergency-salbutamol-inhalers-schools) The guidance covers issues such as arrangements for storage, care and disposal of medication within the school environment. Although these guidance documents are mainly specific for England and Wales the principles of safe usage are, however, universal. Schools in Scotland should contact their own regulator Education Scotland for further guidance on this where required (www.education.gov.scot)

WHERE CAN I LOCATE INFORMATION ON A SCHOOL INCLUDING HEAD TEACHER/PRINCIPAL DETAILS IF REQUIRED?

There is no centralised database containing details of schools and head teachers across Great Britain. Possible sources of information would include:

* Department for Education's register of educational establishments in England and Wales (https://get-information-schools.service.gov.uk/)

* Ofsted reports (www.reports.ofsted.gov.uk)

* Information on the individual school's website.

FURTHER READING

Royal Pharmaceutical Society
Supporting patients with asthma – quick reference guide.
www.rpharms.com

Department for Education
Statutory framework for the early years foundation stage. 2017.
www.foundationyears.org.uk

Department for Education
Supporting pupils at school with medical conditions. 2014.
www.gov.uk

Department of Health
Guidance on the use of emergency salbutamol inhalers in schools. 2015. www.gov.uk

Scottish Executive
Supporting children and young people with healthcare needs in Schools. 2017 www.gov.scot/Publications

Scottish Government
Supporting children and young people with healthcare needs in schools: guidance. 2017. www.gov.scot

Welsh Government
Supporting learners with healthcare needs. 2017. https://gov.wales/sites/default/files/publications/2018-12/supporting-learners-with-healthcare-needs.pdf

Welsh Government
Use of emergency salbutamol inhalers in schools. 2017. https://gov.wales/use-emergency-salbutamol-inhalers-schools

3.3.10.6
SUPPLY OF ADRENALINE AUTO-INJECTORS (AAI) TO SCHOOLS

Since October 2017 schools can purchase AAIs, without a prescription for use in emergencies, from a pharmacy in small quantities provided this takes place on an occasional basis and is not for profit.

WHO CAN PROVIDE A SIGNED ORDER FOR AAIS FOR A SCHOOL?

A written order signed by the principal or head teacher at the school is needed to enable a supply to be made to the school.

WHAT INFORMATION SHOULD BE INCLUDED IN THE SIGNED ORDER?

The order needs to state the name of the school, the purpose for the product and the total quantity required.

Ideally appropriately headed paper should be used, however this is not a legislative requirement.

A suggested letter template to Pharmacy to obtain an AAI for schools is included in the Department of Health Guidance on the use of adrenaline

auto-injectors in schools (www.gov.uk/government/publications/using-emergency-adrenaline-auto-injectors-in-schools).

HOW MANY AAIS CAN A SCHOOL OBTAIN?

The number of AAIs that can be obtained by individual schools is not specified in legislation. Schools will be able to purchase AAIs from a pharmacy in small quantities provided this takes place on an occasional basis and is not for profit, thus in line with MHRA guidance for pharmacists on the repeal of section 10(7) of the Medicines Act 1968. Pharmacists should exercise their professional judgement when responding to requests for AAIs from schools.

WHAT RECORDS DO I NEED TO KEEP IN THE PHARMACY?

The signed order needs to be retained for two years from the date of supply or an entry made into the POM register. Even where the signed order is retained it is good practice to make a record in the POM register for audit purposes.

In line with normal record keeping requirement an entry in the POM register must include:

- Date the POM was supplied

- Name, quantity and where it is not apparent formulation and strength of POM supplied

- Name and address, trade, business or profession of the person to whom the medicine was supplied

- The purpose for which it was sold or supplied.

WHAT OTHER INFORMATION COULD I BE ASKED TO PROVIDE?

- Pharmacists could be asked to explain the instructions for administration of AAIs and any associated information.

- General advice e.g. on storage, disposal of used, miss fired or expired stock.

- Advising schools on the importance of keeping a record of the spare AAIs held and their expiry date and to ensure they are replaced appropriately.

STRENGTH

The strength required will depend on the patient's age and bodyweight. See BNF and Summary of Product Characteristics (SPC) for each product.

BRANDS

Different brands of AAIs are available, and each brand may have different instructions for administration. See SPC and Patient Information Leaflet (PIL) for each product when counselling the person collecting the AAIs.

The Department of Health advises schools to hold an appropriate quantity of a single brand of AAI device to avoid confusion in administration and training but also that the decision as to how many brands they purchase will depend on local circumstances and is left to the discretion of the school.

WHERE CAN I LOCATE INFORMATION ON A SCHOOL, INCLUDING HEAD TEACHER/ PRINCIPAL DETAILS IF REQUIRED?

There is no centralised database containing details of schools and head teachers across Great Britain.

Possible sources of information would include:

- Ofsted reports (www.reports.ofsted.gov.uk)

- Information on the individual school's website.

FURTHER READING

Royal Pharmaceutical Society
Supply of spare adrenaline auto-injectors – quick reference guide.
www.rpharms.com

Department for Education
Statutory framework for the early years foundation stage. 2017.
www.foundationyears.org.uk

Department for Education
Supporting pupils at school with medical conditions. 2014.
www.gov.uk

Department of Health
Guidance on the use of adrenaline auto-injectors in schools. 2017.
https://assets.publishing.service.gov.uk/government/uploads/system/uploads/attachment_data/file/645476/Adrenaline_auto_injectors_in_schools.pdf

Scottish Government
Supporting children and young people with healthcare needs in schools: guidance. 2017.
www.gov.scot

Welsh Government
Supporting learners with healthcare needs. 2017.
https://gov.wales/sites/default/files/publications/2018-12/supporting-learners-with-healthcare-needs.pdf

3.3.10.7
SUPPLY OF NALOXONE BY INDIVIDUALS EMPLOYED OR ENGAGED IN THE PROVISION OF RECOGNISED DRUG TREATMENT SERVICES

Deaths in the UK involving heroin and/or morphine have significantly increased in recent years. Naloxone is an opioid /opiate antagonist which can completely or partially reverse the central nervous system depression, especially respiratory depression, caused by natural or synthetic opioids and is licensed for the treatment of suspected acute opioid overdose.

Following legislative changes in October 2015, naloxone falls into a unique category. Naloxone remains a POM but the Human Medicines (Amendment) (No.3) Regulations 2015 allow staff engaged or employed in "lawful drug treatment services" to obtain naloxone from a wholesaler and make direct supplies to patients without a prescription, patient group direction (PGD) or patient specific direction (PSD). From February 2019 this included nasal naloxone. Lawful drug treatment services is defined as:

"Persons employed or engaged in the provision of drug treatment services provided by, on behalf of or under arrangements made by one of the following bodies:

(a) an NHS body

(b) a local authority

(c) Public Health England, or

(d) Public Health Agency".

This definition extends to commissioned services providing needle and syringe programmes (including those provided by pharmacies) and pharmacies providing drug treatment services (includes instalment and supervised dispensing of Opiate Substitute Therapies (OST).

Anyone can administer naloxone for the purpose of saving a life (Schedule 19 of the Human Medicines Regulations 2012) and there is evidence for the effectiveness of training family members or peers in how to administer the drug. The 2015 amendments widen the groups of people who are eligible to receive supplies of naloxone. This has been extended to cover people likely to witness an overdose and includes family members, peers and staff in regular contact with drug users where naloxone may be required for example.

A number of naloxone products are licensed for use in reversing acute opioid overdose. A UKMi In Use Product Safety Assessment Report provides a useful summary of the available products in the UK (March 2016). www.ukmi.nhs.uk/filestore/ukmiaps/Naloxone%20product%20safety%20review_FINAL.pdf

A pharmacy may be commissioned to participate in a local take home naloxone scheme.

Please note: This is a service that can continue to be provided by appropriately trained staff in the absence of the RP.

FURTHER READING

Department of Health. Clinical Guidelines on Drug Misuse and Dependence Update 2017 Independent Expert Working Group
Drug misuse and dependence: UK guidelines on clinical management. 2017. www.gov.uk/government/publications/drug-misuse-and-dependence-uk-guidelines-on-clinical-management

Department of Health, Medicines and Healthcare products Regulatory Agency (MHRA) and Public Health England.
Widening the availability of naloxone. 2019. www.gov.uk/government/publications/widening-the-availability-of-naloxone

Specialist Pharmacy Service
What naloxone doses should be used in adults to reverse urgently the effects opioids or opiates? www.sps.nhs.uk/articles/what-naloxone-doses-should-be-used-in-adults-to-reverse-urgently-the-effects-of-opioids-or-opiates/

3.3.11
DISPENSING SELF-PRESCRIBED PRESCRIPTIONS AND PRESCRIPTIONS FOR CLOSE FRIENDS AND FAMILY

Pharmacists are occasionally requested to dispense medicines that have been self-prescribed by a prescriber or have been prescribed for close family and friends of the prescriber.

Although a prescription (including one for CDs) in these circumstances may fulfil the usual legal requirements, pharmacists should consider the following before making a supply:

- It is generally considered poor practice to self-prescribe or to prescribe for persons for whom there is a close personal relationship

- The professional judgement of the prescriber may be impaired or influenced by the person they are prescribing for

- It may not be possible for a prescriber to conduct a proper clinical assessment on themselves or on close friends or family

- The regulatory body for doctors (General Medical Council) advises within the Good Medical Practice that doctors must wherever possible avoid prescribing for themselves or anyone with whom they have a close personal relationship

- The regulatory body for nurses (Nursing and Midwifery Council) advises within the document Standards of proficiency for nurse and midwife prescribers that nurses and midwives must not prescribe for themselves and, other than in exceptional circumstances, should not prescribe for anyone with whom they have a close personal or emotional relationship.

- Pharmacist prescribers should be aware of the following documents:

  - Department of Health *Improving Patients' Access to Medicines: A Guide to Implementing Nurse and Pharmacist Independent Prescribing within the NHS in England (April 2006)* states 'Pharmacist Independent Prescribers must not prescribe any medicine for themselves. Neither should they prescribe a medicine for anyone with whom they have a close personal or emotional relationship, other than in an exceptional circumstance'

- NHS Education for Scotland A guide to good prescribing practice for prescribing pharmacists in NHS Scotland (July 2012) states 'You must not prescribe for yourself or for anyone with whom you have a close personal or emotional relationship'

- The existence and content of any local trust, board or hospital policy covering self-prescribing

- The abuse potential of the drug being requested

- CDs should only be supplied in exceptional circumstances and details documented. Where appropriate, the supply or request may prompt referral to the local CD accountable officer.

In an emergency, after exercising professional judgement, a pharmacist may decide that it is appropriate to dispense a medicine that has been self-prescribed or prescribed for persons with whom the prescriber has a close personal relationship.

In the circumstance that refusing to supply is the most appropriate action, be prepared for the person requesting the supply to be disappointed. One strategy would be to clearly and calmly explain that in your professional judgement it would not be appropriate to supply the medicine.

In some circumstances where there is a risk of harm to patients or the public, there may be a duty to raise concerns to the appropriate body (e.g. General Medical Council)

See Appendix 5 for GPhC guidance on raising concerns.

FURTHER READING

Royal Pharmaceutical Society
Practical guide for pharmacist prescribers. 2018.
www.rpharms.com
See case study on *Prescribing for yourself or close family and friends*

General Medical Council
Good practice in prescribing and managing medicines and devices. 2013.
www.gmc-uk.org

General Medical Council
Guidance on assessing the seriousness or concerns relating to self-prescribing, or prescribing to those in close personal relationships with doctors. 2013.
www.gmc-uk.org

NHS Education for Scotland
A guide to good prescribing practice for prescribing pharmacists in NHS Scotland. 2012.
www.nes.scot.nhs.uk

Nursing and Midwifery Council
Standards of proficiency for nurse and midwife prescribers. 2006.
www.nmc.org.uk

3.3.12
SUPPLYING ORAL RETINOIDS AND PREGNANCY PREVENTION

Oral retinoids (include isotretinoin, alitretinoin and acitretin) are used for severe skin conditions. They have has a high risk of causing severe and serious foetal malformations and can increase the risk of spontaneous abortion.

Pharmacists can help patients by ensuring oral retinoids are not dispensed for women who might be pregnant or are considering becoming pregnant. A Pregnancy Prevention Programme (PPP) is in place to protect female patients at risk of pregnancy from becoming pregnant whilst using oral retinoids, and for at least one month after stopping oral retinoids (specific drug specifications for exactly how long).

The programme is a combination of education for healthcare professionals and patients, therapy management (including pregnancy testing before during and after treatment, contraception requirements) and distribution control.

Therapy should only be initiated by or under the supervision of a consultant dermatologist and under the conditions of the PPP. The prescriber must check that the patient complies with, understands and acknowledges the reasons for pregnancy prevention and agrees to monthly follow-up, contraceptive precautions and pregnancy testing.

Female patients should comply with the PPP conditions unless the prescriber agrees that there are compelling reasons that indicate there is no risk of pregnancy.

Reasons may include persons who cannot become pregnant, e.g. following a hysterectomy or a female who is not sexually active (and there is certainty that sexual activity will not start during the period of teratogenic risk).

SPECIAL DISTRIBUTION CONTROLS FOR FEMALES AT RISK OF PREGNANCY

1 **Prescription Validity**

   Under the PPP, prescriptions are valid only for seven days and ideally should be dispensed on the date the prescription is written. Prescriptions which are presented after seven days should be considered expired and the patient should be referred back to the prescriber for a new prescription. Pregnancy status may need to be reconfirmed by a further negative pregnancy test.

2 **Quantity**

   Check that the quantity is for a maximum of 30 days' supply. A quantity for more than 30 days can only be dispensed if the patient is confirmed by the prescriber as not being under the PPP.

In accordance with MHRA approved guidance, pharmacists should not accept repeat prescriptions, free sample distribution, or faxed prescriptions for oral retinoids. A telephone request should only be accepted if this is an emergency supply at the request of a PPP specialist prescriber together with confirmation that pregnancy status has been established as negative within the preceding seven days.

FURTHER READING

Royal Pharmaceutical Society
Dispensing oral isotretinoin and pregnancy prevention – quick reference guide.
www.rpharms.com

Electronic Medicines Compendium
Full details of isotretinoin pregnancy prevention programmes are available on the 'Summary of Product Characteristics' for the oral retinoid preparations.
www.medicines.org.uk

Medicines and Healthcare products Regulatory Agency
Oral retinoids: pregnancy prevention – reminder of measures to minimise teratogenic risk.
www.gov.uk

3.3.13
DISPENSING VALPROATE FOR GIRLS AND WOMEN

Valproate is used to treat epilepsy, bipolar disorder and for preventing migraine (unlicensed). However valproate can seriously harm an unborn child when taken during pregnancy and should be not taken by women and girls unless nothing else works and the person taking valproate is part of a pregnancy prevention programme (PPP).

WHAT PHARMACISTS SHOULD DO:

- Have a conversation with female patients of child-bearing age who are prescribed valproate to find out if they have had a review with their doctor, are aware of the risks and are on a PPP

- Those planning pregnancy should be advised to schedule an appointment with their prescriber to review treatment and to continue with contraception and valproate treatment in the meantime

- If there is an unplanned pregnancy whilst a patient is taking valproate medicines advise the patient NOT to stop their treatment and to arrange to see their prescriber urgently to review treatment

- Report any suspected side effects to valproate medicines via the Yellow Card Scheme (see section 3.7.7 Reporting adverse events)

FURTHER READING

Royal Pharmaceutical Society
Dispensing valproate for girls and women –
quick reference guide.
www.rpharms.com

Medical Royal Colleges
Guidance document on valproate use in women
and girls of child bearing age. (endorsed by RPS).
www.rcog.org.uk/globalassets/documents/
guidelines/valproate-guidance-march-2019.pdf

Medicines and Healthcare products
Regulatory Agency
Drug Safety Update – Valproate medicines
(Epilim, Depakote): contraindicated in women
and girls of childbearing potential unless conditions
of Pregnancy Prevention Programme are met.
www.gov.uk

Medicines and Healthcare products
Regulatory Agency
Valproate use by women and girls.
www.gov.uk

National Institute for Health and Care Excellence
Special considerations for girls and women
with epilepsy. Interactive flowchart. 2019.
www.nice.org.uk

3.3.14
EXPLAINING BIOSIMILAR MEDICINES

Advances in biotechnology have resulted in an increasing number of biological molecules and materials being used as medicines. This is a trend that is expected to continue, at least for the foreseeable future. A number of patents and periods of marketing exclusivity for biological medicines are expiring and biosimilar versions of the medicines are becoming more widely available e.g. insulin glargine. The introduction of biosimilars offers potential benefits in terms of cost savings for the NHS and increased access to treatments for patients. Biosimilars are not the same as a generic medicine and as a pharmacist you will need to be aware of the guidance around the use of biosimilars in order to ensure their safe and effective use.

WHAT IS A BIOLOGIC?
A biologic is a medicine made from a variety of natural sources that may be human, animal or microorganism in origin. Examples of a biologic include vaccines, blood and blood products, somatic cells, DNA, human cells and tissues and therapeutic proteins. In general, the first or original biologic on the market is termed the originator or reference product.

WHAT IS A BIOSIMILAR?
A biosimilar is a biologic medicine that is similar to an already licensed biologic medicine in terms of quality, safety and efficacy. A biosimilar is specifically developed and licensed to treat the same disease(s) as the original innovator product. A biosimilar can only be marketed after the patent protecting the originator product and any period of marketing exclusivity have expired.

WHY IS A BIOSIMILAR MEDICINE NOT A GENERIC MEDICINE?
Due to the complexity of structure and greater size of biologics as well as their inherent heterogeneity resulting from their production methods, it is not possible to make an identical copy of the originator biologic. Biosimilars are licensed for use based on extensive data on quality, safety and efficacy compared to the originator product. It is not possible to characterise a biologic to the same extent as a small molecule drug, where an identical copy can be produced, known as a generic medicine.

IS IT POSSIBLE TO SWITCH BETWEEN AN ORIGINATOR BIOLOGIC AND A BIOSIMILAR?
Any decision to change the brand of a biologic used to treat a patient must only be made by a prescriber following discussions with the patient. It is recommended that, at the point of dispensing, the pharmacist confirms the patient has received the biologic they expect and that they are aware of how to store and use the medicine.

HOW WILL A BIOSIMILAR BE PRESCRIBED?
In contrast to generic products, all biosimilars will have their own unique brand name.
The MHRA has recommended that all biologics should be prescribed by brand to avoid automatic substitution.

TABLE 3: TABLE SHOWING EXAMPLES OF BIOLOGICS AND BIOSIMILARS

BIOLOGICS		
NON PROPRIETARY NAME	ORIGINATOR PRODUCT	EXAMPLE OF BIOSIMILAR
insulin glargine	Lantus	Abasaglar
infliximab	Remicade	Inflectra/Remsima
filgrastim	Neupogen	Nivestim/Tevagrastim
epoetin alfa	Eprex	Binocrit/Retacrit
somatropin	Genotropin	Omnitrope

HOW ARE ADVERSE DRUG REACTIONS TO BIOSIMILARS REPORTED?

It is important that both the brand name and batch number of a biologic medicine are provided when reporting suspected adverse drug reactions to biologics to facilitate effective safety monitoring. To support patient safety, pharmacists should consider it good practice to record the brand name and batch number of any biologic medicine (including biosimilars) supplied to a patient.

FURTHER READING

Royal Pharmaceutical Society
Explaining biosimilar medicines –
quick reference guide.
www.rpharms.com

British Biosimilars Association
Various online resources available.
https://britishbiosimilars.co.uk

British National Formulary
www.medicinescomplete.com
or www.evidence.nhs.uk

European Medicines Agency
Various online resources available.
www.ema.europa.eu/en

Healthcare Improvement Scotland and NHS Scotland
Biosimilar medicines: A national
prescribing framework. 2018.
www.healthcareimprovementscotland.org

International Federation of Pharmaceutical Manufacturers and Association
Considerations for physicians
on switching decisions regarding
biosimilars. Joint position paper. 2017.
www.ifpma.org

Medicines and Healthcare products Regulatory Agency (MHRA)
Drug Safety Update – High strength,
fixed combination and biosimilar
insulin products: minimising the risk
of medication error. 2015.
www.gov.uk

Medicines and Healthcare products Regulatory Agency (MHRA)
What is a biosimilar medicine? 2015.
www.gov.uk

Medicines for Europe
Various online resources available.
www.medicinesforeurope.com/

National Institute for Health and Care Excellence (NICE)
Biosimilar medicines.
Key therapeutic topic. 2016.
www.nice.org.uk

NHS England
Biosimilar medicines.
www.england.nhs.uk

3.3.15
SUMMARY OF PRESCRIBER TYPES AND PRESCRIBING RESTRICTIONS

TABLE 4: THE DIFFERENT TYPES OF PRESCRIBER AND RESTRICTIONS ON WHAT CAN BE PRESCRIBED

TYPE OF PRESCRIBER	CAN PRESCRIBE CONTROLLED DRUGS (SCHEDULE 2 TO 5 ON A PRESCRIPTION)	CAN PRESCRIBE UNLICENSED MEDICINES	OTHER APPLICABLE CONSIDERATIONS	CAN AUTHORISE AN EMERGENCY SUPPLY FOR ITEMS WHICH CAN BE PRESCRIBED
DOCTOR REGISTERED IN THE UK	Yes. A Home Office licence is required to prescribe cocaine, dipipanone, or diamorphine for treating addiction. Address of prescriber must be within the UK	Yes (subject to accepted clinical good practice)	Clinical expertise	Yes. Includes phenobarbital for epilepsy but not Schedule 1, 2 and 3 CDs (see section 3.3.10.2)
PHARMACIST INDEPENDENT PRESCRIBER	Yes (but not cocaine, dipipanone or diamorphine for treating addiction). Address of prescriber must be within the UK	Yes (subject to accepted clinical good practice)	Medicines for any medical condition within their competence	Yes. Includes phenobarbital for epilepsy but not Schedule 1, 2 and 3 CDs (see section 3.3.10.2)
PHYSIOTHERAPIST INDEPENDENT PRESCRIBER	Only the following CDs: diazepam, dihydrocodeine, lorazepam, oxycodone and temazepam for oral administration only; morphine for oral administration or for injection; fentanyl for transdermal administration[1]	Only 'off-label' medicines subject to accepted clinical good practice	Medicines for any medical condition within their competence	Yes, but not Schedule 1, 2, and 3 CDs, including phenobarbital (see section 3.3.10.2)
PODIATRIST INDEPENDENT PRESCRIBER	Only the following CDs for oral administration: diazepam, dihydrocodeine, lorazepam and temazepam[1]	Only 'off-label' medicines subject to accepted clinical good practice	Medicines for any medical condition within their competence	Yes, but not Schedule 1, 2, and 3 CDs, including phenobarbital (see section 3.3.10.2)

TYPE OF PRESCRIBER	CAN PRESCRIBE CONTROLLED DRUGS (SCHEDULE 2 TO 5 ON A PRESCRIPTION)	CAN PRESCRIBE UNLICENSED MEDICINES	OTHER APPLICABLE CONSIDERATIONS	CAN AUTHORISE AN EMERGENCY SUPPLY FOR ITEMS WHICH CAN BE PRESCRIBED
DENTIST REGISTERED IN THE UK	Yes (but not cocaine, dipipanone or diamorphine for treating addiction) Address of prescriber must be within the UK unless prescribing Schedule 4 or 5 CDs	Yes (subject to accepted clinical good practice)	Should restrict prescribing to treatment of dental conditions but legally can prescribe within clinical expertise. NHS dental prescriptions are restricted to medicines within the Dental Formulary (See BNF)	Yes. Includes phenobarbital for epilepsy but not Schedule 1, 2 and 3 CDs (see section 3.3.10.2)
SUPPLEMENTARY PRESCRIBER (PHARMACIST, MIDWIFE, NURSE, CHIROPODIST, DIETITIAN, PODIATRIST, PHYSIOTHERAPIST, RADIOGRAPHER OR OPTOMETRIST)	Yes (but not cocaine, dipipanone or diamorphine for treating addiction) Address of prescriber must be within the UK unless prescribing Schedule 4 or 5 CDs	Yes (subject to accepted clinical good practice)	Prescribed items are subject to clinical competence and inclusion within a clinical management plan agreed	Yes. Includes phenobarbital for epilepsy but not Schedule 1, 2 and 3 CDs (see section 3.3.10.2)
NURSE INDEPENDENT PRESCRIBER	Yes (but not cocaine, dipipanone or diamorphine for treating addiction) Address of prescriber must be within the UK unless prescribing Schedule 4 or 5 CDs	Unlicensed medicines are excluded from the Nurse Prescribing Formulary in Scotland and therefore not reimbursed on NHS prescriptions	Medicines for any medical condition within their competence	Yes. Includes phenobarbital for epilepsy but not Schedule 1, 2 and 3 CDs (see section 3.3.10.2)
OPTOMETRIST INDEPENDENT PRESCRIBER	No	Only 'off-label' medicines subject to accepted clinical good practice	For ocular conditions affecting the eye and surrounding tissue only	Yes
THERAPEUTIC RADIOGRAPHER INDEPENDENT PRESCRIBER	At the time of writing proposed changes to legislation in relation to the use of certain CDs were still to be considered by the Home Office	Only 'off label' medicines subject to accepted clinical good practice	Medicines for any medical condition within their competence	Yes, but not Schedule 1, 2 and 3 CDs, including phenobarbital (see section 3.3.10.2)

TYPE OF PRESCRIBER	CAN PRESCRIBE CONTROLLED DRUGS (SCHEDULE 2 TO 5 ON A PRESCRIPTION)	CAN PRESCRIBE UNLICENSED MEDICINES	OTHER APPLICABLE CONSIDERATIONS	CAN AUTHORISE AN EMERGENCY SUPPLY FOR ITEMS WHICH CAN BE PRESCRIBED
VETERINARY SURGEON AND VETERINARY PRACTITIONER	Yes (for the treatment of animals) Address of prescriber must be within the UK unless prescribing Schedule 4 or 5 CDs Prescriptions for Schedule 2 and 3 CDs must include the Royal College of Veterinary Surgeons registration number of the prescriber	Yes (for the treatment of animals – subject to the veterinary Cascade, see section 3.5.2)	For the treatment of animals only	Not applicable
EEA OR SWISS REGISTERED APPROPRIATE PRACTITIONER	Schedule 4 and 5 CDs only	No	Can only prescribe items which have a recognised marketing authorisation within the UK	Yes
COMMUNITY PRACTITIONER NURSE	No	No	Restricted to dressings, appliances and licensed medicines which are listed in the Nurse Prescribers' Formulary (see BNF)	Yes
PARAMEDIC INDEPENDENT PRESCRIBER	Subjective to legislative changes	Only 'off-label' medicines subject to accepted clinical good practice	Medicines for any medical condition within their competence	Yes, but not Schedule 1, 2 and 3 CDs, including phenobarbital (see section 3.3.10.2)

[1] Health and Care Professionals Council (HCPC) and NHS England have issued a joint statement (www.hcpc-uk.org/registrants/updates/2019/reclassification-of-gabapentin-and-pregabalin/) on the reclassification of gabapentin and pregabalin giving details of which prescribers can issue prescriptions for CDs.

NB: Schedule 1 CDs can only be prescribed under Home Office licence.

3.3.16
CHECKING REGISTRATION OF HEALTHCARE PROFESSIONALS AND ADDITIONAL INFORMATION ON CONDITIONS OF SUPPLY

Pharmacists may need to verify the registration status of other pharmacists and other healthcare professionals as part of the due diligence process when checking whether a person can prescribe or whether they can be wholesaled to. Table 5 provides details on where registration information can be verified (along with additional relevant notes) for several types of healthcare professional.

TABLE 5: HOW TO CHECK REGISTRATION FOR HEALTHCARE PROFESSIONALS

HEALTHCARE PROFESSIONAL	WHERE TO CHECK REGISTRATION	COMMON ISSUES
PHARMACISTS	General Pharmaceutical Council www.pharmacyregulation.org 020 3713 8000	There are pharmacists with further qualifications, such as independent or supplementary prescribers, and this is reflected in the register. Supplementary prescribers can prescribe all medicines included in a clinical management plan agreed with a prescriber and the patient. This includes CDs and unlicensed medicines. Independent prescribers can prescribe unlicensed medicines and CDs. Prescribing should be restricted to areas of clinical competence. Further information on non-medical prescribing, including FAQs, guidance and clinical management plans is available on the Department of Health website (National Archives) (https://webarchive.nationalarchives.gov.uk/+/http://www.dh.gov.uk/en/Healthcare/Medicinespharmacyandindustry/Prescriptions/TheNon-MedicalPrescribingProgramme/DH_099234) and the NHS Education for Scotland website (www.nes.scot.nhs.uk/education-and-training/by-discipline/pharmacy/pharmacists/prescribing-and-clinical-skills/resources.aspx).
PHARMACY TECHNICIANS	General Pharmaceutical Council www.pharmacyregulation.org 020 3713 8000	
DOCTORS	General Medical Council www.gmc-uk.org 0161 923 6602	To practise medicine in the UK, doctors are required to be registered with the GMC and hold a licence to practise.

HEALTHCARE PROFESSIONAL	WHERE TO CHECK REGISTRATION	COMMON ISSUES
DENTISTS	General Dental Council www.gdc-uk.org 020 7167 6000	Dentists can legally write prescriptions for any medicine but they should restrict their prescribing to areas in which they are competent. Therefore they should, generally, only prescribe medicines that have uses in dentistry. When prescribing on an NHS dental prescription, dentists are restricted to the medicines listed in the Dental Practitioners' Formulary (part 8a of the Drug Tariff for Scotland or part XVIIa of the Drug Tariff for England and Wales).
NURSES	Nursing and Midwifery Council www.nmc.org.uk 020 7333 9333	Nurses can have a range of further qualifications, which are annotated on the NMC register. Prescribing should be restricted to areas of clinical competency. Further information on non-medical prescribing, including FAQs, guidance and clinical management plans is available on the Department of Health website (National Archives) (https://webarchive.nationalarchives.gov.uk/+/http://www.dh.gov.uk/en/Healthcare/Medicinespharmacyandindustry/Prescriptions/TheNon-MedicalPrescribingProgramme/DH_099234)
VETERINARY SURGEONS	Royal College of Veterinary Surgeons www.rcvs.org.uk 020 7222 2001	Veterinary surgeons can prescribe and requisition all human and animal medicines, including CDs for the treatment of animals. Where CDs are involved, these do not need to be on standardised forms. Where the medicine is not licensed for the animal, then this needs to be prescribed under the veterinary Cascade (see section 3.5 for further details)
PARAMEDICS	Health and Care Professions Council www.hcpc-uk.org 0300 500 6184	A Home Office group authority has been issued that allows paramedics to possess and supply certain CDs under certain conditions. The Home Office has the authority to revoke or modify the authority at any time. A full list of medicines that a paramedic can obtain for the purposes of administration is available on the MHRA website (www.gov.uk/government/publications/rules-for-the-sale-supply-and-administration-of-medicines) *continues overleaf*

HEALTHCARE PROFESSIONAL	WHERE TO CHECK REGISTRATION	COMMON ISSUES
PARAMEDICS *continued*	Health and Care Professions Council www.hcpc-uk.org 0300 500 6184	Advanced paramedics are now able to prescribe legally, bringing huge benefits to patients and the NHS across the UK. These highly skilled paramedics, after undertaking additional training, will be able to prescribe medicines to patients. This is likely to happen in practice in 2019 www.england.nhs.uk/ahp/med-project/paramedics/.
CHIROPODISTS OR PODIATRISTS	Health and Care Professions Council www.hcpc-uk.org 0300 500 6184	Registered chiropodists and podiatrists can obtain additional qualifications that allow them to sell or supply and administer a larger range of medicines A full list of medicines that a chiropodist can sell, supply or administer is available on the MHRA website (www.gov.uk/government/publications/rules-for-the-sale-supply-and-administration-of-medicines)
PHYSIO-THERAPISTS	Health and Care Professions Council www.hcpc-uk.org 0300 500 6184	
OPTOMETRISTS	General Optical Council www.optical.org 020 7580 3898	Optometrists can take further qualifications to become an 'additional supply optometrist' – this increases the range of medicines that they can sell or supply to patients (and therefore obtain a supply of from a pharmacy). A full list of the medicines that can be obtained is available from the MHRA website (www.gov.uk/government/publications/rules-for-the-sale-supply-and-administration-of-medicines) Further information on non-medical prescribing, including FAQs, guidance and clinical management plans is available on the Department of Health website (National Archives) (https://webarchive.nationalarchives.gov.uk/+/http://www.dh.gov.uk/en/Healthcare/Medicinespharmacyandindustry/Prescriptions/TheNon-MedicalPrescribingProgramme/DH_099234)

HEALTHCARE PROFESSIONAL	WHERE TO CHECK REGISTRATION	COMMON ISSUES
DIETITIANS	Health and Care Professions Council www.hcpc-uk.org 0300 500 6184	
ORTHOPTISTS	Health and Care Professions Council www.hcpc-uk.org 0300 500 6184	Registered orthoptists who undertake additional training and obtain the relevant annotation on the Health and Care Professions Council (HCPC) register can sell, supply and administer certain medicines in the course of their professional practice. A full list of these medicines is available in Schedule 17 of the Human Medicines Regulations 2012 [SI 2016/186] as amended: (www.legislation.gov.uk/ uksi/2016/186/contents/made)
RADIOGRAPHERS	Health and Care Professions Council www.hcpc-uk.org 0300 500 6184	

3.3.17
PRESCRIBING AND DISPENSING TO THE SAME PERSON

The initial prescribing, and supply of medicines prescribed, should normally remain separate functions performed by separate healthcare professionals in order to protect patient safety.

Patient safety is improved by the opportunity for a second healthcare professional to check clinical appropriateness and to interact with the patient.

Where exceptionally it is in the interests of the patient for the same pharmacist prescriber to be responsible for prescribing, clinical check and supply of medicines on the same occasion it would be good practice to maintain an audit trail and to document reasons.

FURTHER READING

Royal Pharmaceutical Society
Practical guide for pharmacist prescribers. 2018.
www.rpharms.com

General Medical Council
Good practice in prescribing and managing medicines and devices. 2013.
www.gmc-uk.org

General Medical Council
Guidance on assessing the seriousness or concerns relating to self-prescribing, or prescribing to those in close personal relationships with doctors. 2013.
www.gmc-uk.org

NHS Education in Scotland (NES)
A guide to good prescribing practice for prescribing pharmacist in NHS Scotland. 2012.
www.nes.scot.nhs.uk

Nursing and Midwifery Council
Standards of proficiency for nurse and midwife prescribers. 2006.
www.nmc.org.uk

3.3.18
MAKING THINGS RIGHT WHEN THERE'S BEEN A DISPENSING ERROR

Professionalism and a culture of candour are vital for patient safety, this is why it is important that pharmacists report, learn, share, act and review instances when there has been dispensing errors or near misses. Pharmacists report various reasons why they find it difficult to report and learn from mistakes. It is estimated that 20% of under reporting is because of fear of prosecution.

Legislation introducing new legal defences to prevent the automatic criminalisation of inadvertent dispensing errors "The Pharmacy (Preparation and Dispensing Errors – Registered Pharmacies) Order 2018" came into force on the 16th April 2018. It is hoped this will reduce the risk of prosecution in the profession, leading to a professional increase in the reporting of dispensing errors, the learning from which could prevent the same error occurring in the future. The sharing and review of data from dispensing error reporting will result in improvements to patient safety across the healthcare system.

WHEN YOU BECOME AWARE OF A DISPENSING ERROR

Whether you are the person who made the error or another member of the pharmacy team, once you become aware, you need to promptly take all reasonable steps to let the patient know and to make things right, unless the circumstances mean it is not necessary or appropriate to. Keeping records can also help to justify your decision.

1 Take steps to let the patient know promptly

2 Make things right (this may involve contacting the prescriber)

3 Offer an apology

4 Let colleagues involved in the error know

WHAT THE DEFENCE MEANS TO ME?
The new defence is expected to reduce fear of prosecution, underpinning professionalism and confidence so that patient safety is best protected.

The defence to the section 64 'dispensing error' offence can be used when the dispensing error has been:

1 Dispensed in a registered pharmacy

2 Dispensed by or under the supervision of a registered pharmacist

3 Supplied against a prescription, PGD or direction from a prescriber

4 Promptly notified to the patient once the pharmacy team are aware of the error

At the time of writing the work of the Rebalancing Programme Board included developing a similar defence for hospital pharmacy and other non-registered pharmacy settings.

FURTHER READING

Royal Pharmaceutical Society (RPS)
Near miss errors – quick reference guide.
www.rpharms.com

Royal Pharmaceutical Society (RPS)
Professional standards for the reporting, learning, sharing, taking action and review of incidents.
www.rpharms.com

Bellingham C.
How medication errors can be avoided.
The Pharmaceutical Journal, January 2004, online.
www.pharmaceutical-journal.com (URI: 20011072)

General Pharmaceutical Council
Joint statement on professional duty of candour.
www.pharmacyregulation.org

General Pharmaceutical Council
Responding to complaints and concerns: guidance note. 2010.
www.pharmacyregulation.org

General Pharmaceutical Council
Standards for pharmacy professionals.
(See Standard 8.) 2017.
www.pharmacyregulation.org
(see MEP Appendix 1)

SEE ALSO:
Pharmacy (Preparation and Dispensing Errors – Registered Pharmacies) Order 2018
www.legislation.gov.uk/uksi/2018/181/contents/made

Rebalancing Medicines Legislation and Pharmacy Regulation Programme Board
www.gov.uk/government/groups/pharmacy-regulation-programme-board#minutes-and-associated-papers

3.4
Wholesale dealing

The MHRA is the regulatory body with responsibility for oversight and enforcement of the wholesale of medicines. In July 2012, MHRA issued regulatory guidance to support changes in legislation related to pharmacy wholesale activities.

This is reproduced with permission from MHRA: www.gov.uk/government/publications/repeal-of-wholesale-dealer-licence-exemption-for-pharmacists

3.4.1
MHRA STATEMENT
GUIDANCE FOR PHARMACISTS ON THE REPEAL OF SECTION 10(7) OF THE MEDICINES ACT 1968

With effect from 14 August 2012, Section 10(7) of the Medicines Act 1968 has been repealed. Section 10(7) provided an exemption in UK law from the requirement for a pharmacist to hold a Wholesale Dealer's Licence (WDA(H)) if they trade in medicines in certain circumstances. Its repeal was necessary in order to comply with EU legislation, in particular, Articles 77(1) and 77(2) of Directive 2001/83/EC which require anyone undertaking wholesale dealing activities to hold an authorisation.

This note provides guidance for pharmacists working in registered pharmacies and in hospitals on how MHRA, as the regulator responsible for the enforcement of EU legislation, will address the implications of the necessary repeal of Section 10(7) for the supply of licensed medicines by pharmacy other than direct to the public.

THE LEGISLATION GOVERNING SUPPLY OF MEDICINES

The legislation and underpinning guidance requires persons trading in medicines to hold a WDA(H) and to apply Good Distribution Practice (GDP) standards and have a suitably experienced 'Responsible Person' named on the licence to ensure that medicines are procured, stored and distributed appropriately. The legislation also ensures that medicines can only be supplied to other wholesale dealers, pharmacists or other persons authorised or entitled to supply medicines to the public. These rules also serve to provide confidence in the medicines supply chain by regulating the transit of medicines from manufacturer to patient.

HOW THIS APPLIES TO SUPPLY OF MEDICINES BY PHARMACY IN THE UK

MHRA is concerned to ensure that the repeal of the Section 10(7) exemption does not adversely impact on arrangements for supply of medicines in the UK. In determining how to address this issue, MHRA has taken careful account of the particular arrangements for delivery of healthcare in the UK which involve a wide range of individuals and in a diverse range of locations. In particular:

- Many healthcare professionals and others authorised or entitled to supply medicines to the public in the UK need to hold small quantities of medicines for local healthcare provision and look to a local community or hospital pharmacy to supply them as part of their professional practice

- In contrast, some pharmacies engage in commercial trade in medicines, not solely as part of their professional practice within the UK healthcare system

- Pharmacists may also occasionally need to obtain small quantities of a particular medicine or medicines from another pharmacist in order to meet the needs of individual patients.

MHRA ENFORCEMENT

MHRA takes the view that the supply of medicines by community and hospital pharmacies to other healthcare professionals in the UK who need to hold small quantities of medicines for treatment of or onward supply to their patients represents an important and appropriate part of the professional practice of both community and hospital pharmacy. Also community and hospital pharmacies may need to obtain small quantities of a medicine from other pharmacies to meet a patient's individual needs.

Both these activities are considered by MHRA to fall within the definition of provision of healthcare services. In such circumstances, provided the transaction meets all of the following criteria MHRA will not deem such transactions as commercial dealing and pharmacies will not be required to hold a WDA(H):

- It takes place on an occasional basis

- The quantity of medicines supplied is small

- The supply is made on a not for profit basis

- The supply is not for onward wholesale distribution.

Conversely, pharmacies who wish to engage in commercial trading in medicines are entitled to do so only if they hold a WDA(H) and comply with all the relevant requirements. As the authority responsible for enforcement MHRA will take appropriate action to enforce the requirement of the legislation and will require any commercial trade in medicines to be undertaken only by holders of a WDA(H).

These restrictions do not apply to the exchange of stock between pharmacies that are part of the same legal entity, although where a legal entity holds a WDA(H) as one (or more) of its pharmacies is involved in the commercial trade of medicines, the supplying pharmacy must also be named on

the WDA(H) if the stock supplied is for the purposes of wholesale.

Guidance on the need for a WDA(H), the application process and a downloadable application form are available on MHRA's website.

Please note:
If you are making a supply outside of the scope of this regulatory statement will probably be required

to obtain a Wholesale Distribution Authorisation for Human use (WDA(H)). This is the revised term for Wholesale Dealer's Licence. Further information about WDA(H) can be obtained from the MHRA: www.gov.uk/government/organisations/medicines-and-healthcare-products-regulatory-agency

3.4.2
WHOLESALE DEALING OF CONTROLLED DRUGS

The Home Office and MHRA have advised that if a WDA(H) is required, this also means that, if supplies include CDs in Schedules 2 to 5 to the Misuse of Drugs Regulations 2001, then it is likely that a corresponding Home Office CD licence is also needed by the pharmacy.

The following document Supplementary information on wholesale dealer and CD licences in the Health and Justice System in England and the accompanying letter provide further information on this that is particularly relevant to pharmacists working in healthcare and secure environment settings. Please note that the requirements to hold WDA(H) and Home Office CD licences apply to all settings and not just those outlined in this document: www.palliativedrugs.com/download/20140711-DH-Wholesalers-Dealer-Liciences-Guidance-FINAL.docx

3.4.3
PERSONS AND ORGANISATIONS THAT CAN RECEIVE MEDICINES

The range of persons and organisations that can receive medicines by wholesale is controlled by legislation and may also be restricted to certain medicines for certain purposes. The full lists are extensive and beyond the scope of this document; however, Table 6 contains signposting information for persons who may commonly approach the pharmacy for medicines, for onward use:

TABLE 6: PERSONS WHO CAN BE SUPPLIED WITH MEDICINAL PRODUCTS

PERSONS

- Doctors
- Dentists
- Registered pharmacies
- Hospitals, clinics and independent medical agencies
- Midwives
- Chiropodists/Podiatrists
- Optometrists and Additional Supply Optometrists
- Paramedics
- Owner or Master of Ship
- Orthoptists
- First aid organisations
- Certified first aiders
- Working for National Lifeboat Institution
- Occupational health schemes
- Drug treatment services
- NHS Trusts

USEFUL REFERENCE SOURCES

Schedule 22 of the Human Medicines Regulations 2012 as amended contains a to z list and organisations who can be supplied with medicines by wholesale

This is available at www.legislation.gov.uk

Schedule 17 of the Human Medicines Regulations 2012 as amended contains information about various persons who have exemptions to sell, supply or administer certain medicines under specified conditions.

These persons can also obtain these medicines by wholesale MHRA have published a summary of rules for the sale, supply and administration of medicines for specific healthcare professionals (www.gov.uk/government/publications/rules-for-the-sale-supply-and-administration-of-medicines/rules-for-the-sale-supply-and-administration-of-medicines-for-specific-healthcare-professionals)

Chapter 9 and 10, Dale and Appelbe's Pharmacy and Medicines Law. 11th edition. 2017 Discusses wholesale dealing

Information about a Controlled Drug Group Authority for paramedics for morphine sulphate and diazepam is available from www.jrcalc.org.uk

Maritime and Coastguard Agency: Ships Medical Stores www.gov.uk/government/publications/ msn-1768-applying-the-ships-medical-stores-regulations-1995

3.4.4
SIGNED ORDERS AND RECORD KEEPING

When a POM is supplied from a registered pharmacy to healthcare professionals or organisations, an entry needs to be made in the POM register or the signed order/invoice needs to be retained for two years from the date of supply. Even where the signed order/invoice is retained, it is good practice to make a record in the POM register for audit purposes.

Schedule 17 of Human Medicines Regulations 2012 states which persons or organisations must provide a written signed order/invoice. For other persons or organisations where a requirement to have a signed order/invoice is not outlined in the legislation, we advise it is good practice to obtain a written signed order/invoice for maintaining an audit trail.

An entry in the POM register must include the:

- Date the POM was supplied

- Name, quantity and, where it is not apparent, formulation and strength of the POM supplied

- Name and address, trade, business or profession of the person to whom the medicine was supplied

- Purpose for which it was sold or supplied.

Legislation does not specify the details that need to be included on a signed order although local standard operating procedures (e.g. local NHS Trust policies or company SOPs) may require templates to be used. It would be advisable for the details required for a POM register entry (i.e. the list above) to be requested as a minimum

for a signed order as this information would be required to complete the POM register.

See section 3.6.6 for details on the requisition requirements for CDs.

If you are making a supply to persons or organisations under a Wholesale Dealer's Licence you will be required to follow Good Distribution Practice (GDP) www.gov.uk/government/ organisations/medicines-and-healthcare-products-regulatory-agency

3.4.5
SUPPLY AND TRADE OF MEDICINES

The Department of Health has published a paper titled Trading Medicines for Human Use: Shortages and Supply Chain Obligations; this document has been endorsed by the RPS. This paper sets out the key legal and ethical obligations on manufacturers, wholesalers, NHS Trusts, registered pharmacies and dispensing doctors in relation to the supply and trading of medicines. Recent increases in the export of medicines are a major contributor to supply problems and risk jeopardising patient care. The full paper can be viewed at www.gov.uk/government/ publications/trading-medicines-for-human-use-shortages-and-supply-chain-obligations--4

Pharmacists can also consider information in the document titled Best Practice Standards for Managing Medicines Shortages in Secondary Care in England. These standards are designed to provide advice to NHS hospitals in managing medicines shortages to minimise risk to patients. Please note: The principles apply to the rest of the UK but the document will require adapting for local structures in Scotland, Wales and N. Ireland. These standards can be viewed at www.rpharms.com

3.4.6
FALSIFIED MEDICINES DIRECTIVE (FMD)

Delegated Regulation to the FMD came into force on 9 February 2019. Including new security features on individual packs and a new electronic scanning authentication process to be undertaken at the point of dispensing/suppling.

The EU Falsified Medicines Directive (FMD) legislation aims to create a system that ensures medicines supplied in the UK are safe. It ensures the trade in medicines is controlled to reduce the risk of fake medicines entering the medicines supply chain and reaching patients.

(We recommend those with Wholesales Dealers Licence refer to any relevant guidance on this from the MHRA.)

For detailed information on FMD see the RPS Falsified Medicines Directive hub on the RPS website www.rpharms.com.

FURTHER READING

Department of Health
Supplementary information on wholesale dealer and Controlled Drugs licences in the health and justice system in England and accompanying letter. 2014.
www.palliativedrugs.com/download/20140711-DH-Wholesalers-Dealer-Liciences-Guidance-FINAL.docx

Medicines and Healthcare products Regulatory Agency
Licences to manufacture or wholesale medicines.
www.gov.uk

Medicines and Healthcare products Regulatory Agency
Rules and guidance for pharmaceutical distributors – The green guide. 2017.
London; Pharmaceutical Press.
www.pharmpress.com/

Medicines and Healthcare products Regulatory Agency
Rules and guidance for pharmaceutical manufacturers and distributors – The orange guide. 10th edition. 2017.
London; Pharmaceutical Press.
www.pharmpress.com/

Wingfield J, Pitchford K, editors
Dale and Appelbe's Pharmacy and Medicines Law. 11th edition. 2017.
London; Pharmaceutical Press.
www.pharmpress.com/

3.5
Veterinary medicines

Pharmacists working in registered premises are authorised to supply veterinary medicines for use in animals under certain circumstances (e.g. when there is a valid prescription) and, as with human medicines, are responsible for any medicines supplied. There are various classes of veterinary medicines, which are summarised in Table 7.

TABLE 7: CATEGORIES OF VETERINARY MEDICINES AND THEIR CHARACTERISTICS

CATEGORY
POM-V

CHARACTERISTIC
Prescription-only medicines that can only be prescribed by a veterinary surgeon and supplied by a veterinary surgeon or a pharmacist with a written prescription

CATEGORY
POM-VPS

CHARACTERISTIC
Prescription-only medicines that can be prescribed and supplied by a veterinary surgeon, a pharmacist or a suitably qualified person on an oral or written prescription. A written prescription is only required if the supplier is not the prescriber

continues overleaf

continued

CATEGORY

NFA-VPS

CHARACTERISTIC

A category of medicine for non-food animals that can be supplied by a veterinary surgeon, a pharmacist or a suitably qualified person. A written prescription is not required

CATEGORY

AVM-GSL

CHARACTERISTIC

An authorised veterinary medicine that is available on general sale

CATEGORY

Exempt medicines under schedule 6 of the veterinary medicines regulations – exemptions for small pet animals (SAES)

CHARACTERISTIC

An unlicensed veterinary medicine that does not require a marketing authorisation because it meets criteria laid out in Schedule 6 of the Veterinary Medicines Regulations - Exemptions for small pet animals. Further details are available in Veterinary Medicines Guidance Exemption from authorisation for medicines for small pet animals (www.gov.uk/guidance/exemption-from-authorisation-for-medicines-for-small-pet-animals)

CATEGORY

Unauthorised veterinary medicine

CHARACTERISTIC

An unlicensed medicine that does not have a marketing authorisation and is not eligible for exemption through the SAES. It can only be prescribed by a veterinary surgeon under the Cascade (see Diagram 10). This includes any human medicine used for animals

3.5.1
PRESCRIPTION REQUIREMENTS FOR POM-V, POM-VPS AND MEDICINES SUPPLIED UNDER THE VETERINARY CASCADE

The following must be present for a veterinary medicine prescription to be valid:

1   Name, address, telephone number, qualification and signature of the prescriber. Where Schedule 2 or 3 CDs have been prescribed, the Royal College of Veterinary Surgeons (RCVS) registration number of the prescriber must also be included.

2   Name and address of the owner.

3   Identification and species of the animal and its address (if different from the owner's address).

4   Date. prescriptions are valid for six months or shorter if indicated by the prescriber (the Veterinary Medicines Directorate (VMD) has confirmed in the case of repeatable prescriptions all supplies must be made within 6 months or shorter if indicated by prescriber). Prescriptions for Schedule 2, 3 and 4 CDs are valid for 28 days.

5   Name, quantity, dose and administration instructions of the required medicine
    NB: The VMD advises that 'as directed' is not an acceptable administration instruction.

6   Any necessary warnings and if relevant the withdrawal period (i.e. the time that must elapse between when an animal receives a medicine and when it can be used for food).

7   Where appropriate, a statement highlighting that the medicine is prescribed under the veterinary Cascade (e.g. 'prescribed under the Cascade' or other wording to the same effect).

8   Where Schedule 2 or 3 CDs have been prescribed, a declaration that 'the item has been prescribed for an animal or herd under the care of the veterinarian' – usual CDs prescription requirements apply (see section 3.6.7).

9   If the prescription is repeatable, the number of times it can be repeated.

DIAGRAM 9: VETERINARY PRESCRIPTION WITH CASCADE WORDING

1 **P.NIGHTINGALE**
MRCVS PRACTICE NAME,
ADDRESS, TOWN, POSTCODE
TELEPHONE NUMBER

Endorsements

3 **PRESCRIPTION FOR SPOT THE DOG**

2 **OWNED BY MRS R SWANN OF**
ADDRESS, TOWN, POSTCODE

5 **SUPPLY PHENYOIN SODIUM**
CAPSULES 100MG X 90
5 CAPSULES
3 TIMES A DAY WITH FOOD
6

9 **REPEAT X4**

7 **PRESCRIBED UNDER THE**
VETERINARY CASCADE

Signature of Prescriber	Date
1 **P.NIGHTINGALE**	4 **30TH MAY 2019**

TABLE 8: SIMILARITIES AND DIFFERENCES BETWEEN VETERINARY AND HUMAN CONTROLLED DRUG PRESCRIPTIONS

DIFFERENCES

- Standardised forms are not required for veterinary prescriptions; however, a statement that the medicines are 'prescribed for the treatment of an animal or herd under my care' is required for Schedule 2 and 3 CDs

- Standardised forms are required for human private prescriptions for Schedule 2 and 3 CDs (see section 3.6.7)

- Veterinary prescriptions should be retained for five years and not submitted to the relevant NHS agency. Original human private prescriptions for Schedule 2 and 3 CDs must be submitted to the relevant NHS agency (see section 3.6.7)

- For all CDs, it is considered good practice for only 28 days' worth of treatment to be prescribed on veterinary prescriptions unless in situations of long term ongoing medication (e.g. when treating epilepsy in dogs). For human prescriptions the maximum quantity of Schedule 2,3 or 4 CDs should not exceed 30 days. If more than 30 days is prescribed the prescriber should be able to justify the quantity requested (see section 3.6.7 under 'Total Quantity' for further detail)

- Veterinary prescriptions for Schedule 2 and 3 CDs must include the Royal College of Veterinary Surgeons (RCVS) registration number of the prescriber. Human private prescriptions for Schedule 2 and 3 CDs must include a prescriber identification number

SIMILARITIES

- Both are valid for 28 days from the appropriate date

- Usual CD prescription content requirements (e.g. Total quantity in words and figures, etc. – see section 3.6.7) apply to both

3.5.2
THE VETERINARY CASCADE

A veterinary medicine with a UK marketing authorisation must be prescribed and supplied where one exists and is clinically appropriate. The Cascade exemption within the Veterinary Medicines Regulations allows the supply of medicines that are not licensed for animals. It is unlawful to supply a human medicine against a veterinary prescription unless it is prescribed by a veterinary surgeon and specifically states that it is 'for administration under the Cascade', or other wording to this effect.

NB: Although the wording on the prescription is a legal requirement, it is important that it reflects the actual Cascade (i.e. if a prescription is written generically for an animal with the Cascade wording present but a licensed veterinary medicine exists, then the Cascade requires the licensed product to be supplied rather than a medicine only licensed for human use).

The exemption specifies that where a licensed veterinary product is not available, other medicines can be considered as shown in Diagram 10.

Veterinary medicines licensed for another species, or for another clinical condition in the same species, extemporaneously prepared medicines or human medicines cannot be supplied against a veterinary prescription unless the prescription specifically states that it is 'for administration under the Cascade', or other wording to this effect.

Veterinary Medicines Guidance *The Cascade: Prescribing Unauthorised Medicines* advises that a human medicine may be used in accordance with the Cascade, assuming that the prescribing veterinary surgeon can justify the course of treatment based on animal welfare. Further detail of the Cascade and additional requirements for food producing animals is available in this guidance on the VMD website (www.gov.uk/government/organisations/veterinary-medicines-directorate).

DIAGRAM 10: VETERINARY CASCADE

WHERE AVAILABLE IT IS A LEGAL REQUIREMENT TO:

SUPPLY A LICENSED VETERINARY MEDICINE

↓

ONLY WHERE THE ABOVE IS NOT POSSIBLE

AN EXISTING LICENSED VETERINARY MEDICINE FOR ANOTHER SPECIES OR DIFFERENT CONDITION CAN BE CONSIDERED

↓

ONLY WHERE THE ABOVE IS NOT POSSIBLE

A LICENSED HUMAN MEDICINE OR AN EU-LICENSED VETERINARY MEDICINE CAN BE CONSIDERED

↓

ONLY WHERE THE ABOVE IS NOT POSSIBLE

EXTEMPORANEOUS OR SPECIALLY MANUFACTURED MEDICINES CAN BE CONSIDERED

SALE OF UNAUTHORISED VETERINARY MEDICINES

It is unlawful to sell or supply unauthorised veterinary medicines (medicines not licensed as veterinary medicines), including human medicines such as GSL and P medicines, for an animal unless this takes place under the veterinary Cascade. This applies even if a veterinary surgeon asks the animal owner verbally to purchase an over-the-counter human product from a pharmacy.

SALE OF NFA-VPS AND POM-VPS MEDICINES

It is a legal requirement for pharmacists who supply NFA-VPS medicines or prescribe POM-VPS medicines to:

* Advise on how to use the product safely
* Advise on any applicable warnings and contraindications on the packaging or label
* Be satisfied that the recipient intends to use the medicine correctly and is competent to do so
* Prescribe or supply the minimum quantity required for treatment.

PHYSICAL PRESENCE OF A PHARMACIST

Unless a transaction has been individually authorised in advance by a pharmacist and the person handing out the medicine is judged to be competent, the physical presence of the pharmacist is required for POM-V, POM-VPS and NFA-VPS medicines to be supplied.

3.5.3 LABELLING

When a medicine is supplied by a pharmacy for use under the Cascade, the following details must appear on the dispensing label unless they already appear on the packaging and are not obscured by the dispensing label:

* Name of the prescribing veterinary surgeon
* Name and address of the animal owner

- Name and address of the pharmacy

- Identification and species of the animal

- Date of supply

- Expiry date of the product

- The name or description of the product or its active ingredients and content quantity

- Dosage and administration instructions

- If appropriate, special storage instructions

- Any necessary warnings for the user (e.g. relating to administration, disposal, target species, etc)

- Any applicable withdrawal period (i.e. The time between when an animal receives a medicine and when it can safely be used for food)

- The words: 'For animal treatment only'

- The words: 'Keep out of reach of children'.

  Please note that the RPS recommends that the wording 'Keep out of the reach and sight of children' is included on the dispensing label. If the medicine is not prescribed under the Cascade, the Veterinary Medicines Regulations do not specify that a dispensing label is required. However, the RPS advises that it would be appropriate to generate a dispensing label for all veterinary medicines, particularly for individual animals (pets).

3.5.4
RECORD KEEPING

It is a requirement to keep records of receipt and supply of POM-V and POM-VPS products showing:

- Name of the medicine

- Date of the receipt or supply

- Batch number

- Quantity

- Name and address of the supplier or recipient

- If there is a written prescription, record the name and address of the prescriber and keep a copy of the prescription

- Pharmacists can either keep all documents that show the required information or can make appropriate records in their private prescription book

- Records can be kept electronically

- Records and documents must be kept for at least five years

- Pharmacies that supply POM-V and POM-VPS medicines must undertake an annual audit.

ADVERSE REACTIONS

Pharmacists are increasingly supplying veterinary medicines for companion animals and should be mindful to the possibility that veterinary medicines can cause adverse reactions in humans as well as in animals exposed to a veterinary medicine. Suspect adverse drug reactions (SADRs) in humans are often associated with a failure to read and/or adequately follow product guidance information. Examples include animal sprays and 'spot-ons' onto human skin. The adverse reaction scheme for veterinary medicines is the equivalent of the 'yellow card' scheme for human medicines. Both animal adverse reactions and human adverse reactions to veterinary medicinal products should be reported. Additionally report a suspected problem with a microchip. Details of the scheme and reporting forms are available at www.gov.uk/report-veterinary-medicine-problem or directly from VMD on tel: 01932 336911.

3.5.5
WHOLESALE DEALING

VETERINARY MEDICINES
The VMD provides the following information in Veterinary Medicines Guidance Retail of Veterinary Medicines.

'Only the manufacturer of a veterinary medicine or a holder of a wholesale dealer's authorisation (WDA) may routinely supply authorised retailers with veterinary medicines'.

This guidance also states that 'An authorised retailer of veterinary medicines may supply products they are qualified to supply to another authorised retailer to relieve a temporary supply shortage, without a WDA. This exemption from the VMR is intended to prevent shortages of available medicines causing animal welfare problems. It is not intended to exempt wholesale supply from the need for a WDA.'

Further information is available in Veterinary Medicines Guidance Retail of Veterinary Medicines and Veterinary Medicines Wholesale Dealer's Authorisation (WDA): www.gov.uk/government/collections/veterinary-medicines-guidance-notes-vmgns

HUMAN MEDICINES FOR VETERINARY USE UNDER THE CASCADE

The MHRA statement 'Guidance for pharmacists on the repeal of Section 10(7) of the Medicines Act' that has been reproduced in section 3.4 also applies to the wholesale supply of human medicines to veterinary surgeons for use in animals under the Cascade.

FURTHER READING

Harper Adams University
Veterinary pharmacy post-graduate training – various courses available.
www.harper-adams.ac.uk

Kayne S
An introduction to veterinary medicine. 2011.
Saltire Books.

National Office of Animal Health
NOAH Compendium
Access up-to-date datasheets
of authorised veterinary medicines
www.noahcompendium.co.uk

Veterinary Medicines Directorate
Accredited internet retailer scheme (AIRS) –
list of accredited internet retailers.
www.vmd.defra.gov.uk/InternetRetailers/accredited-retailers.aspx

Veterinary Medicines Directorate
Guidance on prescribing or supplying
veterinary medicines including requirements
for registration and inspections of premises.
www.gov.uk/guidance/retail-of-veterinary-medicines

Veterinary Medicines Directorate
Various additional online resources – including a database of veterinary medicinal products.
www.gov.uk/government/organisations/veterinary-medicines-directorate

Wingfield J, Pitchford K, editors
Dale and Appelbe's Pharmacy and Medicines Law.
11th edition. 2017.
London; Pharmaceutical Press.
www.pharmpress.com

Online MAVIS 'Hub' accessible via a quick link on GOV.UK homepage (at time of writing this edition the online hub was not available on website).

3.6
Controlled drugs

CONTROLLED DRUGS RESOURCES

Accountable Officers Network Scotland
A guide to good practice in the management of Controlled Drugs in primary care – Scotland. 2014.
www.knowledge.scot.nhs.uk/accountableofficers/resources.aspx

Care Quality Commission
Controlled Drugs governance self assessment tools (for primary care and secondary care).
www.cqc.org.uk/guidance-providers/controlled-drugs/controlled-drugs-accountable-officers

Care Quality Commission
The safer management of Controlled Drugs annual report.
www.cqc.org.uk/content/controlled-drugs

Department of Health (archived)
Safer management of Controlled Drugs: a guide to good practice in secondary care (England). 2007.
https://webarchive.nationalarchives.gov.uk/+/www.dh.gov.uk/prod_consum_dh/groups/dh_digitalassets/@dh/@en/documents/digitalasset/dh_074511.pdf

Department of Health. Clinical Guidelines on Drug Misuse and Dependence Update 2017 Independent Expert Working Group
Drug misuse and dependence: UK guidelines on clinical management. 2017.
https://assets.publishing.service.gov.uk/government/uploads/system/uploads/attachment_data/file/673978/clinical_guidelines_2017.pdf

Faculty of Pain Medicine
Opioids Aware: A resource for patients and healthcare professionals to support prescribing of opioid medicines for pain
www.rcoa.ac.uk/faculty-of-pain-medicine/opioids-aware

Home Office
Guidance for the safe custody of Controlled Drugs and drug precursors in transit. 2018.
https://assets.publishing.service.gov.uk/government/uploads/system/uploads/attachment_data/file/758746/transit-guidance-v1.3-nov-2018.pdf

Home Office
Security guidance for all existing or prospective Home Office Controlled Drug licensees and/or Precursor Chemical licensees and registrants. 2018.
https://assets.publishing.service.gov.uk/government/uploads/system/uploads/attachment_data/file/758776/security-guidance-businesses-other-organisationsv1.3-nov-2018.pdf

Ministry of Justice
PSI 45/2010: Prison Service Order for Integrated Drug Treatment System. 2010.
www.justice.gov.uk

My Live Well with pain
Useful patient information
http://my.livewellwithpain.co.uk/

National Patient Safety Alerts
Archived alerts (published before 1st April 2012)
https://webarchive.nationalarchives.gov.uk/20171030124143/http://www.nrls.npsa.nhs.uk/resources/type/alerts/

National Institute for Health and Care Excellence
Controlled drugs: safe use and management. NICE guideline. 2016.
www.nice.org.uk

National Institute for Health and Care Excellence
Managing medicines in care homes. Social care guideline. 2014
www.nice.org.uk

National Prescribing Centre (archived)
A guide to good practice in the management of Controlled Drugs in primary care (England). 2009.
www.webarchive.org.uk/wayback/archive/20140627111125/http:/www.npc.nhs.uk/controlled_drugs/resources/controlled_drugs_third_edition.pdf

National Prescribing Centre (archived)
Handbook for Controlled Drugs accountable officers in England. 2011.
www.webarchive.org.uk/wayback/archive/20140627111322/http://www.npc.nhs.uk/controlled_drugs

NHS Improvement
Patient Safety Alerts (published on or after 1st April 2012)
https://improvement.nhs.uk/news-alerts/?keywords=&articletype=patient-safety-alert&after=&before=

Scottish Government
Safer management of controlled drugs:
A Guide to Good Practice in Secondary Care
(Scotland). 2008. www.sehd.scot.nhs.uk

Wingfield J, Pitchford K, editors
Dale and Appelbe's Pharmacy
and Medicines Law. 11th edition. 2017.
London; Pharmaceutical Press.
www.pharmpress.com

* These resources are archived and refer to
The Controlled Drugs (Supervision of Management
and Use) Regulations 2006 which have now been
replaced by The Controlled Drugs (Supervision of
Management and Use) Regulations 2013. The 2013
Regulations provide less detail of specific standard
operating procedures and are focused on
ensuring that adequate monitoring of Controlled
Drugs is undertaken.

3.6.1
BACKGROUND

Legislation applicable to CDs and
pharmacy include:

- The Misuse of Drugs Act 1971 as amended
  (herein referred to as 'the 1971 Act')

- The Misuse of Drugs Regulations 2001 as amended
  (herein referred to as 'the 2001 Regulations')

- The Misuse of Drugs (Safe Custody) Regulations
  1973 as amended (herein referred to as 'Safe
  Custody Regulations')

- The Health Act 2006

- Controlled Drugs (Supervision of Management
  and Use) Regulations 2013 which affect England
  and Scotland.

The 1971 Act imposes prohibitions on the possession,
supply, manufacture, import and export of CDs –
except where permitted by the 2001 Regulations or
under licence from the Secretary of State. The Safe
Custody Regulations detail the storage and safe
custody requirements for CDs.

The enforcement body for CDs offences is the
Home Office, via the police.

The Health Act 2006 introduced the concept
of an 'accountable officer' (see section 3.6.10)
and requires healthcare organisations, and those

providing services to healthcare organisations,
to have standard operating procedures in place
for using and managing CDs.

For registered pharmacies, the Responsible
Pharmacist Regulations 2008 also require that
a range of pharmacy procedures are established –
including procedures for CDs (see Chapter 4).

At the time of writing this edition of MEP we are
waiting for changes in the Pharmacy (Responsible
Pharmacists, Superintendent Pharmacists etc.)
Order 2018 affecting the future role Responsible
Pharmacists have with pharmacy procedures.

Pharmacists should ensure that they are
familiar with the standard operating procedures
for managing CDs in their pharmacies and the
steps that they should take should an incident
or concern relating to CDs arise.

GOSPORT REPORT
At least 450 patients are thought to have died
after the administration of inappropriately high
doses of opioids between 1988 and 2000 at Gosport
War Memorial Hospital. In June 2018, the report
of the Gosport Independent Panel into failures
of care was published.

In November 2018, the Government responded
to the report of the Gosport Independent Panel
www.gov.uk/government/publications/gosport-
independent-panel-report-government-response.
This discussion paper focuses on pharmacy
services and was developed primarily from the
views of the RPS's Hospital Expert Advisory Group.
It discusses the issues the Gosport report raises
for providers of pharmacy services and lessons
to be learnt.

Whilst practice has improved and there are now
professional standards for hospital pharmacy
services (www.rpharms.com/recognition/setting-
professional-standards/professional-standards-
for-hospital-pharmacy), pharmacy teams are
urged to continue to be medicine safety advocates
for the public and support a culture of listening,
speaking up and being heard.

Further information can be viewed on the
RPS website at www.rpharms.com.

ACCOUNTABLE OFFICERS
Accountable officers are responsible for
supervising and managing the use of CDs

in their organisation or setting. Their roles and responsibilities include:

- Oversight of the monitoring and auditing of the management, prescribing and use of CDs

- Ensuring that systems are in place for recording concerns and incidents involving CDs and the operation of these systems

- Attendance of Local Intelligence Network meetings

- Submission of occurrence reports which describe the details of any concerns the organisation has had regarding the management of CDs in a required time frame

- The appointment of authorised witnesses for the destruction of CDs

Further information on the types of individuals who can become authorised witnesses can be found in the documents *The Controlled Drugs (Supervision of Management and Use) Regulations 2013 NHS England Single Operating Model* (www.england.nhs.uk/publications) and *A Guide to Good Practice in the Management of Controlled Drugs in Primary Care – Scotland* (www.knowledge.scot.nhs.uk/accountableofficers/resources-library/resource-detail.aspx?id=4055959). Sources of further information on the duties of accountable officers are specified in Table 9.

TABLE 9: SOURCES OF INFORMATION ON THE DUTIES OF ACCOUNTABLE OFFICERS

COUNTRY

ENGLAND

SOURCE OF INFORMATION

The National Prescribing Centre has published a document that describes the core role of accountable officers. The resource is entitled the Handbook of Controlled Drug accountable officers in England (1st edition) and is available on the UK Web Archive: www.webarchive.org.uk/wayback/archive/20140627111322/http://www.npc.nhs.uk/controlled_drugs/

NHS England have also published guidance *The Controlled Drugs (Supervision of Management and Use Regulations 2013 NHS England Single Operating Model*: www.england.nhs.uk/publications

A register of accountable officers in England is published on the Care Quality Commission website: www.cqc.org.uk

COUNTRY

SCOTLAND

SOURCE OF INFORMATION

Information on the role of accountable officers and a list of accountable officers in Scotland is available on the Healthcare Improvement Scotland website: www.healthcareimprovementscotland.org/our_work/governance_and_assurance/controlled_drugs.aspx

COUNTRY

WALES

SOURCE OF INFORMATION

Information regarding the role of accountable officers in Wales and a list of accountable officers is available on the Healthcare Inspectorate Wales website: www.hiw.org.uk

3.6.2
CLASSIFICATION

The 2001 Regulations classify CDs into five Schedules according to the different levels of control attributed to each:

- Schedule 1 (CD Lic POM)

- Schedule 2 (CD POM)

- Schedule 3 (CD No Register POM)

- Schedule 4 (CD Benz POM and CD Anab POM)

- Schedule 5 (CD INV P and CD INV POM).

The BNF includes CD classification information for Schedule 1 to 4 medicines within the monograph.

SCHEDULE 1
(CD LIC POM)

Most Schedule 1 drugs have no therapeutic use and a licence is generally required for their production, possession or supply. Examples include hallucinogenic drugs (e.g. 'LSD'), ecstasy-type substances, raw opium and cannabis (for further information see section '3.6.15 Cannabis-based products for medicinal use in humans', moving some cannabis products from Schedule 1 to Schedule 2).

SCHEDULE 2
(CD POM)

Pharmacists and other classes of person named in the 2001 Regulations have a general authority to possess, supply and procure Schedule 2 CDs when acting in that capacity.

Schedule 2 includes opiates (e.g. diamorphine, morphine, methadone, oxycodone, pethidine), major stimulants (e.g. amfetamines), quinalbarbitone and ketamine.

SCHEDULE 3
(CD NO REGISTER POM)

Schedule 3 CDs include minor stimulants and other drugs (such as buprenorphine, temazepam, tramadol, midazolam and phenobarbital) that are less likely to be misused (and less harmful if misused) than those in Schedule 2.

From 1st April 2019, gabapentin and pregabalin were rescheduled as Schedule 3 CDs.

SCHEDULE 4
(CD BENZ POM OR CD ANAB POM)

Schedule 4 is split into two parts:

- **Part I (CD Benz POM)**

  Contains most of the benzodiazepines (such as diazepam), non-benzodiazepine hypnotics (such as zopiclone), and Sativex (a cannabinoid oromucosal mouth spray)

- **Part II (CD Anab POM)**

  Contains most of the anabolic and androgenic steroids, together with clenbuterol (an adrenoceptor stimulant) and growth hormones.

SCHEDULE 5
(CD INV POM OR CD INV P)

Schedule 5 contains preparations of certain CDs (such as codeine, pholcodine and morphine) that are exempt from full control when present in medicinal products of specifically low strengths.

Table 10 summarises the various characteristics of CDs.

TABLE 10: SUMMARY OF VARIOUS CHARACTERISTICS OF CONTROLLED DRUGS

	SCHEDULE 2	SCHEDULE 3	SCHEDULE 4 (PART 1)	SCHEDULE 4 (PART 2)	SCHEDULE 5
DESIGNATION	CD POM	CD No Reg POM	CD Benz POM	CD Anab POM	CD INV P or CD INV POM
PRESCRIPTION REQUIREMENTS – SEE SECTION 3.6.7	Yes	Yes	No	No	No
PRESCRIPTION VALID FOR	28 days after appropriate date	28 days after appropriate date	28 days after appropriate date	28 days after appropriate date	6 months
ADDRESS OF PRESCRIBER REQUIRED TO BE WITHIN THE UK	Yes	Yes	No	No	No

	SCHEDULE 2	SCHEDULE 3	SCHEDULE 4 (PART 1)	SCHEDULE 4 (PART 2)	SCHEDULE 5
EEA AND SWISS PRESCRIBERS CAN LEGALLY PRESCRIBE	No	No	Yes	Yes	Yes
PRESCRIPTION IS REPEATABLE*	No	No	Yes	Yes	Yes
EMERGENCY SUPPLY	No	No *(except phenobarbital [also known as phenobarbitone or phenobarbitone sodium] for epilepsy by a UK-registered prescriber)*	Yes	Yes	Yes
REQUISITION NECESSARY	Yes	Yes	No	No	No
REQUISITION TO BE MARKED BY THE SUPPLIER	Yes	Yes	No	No	No
INVOICES TO BE RETAINED FOR TWO YEARS**	No	Yes	No	No	Yes
LICENCE REQUIRED TO IMPORT OR EXPORT	Yes	Yes	Yes	Yes *(unless the substance is imported or exported by a person for self-administration)*	No

*By 'repeatable' we mean the instance where the prescriber adds an instruction on the main prescription for the prescribed item to be repeated, e.g. repeat x 3. This does not refer to the prescription counterpart which is sometimes used as a patient repeat request to the prescriber.

NHS prescriptions are not repeatable (see section 3.3.1 under repeatable prescriptions).

**NICE advise that organisations should consider retaining all CDs invoices for six years for the purpose of HM Revenue and Customs.

3.6.3
POSSESSION AND SUPPLY

Pharmacists, doctors and dentists, when acting in these capacities, are among those empowered by the 2001 Regulations under a general authority to possess, supply and procure Schedule 2, 3, 4 and 5 CDs.

Other mechanisms for the lawful possession of CDs include:

- **Home Office licence**
  Persons who have an applicable Home Office licence can possess and supply CDs in accordance with the terms of the licence (e.g. the RPS museum holds a Home Office licence to possess CDs for the purposes of the museum)

- **Home Office group authority**
  Persons who are covered by an applicable Home Office licence group authority can possess and supply CDs in accordance with the terms of the group authority (e.g. there is currently a group authority covering paramedics that allows them to possess and supply certain CDs)

- **Legislation: class of person**
  Other classes of person specified in the 2001 Regulations, provided they are acting in the capacity of the specified class (e.g. a postal operator or, for specified CDs, a registered practising midwife)

- **Legislation: class of drug**
  The 2001 Regulations indicate that possessing certain classes of CDs is lawful (e.g. Schedule 4 part II drugs when contained in medicinal products and Schedule 5 drugs)

- **Patients**
  Persons who have been prescribed a CD by a doctor, supplementary prescriber, nurse independent prescriber, pharmacist independent prescriber, dentist or veterinary surgeon (for an animal).

A comprehensive analysis of the multiple classes of persons who, and organisations that, can possess and supply CDs is outside the scope of this document. However, this has been summarised within Chapter 17 of *Pharmacy and Medicines Law* (11th edition. 2017) or can be found in the 2001 Regulations.

POSSESSION OF SCHEDULE 1 CONTROLLED DRUGS

A Home Office licence would be required to possess Schedule 1 CDs. However, some pharmacists, particularly those working within a hospital, may be asked to deal with substances removed from patients on admission, which may be Schedule 1 products (e.g. cannabis).

A pharmacist, under two specific exemptions, can take possession of such CDs. The first exemption is when possession is taken for the purpose of destruction. The second is for the purpose of handing over to a police officer. You should refer to your organisation policy for further detailed information on this.

The patient's confidentiality should normally be maintained and the police should be called on the understanding that the source will not be identified. If, however, the quantity is so large that the drug could not be purely for personal use the pharmacist may decide that the greater interests of the public require identification of the source. Such a decision should not be taken without first considering discussing the situation with the other health professionals involved in the patient's care and taking advice from the pharmacist's professional indemnity insurer's legal adviser.

The patient should give authority for the drug to be removed and destroyed. If the patient refuses, the pharmacist may feel that he or she has no alternative other than to call in the police. Under no circumstances can a suspected illicit drug be handed back to a patient.

3.6.4
ADMINISTRATION

Schedule 1 CDs may only be administered, or prescribed under a Home Office licence. Schedule 2, 3 or 4 CDs can be administered to a patient by:

- A doctor, dentist, pharmacist independent prescriber or nurse independent prescriber acting in their own right

- A supplementary prescriber (including a pharmacist supplementary prescriber) acting in accordance with a clinical management plan

- A person acting in accordance with the directions of a prescriber entitled to prescribe CDs (including pharmacist independent prescribers).

Only medical prescribers who hold a special licence from the Home Secretary or Scottish Government's Chief Medical Officer can prescribe cocaine, diamorphine or dipipanone for treating addiction. This special licence is not required if treating organic disease or injury. Pharmacist independent prescribers, nurse independent prescribers and supplementary prescribers may not prescribe cocaine, diamorphine or dipipanone for treating addiction, but may prescribe these medicines for treating organic disease or injury.

NB: In healthcare environments, including secure environments, additional requirements and restrictions regarding who may administer or witness the administration of medicines may exist to satisfy medicines management, governance and patient safety considerations.

3.6.5
IMPORT, EXPORT AND TRAVELLERS

A licence is needed for a pharmacy to import or export Schedule 1, 2, 3 and 4 (part 1) CDs. A licence is needed for Schedule 4 (part II) CDs, unless the substance is imported or exported by a person for self-administration. There are no restrictions on the import or export of Schedule 5 CDs (see Table 10). Pharmacists are often asked about arrangements for patients who are taking CDs abroad. The Home Office is the regulatory body in this instance and may require individuals to apply for personal licences in certain circumstances. Information can be found on the Home Office website (www.gov.uk/government/organisations/home-office) and *'Drug misuse and dependence – UK guidelines on clinical management'* (https://assets.publishing.service.gov.uk/government/uploads/system/uploads/attachment_data/file/673978/clinical_guidelines_2017.pdf)

TRAVELLERS

At the time of writing, a personal licence was not required by the Home Office if a person travelling is carrying less than three months' supply of a CDs. However, it is advised that a covering letter signed by the prescriber is obtained that confirms the name of the patient, travel plans, name of the prescribed CDs, total quantities and dose.

The patient should also check with the embassies or high commissions for the countries they will be travelling through to ensure that the import and export regulations in those countries are complied with.

It would be prudent for patients to check any additional requirements that their travel operator/airline company may impose.

The patient may also want to refer to the NHS website 'Can I take my medicines abroad' www.nhs.uk for further guidance

3.6.6
OBTAINING CONTROLLED DRUGS – REQUISITION REQUIREMENTS FOR SCHEDULE 1, 2 AND 3 CONTROLLED DRUGS

On 30 November 2015, amendments to the Misuse of Drugs Regulations 2001 made the use of an approved form for the requisitioning of Schedule 2 and 3 CDs in the community mandatory. This applies to both requisitions for human and for veterinary use. Hospices and prisons are exempt from the requirement to use the approved form.

The introduction of an approved mandatory requisition form is a remaining Shipman Inquiry recommendation aimed at ensuring the purchase of all stocks of Schedule 2 and 3 CDs by healthcare professionals within the community can be monitored.

THE LEGAL REQUIREMENTS FOR A CONTROLLED DRUG REQUISITION ARE:

1   Signature of the recipient

2   Name of the recipient

3   Address of the recipient

4   Profession or occupation

5   Total quantity of drug

6   Purpose of the requisition

DIAGRAM 11: SUMMARY OF WHEN AN APPROVED MANDATORY REQUISITION FORM MUST BE USED TO REQUEST STOCK OF SCHEDULE 2 AND 3 CONTROLLED DRUGS

RECEIVED BY HOSPITAL PHARMACY
↓
IS THE REQUEST ON BEHALF OF A WARD OR DEPARTMENT WHITHIN THE SAME LEGAL ENTITY?
↓   ↓
YES   NO →
↓
APPROVED FORM NOT REQUIRED – MAY CONTINUE WITH CURRENT REQUISITION ARRANGEMENTS

RECEIVED BY COMMUNITY PHARMACY
↓
REQUEST FROM A HOSPITAL, COMMUNITY, HEALTH PROVIDER (E.G.GP) OR VETERINARY SURGEON
↓
APPROVED FORM MUST BE USED* (SEE BELOW FOR FURTHER INSTRUCTIONS)

*Unless the request is from a hospice or a prison

The handling of CDs in prisons requires specific processes. In England these are underpinned by the information currently found in the NPC document (UK Web Archive) Safe Management and Use of Controlled Drugs in Prison Health in England (http://drugslibrary.wordpress.stir.ac.uk/files/2017/07/final_report_safe_management_and_use_of_controlled_drugs_in_prison_health_in_england_final.pdf)

In prisons in England, hospital-style requisition forms (instead of a standardised form) are usually used and are printed in a bound, book format – sequentially numbered with a carbon copy of each requisition to provide a robust audit trail. Although not a legal requirement, prisons in Scotland currently use standardised CDRF forms to request stock.

HOSPITAL REQUISITIONS

Hospital pharmacy requisitions from a ward or department that are presented to a pharmacy that is a separate legal entity must also meet these requirements, including the use of an approved mandatory requisition form. The Home Office has advised that the person in charge or acting in charge of a hospital can issue a yearly 'bulk' or 'global' requisition on the approved mandatory form to the separate legal entity that supplies its wards or departments for the wards or departments to then draw on throughout the year using CDs requisition books with duplicate pages. The full Home Office guidance specific to this scenario can be accessed on the NHSBSA website (www.nhsbsa.nhs.uk/ PrescriptionServices/1120.aspx). Where the person in charge, or acting in charge of a hospital issues and signs a requisition, this must also be signed by a doctor or dentist employed or engaged in that hospital.

PRACTICE ISSUES

- Supplies made against a faxed or photocopied requisition are not acceptable

- Legislation requires that a requisition in writing must be obtained by the supplier (i.e. the pharmacy) before delivery of any Schedule 2 or 3 CDs to the following recipients – practitioners, hospitals, care homes, ship and offshore installation personnel, senior registered nurses in charge of wards, theatres and other hospital departments. Some recipients (such as GPhC registered pharmacies) are not included in this legal requirement. However, the Home Office advises that supplies from one registered pharmacy to another registered pharmacy should only be made after receiving a written requisition on an approved requisition form

- In an emergency, a doctor or dentist can be supplied with a Schedule 2 or 3 CDs on the undertaking that a requisition will be supplied within the next 24 hours. Failure to do so would be an offence on the part of the doctor or dentist

- Where stock is collected by a messenger on behalf of a purchaser, a written authorisation must be provided to the supplying pharmacist that empowers the messenger to receive the medicines on behalf of the purchaser. The supplying pharmacist needs to be reasonably satisfied that the authorisation is genuine and must retain it for two years

- A licence would be required for any healthcare professional to possess Schedule 1 CDs; pharmacists are reminded that they are not able to requisition Schedule 1 CDs

- For further details on wholesale dealing see section 3.4.

PROCESSING REQUISITION FORMS (MARKING AND SENDING)

When a requisition for a Schedule 1, 2 or 3 CD is received, it is a legal requirement to:

- Mark the requisition indelibly with the supplier's name and address (i.e. the name of the pharmacy); where a pharmacy stamp is used this must be clear and legible

- Send the original requisition to the relevant NHS agency.

As a matter of good practice, pharmacies should retain a copy of the requisition for two years from the date of supply.

These processing requirements do not apply when the supply is made:

- By a person responsible for the dispensing and supply of medicines at a hospital, care home, hospice, prison or organisation providing

ambulance services who must mark and retain the original requisition for two years

- By pharmaceutical manufactures or wholesalers

- Against veterinary requisitions (the original requisition should be retained for five years).

MIDWIFE SUPPLY ORDERS

A registered midwife may use a midwife supply order to obtain the following CDs:

- Diamorphine

- Morphine

- Pethidine.

The order must contain the following:

- Name of the midwife

- Occupation of the midwife

- Name of the person to whom the CD is to be administered or supplied

- Purpose for which the CD is required

- Total quantity of the drug to be obtained

- Signature of an appropriate medical officer – a doctor authorised (in writing) by the local supervising authority or the person appointed by the supervising authority to exercise supervision over midwives within the area

For details on checking registration of nurses see section 3.3.16.

TABLE 11: APPROVED MANDATORY REQUISITION FORMS

	ENGLAND	SCOTLAND*	WALES
TYPE OF FORM	FP10CDF	CDRF – for private supplies GP10A – for NHS supplies	WP10CDF
WHERE TO OBTAIN FORMS	Download from NHSBSA website (www.nhsbsa.nhs.uk)	Local NHS health board	Local NHS health board

3.6.7
PRESCRIPTION REQUIREMENTS FOR SCHEDULE 2 AND 3 CONTROLLED DRUGS

The requirements that must be present for a prescription (both NHS and private) for Schedule 2 or 3 CDs to be valid are outlined in Diagram 12 (see section 3.3.1 for the usual prescription requirements which also apply). For private prescriptions see also Table 13 for information on the standardised forms that must be used.

From 1st April 2019, gabapentin and pregabalin were rescheduled as Schedule 3 CDs. The prescription requirements outlined in Diagram 12 below apply to gabapentin and pregabalin. See RPS support alert titled 'Rescheduling of Gabapentin and Pregabalin to Schedule 3 Controlled Drugs from 1 April 2019' (www.rpharms.com/about-us/news/details/rescheduling-of-gabapentin-and-pregabalin-to-schedule-3-controlled-drugs-from-1-april-2019).

DIAGRAM 12: CONTROLLED DRUG PRESCRIPTION REQUIREMENTS FOR SCHEDULE 2 OR 3 CONTROLLED DRUGS

Pharmacy Stamp	Age	Title, Forename, Surname & Address:
	D.o.B.	9 **PATIENT NAME** 10 **PATIENT ADDRESS**

Please don't stamp over age box

Number of days' treatment NB Ensure dose is stated		NHS Number:

Endorsements

4 **DOSE**

5 **FORM**

6 **STRENGTH**

7 **TOTAL QUANTITY**

8 **QUANTITY PRESCRIBED**

11 **DENTAL WORDING WHERE APPROPRIATE**

12 **INSTALMENT WORDING WHERE APPROPRIATE**

Signature of Prescriber	Date
1 **SIGNATURE OF PRESCRIBER**	2 **DATE**

For dispenser No. of Prescns. on form	3 **ADDRESS OF PRESCRIBER**

NHS

1 **Signature**

The prescription needs to be signed by the prescriber with their usual signature. The pharmacist should either recognise the signature (and believe it to be genuine) or take reasonable steps to satisfy themselves that it is genuine. The prescription may be signed by another prescriber other than the named prescriber and still be legally valid. However, the address of the prescriber needs to be applicable to the signatory for the prescription to be legally compliant. The CD register entry should record the details of the actual prescriber (the signatory) rather than the named prescriber. Doctors, dentists, vets, supplementary nurse or pharmacist prescribers (subject to a clinical management plan), independent nurse prescribers and pharmacist independent prescribers can prescribe CDs. Advanced electronic signatures can be accepted for Schedule 2 and 3 CDs where the Electronic Prescribing Service (EPS) is used, see the pink box overleaf for further information.

2 **Date**

The prescription needs to include the date on which it was signed. CD prescriptions are valid for 28 days after the appropriate date on the prescription. The appropriate date is either the signature date or any other date indicated on the prescription (by the prescriber) as a date before which the drugs should not be supplied – whichever is later. The 28 day restriction includes prescriptions for Schedule 4 CDs and any owing balances (see section 3.3.1 for details on the validity of owings).

3 **Prescriber's address**

The address of the prescriber must be included on the prescription and must be within the UK.

4 **Dose**

The dose does not need to be in both words and figures; however, it must be clearly defined (see Table 12).

5 **Form**

The formulation must be stated; the abbreviations 'tabs' and 'caps' are acceptable. It should be clear and unambiguous if the prescriber intends a supply of m/r , s/r etc.

6 **Strength**

The strength only needs to be written on the

prescription if the medicine is available in more than one strength. To avoid ambiguity, where a prescription requests multiple strengths of a medicine, each strength should be prescribed separately (i.e. separate dose, total quantity, etc.).

7 **Total quantity**
The total quantity must be written in both words and figures. For tablets, capsules, ampoules, etc. the quantity can be expressed as either

- the total number of dosage units required e.g. 10mg x 10 (ten);

- or the total quantity of drug as milligrams e.g. 100 (one-hundred) mg.

- The total quantity for liquid preparations should be the volume required e.g. 100 millilitres.

Both of the above are legal. The RPS advises where the CD is available as a dosage unit it is preferable to prescribe in dosage units, as this helps reduce the risk of arithmetic errors in prescribing or dispensing.

The total quantity of dosage units may be expressed either as the total number of dosage units e.g. 'sixty 10mg tablets' or as the multiplication of two numbers provided both components are written in words and figures, e.g. '10mg tablets, 2 packs of 30 tablets [two packs of thirty tablets]'. However, using pack sizes may introduce unnecessary complexity if products are supplied in different pack sizes, or the pack size prescribed is unavailable. Whichever form is used, the pharmacist must be satisfied that the total quantity is unambiguous.

The Home Office advise:

"If there are different strength tablets, the quantities for each strength must be listed in words and figures, either as:

- *'numbers of tablets' e.g. : 7 (seven) x 8mg tabs, 14 (fourteen) x 2mg tabs or as:*

- *'milligrams' e.g. 56 (fifty-six) mg as 8mg tablets 28 (twenty-eight) mg as 2mg tablets*

For clarity, the name of the drug should also appear each time for each different strength so that there can be no ambiguity. If there is only one strength of tablets specified,

the total can be provided simply in numbers of tablets or milligrams e.g. as: 112 (one hundred and twelve) mg, or 14 (fourteen) tablets."

For further information see *Drug misuse and dependence UK guidelines on clinical management*, update 2017, (www.gov.uk/government/publications/drug-misuse-and-dependence-uk-guidelines-on-clinical-management).

8 **Quantity prescribed**
The Department of Health and the Scottish Government have issued strong recommendations that the maximum quantity of Schedule 2, 3 or 4 CDs prescribed should not exceed 30 days. This is not a legal restriction but prescribers should be able to justify the quantity requested (on a clinical basis) if more than 30 days' supply is prescribed. There may be genuine circumstances for which medicines need to be prescribed in this way.

9 **Name of patient**

10 **Address of patient**
If the patient does not have a fixed address (e.g. because he or she is homeless or under a witness protection scheme), 'no fixed abode' or 'NFA' is acceptable. Use of a PO Box is not acceptable.

11 **Dental prescriptions**
Where the CD prescription is written by a dentist, the words 'for dental treatment only' must be present.

12 **Instalment direction**
Where the prescription is intended to be supplied in instalments a valid instalment direction is required. (For further information see 'Instalment direction for Schedule 2 or Controlled Drugs').

Additional requirements
When the CDs is supplied, it is a requirement to mark the prescription with the date of supply at the time the supply is made. The prescription needs to be written in indelible ink and can be computer generated.

Sugar free products
Pharmacists are reminded that sugar free and/or colour free products have a greater potential for abuse; therefore the RPS advise that these are only supplied when specifically prescribed.

NAME OF THE MEDICINE

The name of the prescribed medicine is necessary on a prescription to identify which medicine is being requested. However, it is not a legal requirement. It is good practice to write the name of the medicine in full as it appears in the manufacturer's summary of product characteristics.

TABLE 12: EXAMPLES OF DOSES THAT ARE, AND ARE NOT, LEGALLY ACCEPTABLE (NOT EXHAUSTIVE)

EXAMPLES OF DOSES THAT ARE NOT LEGALLY ACCEPTABLE

- As directed
- When required
- PRN
- As per chart
- Titration dose
- Weekly (this is just a frequency and not a dose)
- Decrease dose by 3.5ml every four days
- Twice a day

EXAMPLES OF DOSES THAT ARE LEGALLY ACCEPTABLE (NB: LEGAL ACCEPTABILITY DOES NOT AUTOMATICALLY INDICATE CLINICAL APPROPRIATENESS)

- One as directed
- Two when required
- One PRN
- Three ampoules to be given as directed (better still – three ampoules to be given over 24 hours as directed)
- One to two when required

CONTROLLED DRUGS ELECTRONIC PRESCRIPTIONS

At the time of writing, the national roll out of CDs in EPS was underway. Further information on this can be viewed on the NHS Digital website https://digital.nhs.uk/services/electronic-prescription-service/controlled-drugs#summary

The PSNC has published information on EPS and CDs including a FAQ factsheet and dispensing and supplying CDs via EPS http://psnc.org.uk/dispensing-supply/eps/dispensing-in-eps-release-2/eps-legality-and-scope/eps-and-controlled-drugs/

INSTALMENT DIRECTION FOR SCHEDULE 2 OR 3 CONTROLLED DRUGS

An instalment direction combines two pieces of information:

1 Amount of medicine per instalment
2 Interval between each time the medicine can be supplied

The Home Office has confirmed that an instalment prescription must have both a dose and an instalment amount specified separately on the prescription.

The first instalment must be dispensed within 28 days of the appropriate date (see Date Diagram 12). The remainder of the instalments should be dispensed in accordance with the instructions (even if this runs beyond 28 days after the appropriate date).

If the only date on the prescription is the date of signing, the first dispensing needs to take place within 28 days of this date. If the prescriber indicates on the prescription a date before which the prescribed medicine should not be dispensed, this would be the appropriate date instead. The prescription must then be marked with the date of each supply.

The instalment direction is a legal requirement and needs to be complied with. However, because there are acknowledged practical difficulties with missed doses and dates when the pharmacy is closed (e.g. bank holidays), the Home Office has approved specific wording to be used that gives pharmacists a degree of flexibility when making a supply and to ensure patient care is not compromised, provided pharmacists are satisfied of the prescriber's intention. If the relevant approved wording is used, a pharmacist can supply:

- the balance of an instalment if the interval date is missed (i.e. if three days' supply was directed to be supplied on day one but it was missed, it allows two days' supply to be issued on day two).

- treatment prior to the start date on the prescription, if this is on a day the pharmacy is closed for example during bank holiday periods.

HOME OFFICE APPROVED WORDING FOR INSTALMENT PRESCRIBING

The Home Office introduced the following set of approved wording for instalment prescribing in November 2015.

HOME OFFICE APPROVED WORDING FOR INSTALMENT PRESCRIBING

1 Please dispense instalments due on pharmacy closed days on a prior suitable day.

2 If an instalment's collection day has been missed, please still dispense the amount due for any remaining day(s) of that instalment.

3 Consult the prescriber if three or more consecutive days of a prescription have been missed.

4 Supervise consumption on collection days.

5 Dispense daily doses in separate containers.

NB: If the prescriber selects instalment intervals that take bank holidays or other closure dates into account, it may not be necessary to include this wording.

NB: If you decide to supply against a prescription that uses wording not approved by the Home Office, it will not provide the same protection from enforcement when making the supply. In this instance, if practical, you should try to get the prescription amended by the prescriber to include the approved Home Office wording.

FURTHER READING

Home Office
Circular 027/2015: Approved mandatory requisition form and Home Office approved wording. 2015.
www.gov.uk/government/publications/circular-0272015-approved-mandatory-requisition-form-and-home-office-approved-wording/circular-0272015-approved-mandatory-requisition-form-and-home-office-approved-wording

MISSED DOSES

If you know a patient has missed three days' prescribed treatment (or the number of days defined by any local agreement with the prescriber), there is a risk that he or she will have lost tolerance to the drug and the usual dose may cause overdose. In the best interests of the patient, consider contacting the prescriber to discuss appropriate next steps.

TECHNICAL ERRORS

Where a prescription for a Schedule 2 or 3 CD contains a minor typographical error or spelling mistake, or where either the words or figures (but not both) of the total quantity has been omitted, a pharmacist can amend the prescription indelibly so that it becomes compliant with legislation.

The pharmacist needs to have exercised due diligence, be satisfied that the prescription is genuine and that the supply is in accordance with the intention of the prescriber. The prescription must also be marked to show that the amendments are attributable to the pharmacist (e.g. name, date, signature and GPhC registration number).

Pharmacists cannot correct other amendments or omissions (e.g. missing date, incorrect dose, form or strength). These should be corrected by the original prescriber or, in an emergency, another prescriber authorised to prescribe CDs.

Amendments cannot be made by covering letter from the prescriber.

Only medical prescribers who hold a special licence from the Home Secretary or Scottish Government's Chief Medical Officer can prescribe cocaine, diamorphine or dipipanone for treating addiction. This special licence is not required if treating organic disease or injury. Pharmacist independent prescribers, nurse independent prescribers and supplementary prescribers may not prescribe cocaine, diamorphine or dipipanone for treating addiction, but may prescribe these medicines for treating organic disease or injury.

The handling of CDs in prisons requires specific processes underpinned by the information currently found in the NPC document (UK Web Archive) Safe Management and Use of Controlled Drugs in Prison Health in England (http://drugslibrary.wordpress.stir.ac.uk/files/2017/07/final_report_safe_management_and_use_of_controlled_drugs_in_prison_health_in_england_final.pdf)

PRIVATE PRESCRIPTION REQUIREMENTS FOR SCHEDULE 2 AND 3 CONTROLLED DRUGS

1 STANDARDISED FORM

Private prescriptions for Schedule 2 or 3 CDs must be written on designated standardised forms. The forms that should be used are described in Table 13.

Private prescriptions that are not on the designated standardised form must not be accepted unless they are veterinary prescriptions. For a hospital pharmacy to lawfully supply a Schedule 2 or 3 CD against a private prescription issued outside that hospital (i.e. outside its legal entity), a standardised form must be used. Where the private prescription is issued and dispensed within the same legal entity, a standardised form is not required.

2 PRESCRIBER IDENTIFICATION NUMBER

A prescriber identification number must be included on standardised private prescriptions. This number is not the prescriber's professional registration number (i.e. the GMC number). It is a number issued by the relevant NHS agency and the prescriber can obtain it from their local primary care organisation. In Scotland, a valid NHS prescriber code is used where available or new ones issued where necessary.

3 SUBMISSION

Pharmacies must submit the original private prescription to the relevant NHS agency (NHS Business Services Authority or equivalent); for veterinary prescriptions see below. This requires an identifying code assigned to the pharmacy for this purpose by the local primary care organisation (an identifying code is not required for Scotland).

VETERINARY PRESCRIPTIONS

Veterinary prescriptions for CDs do not need to be written on standardised forms and do not need to be submitted to the relevant NHS agency. Forms must be retained for five years.

PRACTICE ISSUES: PRESCRIBING OTHER MEDICINES ON THE SAME PRIVATE PRESCRIPTION FORM AS CDS

Medicines that are not CDs should not be prescribed on the same form as a Schedule 2 or 3 CD. This is because the form needs to be sent to the relevant NHS agency so the pharmacist would be unable to comply with the requirement to keep private prescriptions for a POM for two years.

FURTHER READING

Information Services Division Scotland
Private prescribers of Controlled Drugs.
www.isdscotland.org/Health-Topics/Prescribing-and-Medicines/Prescriber-Codes

NHS Business Services Authority
Private CD prescribers.
www.nhsbsa.nhs.uk/PrescriptionServices/3993.aspx

TABLE 13: CONTROLLED DRUGS PRIVATE PRESCRIPTION FORMS

	ENGLAND	SCOTLAND	WALES
TYPE OF FORM	FP10 PCD	PPCD(1)	WP10 PCD
WHERE TO OBTAIN FORMS	Local NHS England area team	Local NHS health board	Local NHS health board

3.6.8
COLLECTION OF DISPENSED CONTROLLED DRUGS

When a Schedule 2 CD is collected from a pharmacy, the pharmacist is legally required to determine whether the person collecting is a patient, patient's representative or healthcare professional.

Depending upon which type of person is collecting, the pharmacist needs to take appropriate action (see Table 14). See also section 3.6.11 for further information on record keeping requirements.

COLLECTION BY A REPRESENTATIVE OF A DRUG MISUSE PATIENT

If a drug misuser wants a representative to collect a dispensed CD on his or her behalf, pharmacists are advised to first obtain a letter from the drug misuser that authorises and names the representative. (This includes those detained in police custody who should supply a letter of authorisation to a police custody officer to present to the pharmacist). A separate letter should be obtained each time the drug misuser sends a representative to collect and the representative should bring identification. The pharmacist must be satisfied that the letter is genuine. It is also good practice to insist on seeing the patient in person at least once a week unless this is known not to be possible. The record of supply in the CD register should include details of the representative. If the directions on the prescription state that the dose must be supervised, the pharmacist should contact the prescriber before the medicine is supplied to the representative – since supervision will not be possible. It is legally acceptable to confirm verbally with the prescriber that they are happy with this arrangement since supervision, while important, is not a legal requirement under the 2001 Regulations. An appropriate record of this conversation should be made. It would not be necessary to contact the prescriber if the person has been detained in police custody and the representative collecting the dose is a police custody officer or a custody healthcare professional. This is because the administration of any Schedule 2 or 3 CD in custody will be supervised by a healthcare professional. If the dose is usually supervised, but has been supplied, the pharmacist should consider annotating the prescription and patient medication records to advise others that the dose has not been supervised in the pharmacy.

TABLE 14: ACTIONS REQUIRED WHEN A DISPENSED SCHEDULE 2 CONTROLLED DRUG IS COLLECTED

PERSON COLLECTING	ACTION	NOTES
PATIENT or PATIENT'S REPRESENTATIVE	Pharmacist may request evidence of that person's identity, unless already known to the pharmacist	The decision whether to supply or not is at the discretion of the supplying pharmacist – based on their professional judgement
*HEALTHCARE PROFESSIONAL ACTING IN THEIR PROFESSIONAL CAPACITY ON BEHALF OF THE PATIENT	Unless already known to the pharmacist, obtain: 1 Name of healthcare professional 2 Address of healthcare professional Also request evidence of identity	Where evidence of identity is not available, the pharmacist has discretion over whether to supply or not – based on their professional judgement

*In this scenario, 'healthcare professional' refers to any person authorised to collect a Schedule 2 CD medication on behalf of the person named on the prescription who is operating under a contract of employment in a health or social care occupation (for example a doctor, nurse or care worker).

PRACTICE ISSUES

• It is good practice for the person collecting a Schedule 2 or 3 CD to sign the space on the reverse of the prescription form that is specifically for this purpose. A supply can be made if this is not signed, subject to the professional judgement of the pharmacist

• Instalment prescriptions only need to be signed once

• A representative, including a delivery driver, can sign on behalf of a patient. However, a robust audit trail should be available to confirm successful delivery of the medicine to the patient.

3.6.9
SAFE CUSTODY

The Safe Custody Regulations refer to the physical security of certain Schedule 2 or 3 CDs. It requires that pharmacies, private hospitals and care homes keep relevant CDs in a 'locked safe, cabinet or room which is constructed as to prevent unauthorised access to the drugs'. For settings other than those listed above, these regulations are considered minimum standards for safe custody.

STRUCTURAL REQUIREMENTS OF SAFES, CABINETS AND ROOMS USED FOR STORING CONTROLLED DRUGS

The structural requirements and technical details with which CD safes, cabinets and rooms must comply are detailed in Schedule 2 of the Safe Custody Regulations. These requirements are of a technical nature requiring expertise and knowledge of construction. We do not endorse or approve individual (or brands of) CD cabinets. When purchasing a safe or cabinet, reassurance should be sought from the vendor or manufacturer that the product specifications comply with the requirements specified in the Safe Custody Regulations.

Alternatively, you must apply for an exemption certificate from the police, which certifies that the safe, cabinet or room provides an adequate degree of security for holding CDs. For further information, contact your local police station.

The Controlled Drugs that must be kept under safe custody are:

• Schedule 1 drugs

• Schedule 2 drugs except some liquid preparations and quinalbarbitone (secobarbital). Details of exempted Schedule 2 CDs are available from the Misuse of Drugs (Safe Custody) Regulations 1973 as amended

• Schedule 3 drugs unless exempted under the Misuse of Drugs (Safe Custody) Regulations 1973 as amended, where the full lists are available. Common exemptions include: phenobarbital, mazindol, meprobamate, midazolam, tramadol, pentazocine and phentermine

• From 1st April 2019, gabapentin and pregabalin were rescheduled as Schedule 3 CDs and are exempt from safe custody requirements

• Common Schedule 3 CDs which require safe custody include temazepam and buprenorphine

SAFE CUSTODY REQUIREMENTS FOR SECURE ENVIRONMENTS AND SECONDARY CARE

Prison building regulations specify details of the robust nature required for all rooms that store CDs. For further information, see the Ministry of Justice's PSI 45/2010 Prison Service Order for Integrated Drug Treatment System (www.justice.gov.uk)

In prisons and hospitals, it is recommended that the CD cabinet should meet the 'Sold secure silver standard'. For further information, see:

Department of Health (National Archives)
Safer management of Controlled Drugs: A guide to good practice in secondary care (England). October 2007.
https://webarchive.nationalarchives.gov.uk/+/www.dh.gov.uk/prod_consum_dh/groups/dh_digitalassets/@dh/@en/documents/digitalasset/dh_074511.pdf

Health Building Notes 00-01 General design principles 14-01 Designing pharmacy and radiopharmacy facilities
www.gov.uk/government/publications/guidance-on-the-design-and-layout-of-pharmacy-and-radiopharmacy-facilities

Welsh Health Building Notes 00-01 General design principles 14-01 Designing pharmacy and radiopharmacy facilities
www.wales.nhs.uk

Some organisations may carry out a risk assessment which determines that CDs in Schedules 3, 4 and 5 should be handled in the same way as CDs in Schedule 2. This may result in CDs other than those that require safe custody by law, being stored in the CDs safe, cabinet or room. This should be included in the relevant policy documents and standard operating procedures.

When CDs requiring safe custody are not kept in the CD cabinet, safe or room (e.g. during the dispensing process), they must be under the 'direct personal supervision' of a pharmacist.

Access to CDs (including handling of 'CD keys') should be documented within a policy. The policy should prevent unauthorised access and be able to identify who has had access to CDs (e.g. the electronic logs from a room or cabinet with electronic access or an audit trail for holders of the CD keys). In community pharmacies, it is common for the pharmacist to hold the CD keys.

A key log could be used to keep an audit trail of who has had access to the keys, including overnight storage in the pharmacy, the transfer of the keys from one pharmacist at the end of a shift to another pharmacist, etc. A template CD key log is available in the quick reference guide Safe custody of Controlled Drugs: www.rpharms.com

PATIENT-RETURNED AND OUT-OF-DATE OR OBSOLETE CONTROLLED DRUGS

Safe custody applies to patient-returned, out-of-date and obsolete CDs until they can be destroyed (see section 3.6.10). To minimise the risk of supplying these to patients, this stock should be segregated from other pharmacy stock and be clearly marked (e.g. mark the stock as 'patient returns waiting to be destroyed' or 'out of date, waiting authorised witness to destroy', etc).

FURTHER READING

Royal Pharmaceutical Society
Safe custody of Controlled Drugs – quick reference guide.
www.rpharms.com

Wingfield J, Pitchford K, editors
Dale and Appelbe's Pharmacy and Medicines Law.
11th edition. 2017. London; Pharmaceutical Press.
www.rpharms.com

3.6.10
DESTRUCTION OF CONTROLLED DRUGS

Pharmacies are required to denature CDs prior to disposal. Usually, this process requires an appropriate licence but pharmacies can register an exemption without needing to obtain a licence.

In England and Wales, an exemption is issued by the Environment Agency and is known as the 'T28 exemption'. This allows pharmacies to sort and dispose of CDs and to comply with the 2001 Regulations by denaturing them prior to disposal. This exemption needs to be registered with the Environment Agency, which can be done on their website: www.gov.uk/government/organisations/environment-agency

In Scotland, the exemption is issued by the Scottish Environment Protection Agency (SEPA), which currently accepts that the denaturing of CDs forms part of the exempt activity of secure storage.

CONTROLLED DRUGS THAT NEED TO BE DENATURED BEFORE DISPOSAL

The Home Office has advised that all CDs in Schedules 2, 3 and 4 (part 1) should be denatured and, therefore, rendered irretrievable before disposal.

PERSONS AUTHORISED TO WITNESS THE DENATURING OF CONTROLLED DRUGS

In some circumstances, the denaturing of CDs needs to be witnessed by an authorised person. Where there is a requirement to make a CD register entry, legislation also requires to have their destruction witnessed. Typically, the destruction of pharmacy stock of Schedule 2 CDs needs to be

TABLE 15: DENATURING AND WITNESS REQUIREMENTS FOR PATIENT-RETURNED AND EXPIRED CONTROLLED DRUGS

	IS DENATURING REQUIRED?	IS AN AUTHORISED WITNESS REQUIRED?	RECORD KEEPING
PATIENT-RETURNED CONTROLLED DRUG	Yes, if Schedule 2, 3 or 4 (part 1)	No. However it is preferable for denaturing to be witnessed by another member of staff familiar with CDs (preferably a registered health professional)	A record should not be made in the CD register but records of patient-returned Schedule 2 CDs and their subsequent destruction should be recorded in a separate record for this purpose
EXPIRED/ OBSOLETE/ UNWANTED STOCK	Yes, if Schedule 2, 3 or 4 (part 1)	Yes, if Schedule 2. For Schedule 3 medicines it would be good practice to have another member of staff witness the denaturing	An entry should be made in the CD register for Schedule 2 CDs

witnessed. The destruction of patient-returned CDs, whether they require denaturing or not, does not require witnessing by an authorised person.

In prisons, to maintain a robust audit trail, use of Schedule 3 CDs (e.g. buprenorphine) should be recorded in the CD register. Therefore, any destruction should also be recorded. It is also recommended that a robust audit trail is maintained for Schedule 4 CDs, such as diazepam and chlordiazepoxide.

Various individuals and classes of person (e.g. police constables) are authorised to witness the destruction of CDs. This authority is derived from the Home Secretary. It can also be derived from the Secretary of State for Health or from an accountable officer (see section 3.6.1). An accountable officer has the power to authorise other persons to witness the destruction of CDs. However, the 2001 Regulations prevent an accountable officer from being an authorised person directly. Persons authorised by the accountable officer are usually senior members of staff who are not involved in the day-to-day management or use of CDs.

NB: If a pharmacy is engaged in manufacturing, compounding, importing or exporting Schedule 3 or 4 CDs then record keeping arrangements apply. Therefore, destruction of these requires an authorised witness.

METHODS OF DENATURING CONTROLLED DRUGS

All medicines should be disposed of in a safe and appropriate manner. Medicines should be disposed of in appropriate waste containers that are then sent for incineration. They should not be disposed of into the sewerage system.

The following generic advice has been agreed with the Home Office. All CDs in Schedule 2, 3 and 4 (part 1) should be destroyed by being denatured and rendered irretrievable before being placed into pharmaceutical waste containers and sent for incineration.

The context of destruction by denaturing and rendering irretrievable is to guard against the misuse of drugs, harm to the environment or people and prevent the supply of easily retrievable CDs to waste carriers. These methods are not expected to render the detection of active ingredients with specialist equipment impossible, or to modify the chemical composition or properties of CDs.

For all forms of denaturing, and particularly if grinding or crushing tablets or breaking containers is involved individuals should work in a well-ventilated area and wear suitable protective gloves, a face mask and goggles as appropriate; following good Health and Safety practice.

Table 16 contains generic advice on methods of denaturing which have been agreed with the Home Office as likely to be compatible with legislative requirements. If additional product specific information is needed speak to the manufacturer of the product or your local Controlled Drug accountable officer.

CD denaturing kits designed specifically for this purpose are widely available and should be used in preference to other materials that were historically used such as cat litter. It is the responsibility of the manufacturer or supplier of the kit to ensure that the kit and the instructions for use are fit-for purpose. Pharmacists are responsible for using a kit that has been obtained from a reputable source and to use those kits in accordance with the manufacturers' instructions – generic advice is also available in Table 16.

TABLE 16: DESTRUCTION OF CONTROLLED DRUGS

DOSAGE FORM	METHOD OF DESTRUCTION
SOLID DOSAGE FORMS, E.G. CAPSULES AND TABLETS	Grind or crush the solid dose formulation before adding to the CD denaturing kit to ensure that whole tablets or capsules are not retrievable. The use of a small amount of water whilst grinding or crushing may assist in minimising particles of dust being released into the air
	Where a CD denaturing kit is not available, an alternative method of denaturing is to crush or grind the solid dose formulation and place it into a small amount of warm, soapy water stirring sufficiently to ensure the drug has been dissolved or dispersed. The resulting mixture is poured onto an appropriate amount of suitable product* and added to an appropriate waste disposal bin supplied by the waste contractor
LIQUID DOSAGE FORMS	Pour into an appropriately-sized CD denaturing kit
	Where a CD denaturing kit is not available, an alternative method is to pour the liquid onto an appropriate amount of suitable product* and add this to an appropriate waste disposal bin
	When a bottle containing a liquid CD has been emptied, small amounts of the pharmaceutical can remain
	Bottles can be rinsed and the liquid disposed using the denaturing kit and then as the correct category of pharmaceutical waste. You may only dispose of rinsings contaminated with pharmaceuticals via the sewerage system IF you have a relevant Trade Effluent Consent from the relevant sewerage undertaker
AMPOULES AND VIALS	For liquid containing ampoules, open the ampoule and empty the contents into a CD denaturing kit, or dispose of in the same manner as liquid dose formulations above. Dispose of the ampoule as sharps pharmaceutical waste
	For powder containing ampoules, open the ampoule and add water to dissolve the powder inside. The resulting mixture can be poured into the CD denaturing kit and the ampoule disposed of as sharps pharmaceutical waste

continues overleaf

DOSAGE FORM	METHOD OF DESTRUCTION
AMPOULES AND VIALS *continued*	An alternative but less preferable, disposal method is where the ampoules are crushed with a pestle inside an empty plastic container. Once broken, a small quantity of warm soapy water (for powder ampoules) or suitable product* (for liquid ampoules) is added. If these methods are used, care should be taken to ensure that the glass does not harm the person destroying the CD. The resulting liquid mixture should then be disposed of in a CD denaturing kit or in the bin that is used for disposal of liquid medicines
PATCHES	Remove the backing and fold the patch over on itself. Place into a waste disposal bin or a CD denaturing kit
AEROSOL FORMULATIONS	Expel into water and dispose of the resulting liquid in accordance with the guidance above on destroying liquid formulations
	If this is not possible because of the nature of the formulation, expel into an absorbent material and dispose of this as pharmaceutical waste
	Alternatively consider if it would be safe to open or to otherwise compromise the container to release the CD safely. The resulting liquid mixture should then be disposed of in a CD denaturing kit and disposed of as pharmaceutical waste

A risk assessment should be carried out to determine whether a product is suitable. A suitable product should render the CD irretrievable without compromising patient safety, the safety of the person carrying out the destruction, or the environment.

3.6.11
RECORD KEEPING AND CONTROLLED DRUGS REGISTERS

A Controlled Drugs register must be used to record details of any Schedule 1 and Schedule 2 CDs received or supplied by a pharmacy.

Pharmacists are also required to keep records of Sativex (which is a Schedule 4 Part 1 CD). The Home Office strongly recommends the use of a CD register for making records relating to Sativex.

For Controlled Drugs received, the following must be recorded:

- Date supply received
- Name and address from whom received
- Quantity received.

For Controlled Drugs supplied, the following must be recorded:

- Date supplied
- Name and address of recipient
- Details of authority to possess – prescriber or licence holder's details
- Quantity supplied
- Details of person collecting Schedule 2 CD – patient, patient's representative or healthcare representative (if the latter, also record their name and address)
- Whether proof of identity was requested of the person collecting
- Whether proof of identity was provided.

These are the minimum fields of information that must be recorded; additional relevant information can be added.

THE NATURE OF THE REGISTER

Legislation requires that the class, strength and form be specified at the head of each page of the CD register. The register is required to be a bound book register (see box overleaf titled Electronic Controlled Drugs register for alternative to bound). It is also a requirement that different classes are kept in a separate part of the register and that, within each class, a separate page is used for different strengths and formulations of each drug. Multiple registers for the same class of CD are allowable if approved by the Home Office.

Prisons have one legally compliant register that records all the details as specified. However, since there are often several areas in each prison where CDs are stored, administered or issued, each of these areas should maintain a CD record book (similar to those used by hospital wards). Also recommended is that the movement of CDs between these areas be recorded by internal requisition so that robust audit trails are maintained.

THE NATURE OF THE ENTRIES

All entries made in CD registers should be:

- Entered chronologically

- Entered promptly – entries must be made on the day of the transaction or on the following day

- In ink or indelible – entries and corrections must be in ink or indelible (or computerised (see below))

- Unaltered – entries must not be cancelled, obliterated or altered. Corrections must be made by dated marginal notes or footnotes. The register should be marked to show who the amendments made are attributable to (e.g. name, initials/signature, GPhC number if applicable).

RECORD KEEPING

The following points regarding record keeping should be adhered to when maintaining CD registers:

- Location – each register should be kept at the premises to which it applies

- Duration – registers should be kept for two years from the date of the last entry

- Form – records can be kept in their original form or copied and kept in an approved computerised form

- Inspection – a copy of the register, and other details of stock, receipts and supplies, must be made available to authorised persons (e.g. a GPhC inspector or CD liaison officer) upon request.

ELECTRONIC CONTROLLED DRUGS REGISTERS

Electronic CD registers are permitted as an alternative to having a bound-book CD register. Legislation requires that computerised entries must be:

- Attributable

- Capable of being audited

- Compliant with best practice.

An electronic CD register must also be accessible from the premises and capable of being printed. Registers may only be kept in computerised form if safeguards are incorporated into the software to ensure all of the following:

- The author of each entry is identifiable

- Entries cannot be altered at a later date

- A log of all data entered is kept and can be recalled for audit purposes.

Access control systems should be in place to minimise the risk of unauthorised or unnecessary access to the data. Adequate backups must be made of computerised registers. Arrangements should be made so that inspectors can examine computerised registers during a visit with minimum disruption to the dispensing process.

RUNNING BALANCES AND STOCK CHECKS

The aim of a running balance is to ensure that irregularities or discrepancies are identified as quickly as possible. There should be SOPs in place for checking stock levels against the running balance and dealing with discrepancies. For most organisations the frequency of stock checks should be at least once a week* but these may be more or less frequent based on risk assessment, volume of CDs dispensing, frequency of past irregularities or incidents, or if there are several different pharmacists in charge over short periods. Liquid balances should be checked visually with periodic volume checks, and checks to confirm the balance on completion of a bottle. Stock checks should be recorded, signed and dated by the healthcare professional carrying out the check and if possible, two people should carry out stock checks.

It is also appropriate to visually check the running balance each time a CD is dispensed (i.e. where the calculated balance in the register visually matches the quantity you can see. If it does not match, you should investigate in more detail).

Some common reasons for stock to be at zero balance could be due to the drug not being reordered, destruction of the drug (i.e. expired and obsolete, see section 3.6.10 for destruction of CDs) or discontinuation of the drug by the manufacturer. Pharmacists can exercise their professional judgement to help decide whether the weekly running balance check for these CDs that have been zero balance for some time should be continued or suspended. Referring to relevant SOP(s) could form part of this process.

A running balance should be maintained as a matter of good practice and is a recommendation from the Shipman Inquiry. (It is intended that once electronic registers are in common use this will become a legal requirement).

*Once a week, not necessarily required to be on the same day every week

PRACTICE ISSUES

- The pharmacist has overall responsibility for maintaining running balances and dealing with discrepancies. However, these tasks can be delegated to competent staff, where appropriate

- If a discrepancy can be resolved following checks, a marginal note or footnote should be made in the register and the discrepancy corrected

- Running balances for liquid CDs can be affected by overage, residue and spillage

- Where a CD register entry has been made for a Schedule 2 CD, the usual requirement to make a record in the POM register does not apply.

3.6.12
PRACTICE ISSUES: DISPOSING OF SPENT METHADONE BOTTLES

Once a methadone bottle is emptied as far as possible, bottles can be rinsed and the liquid added to a denaturing kit and treated as pharmaceutical waste.

Waste medicines should not be discharged to the foul sewer without a trade effluent consent from the sewerage undertaker. Disposal of irretrievable amounts of CDs does not need to be recorded.

Labels and other identifiers should be removed or obliterated and the clean, empty container disposed of into the recycling or general waste.

FURTHER READING

Department of Health
Safe management of healthcare waste. 2013.
https://assets.publishing.service.gov.uk/
government/uploads/system/uploads/attachment_
data/file/167976/HTM_07-01_Final.pdf

National Institute for Health and Care Excellence
Controlled drugs: safe use and management.
NICE guideline. 2016.
www.nice.org.uk

Water UK
National guidance for healthcare waste water discharges. 2014.
www.water.org.uk/publications/
water-industry-guidance

3.6.13
PRACTICE ISSUES: NEEDLE EXCHANGE SCHEME

Pharmacists who are delivering or contemplating on providing a needle exchange service should be aware of national guidelines:

FURTHER READING

National Institute for Health and Care Excellence
Needle and syringe programmes.
Public health guideline. 2014.
www.nice.org.uk

Scottish Government
Guidelines for services providing injecting equipment: Best practice recommendations for commissioners and injecting equipment provision services in Scotland. 2010.
www.gov.scot

3.6.14
EXTEMPORANEOUS METHADONE

The GPhC has published guidance on the preparation of unlicensed medicines, which sets out the key areas that need to be considered by the pharmacy owner and superintendent pharmacist in any registered pharmacy where unlicensed medicines are prepared by a pharmacist or under the supervision of a pharmacist. Every patient has every right to expect that when an unlicensed medicine is prepared, it is of equivalent quality to a licensed medicine.

This guidance also applies when unlicensed methadone is extemporaneously prepared. The guidance explains that pharmacies preparing unlicensed medicines must mitigate risks to patients and meet the GPhC's standards for registered pharmacies.

FURTHER READING

General Pharmaceutical Council
Standards for registered pharmacies. 2018.
www.pharmacyregulation.org
(see MEP Appendix 2)

General Pharmaceutical Council
Guidance for registered pharmacies preparing unlicensed medicines. 2018.
www.pharmacyregulation.org
(see MEP Appendix 9)

3.6.15
CANNABIS-BASED PRODUCTS FOR MEDICINAL USE IN HUMANS

On 1st November 2018 access to cannabis-based products for medicinal use (CBPM) in humans in England, Scotland and Wales widened in legislation. Moving cannabis products from Schedule 1 to Schedule 2 of the Misuse of Drugs Regulations 2001.

This allows defined cannabis-based products for medicinal use and restricts routes of access and limits the prescribing of these products to specialist doctors on the GMC's Specialist Register.

We have worked with the Department of Health and Social Care (DHSC) and Guy's and St Thomas's NHS Foundation Trust to develop this guidance.

CBPMs are Schedule 2 CDs and are currently unlicensed medicines – so must be prescribed and supplied in line with all legal requirements applicable to unlicensed medicines and Schedule 2 CDs.

TYPES OF CANNABIS-BASED PRODUCT
There are a wide range of cannabis-based products, with varying constituents including tetrahydrocannabinol (THC) and covered by different aspects of legislation. These can be broadly categorised as:

1 UNLICENSED CANNABIDIOL (CBD) PRODUCTS
There are a range of products marketed as food supplements. Provided no medicinal claims are made, these products fall outside medicines legislation.

- Such products must not contain THC which remains a controlled substance, under Home Office legislation.

  - *Note:* patients may have bought products over the internet or from non-reputable sources.

2 LICENSED PRODUCTS/SYNTHETICS
There are a range of licensed cannabis-based products and synthetic products that are already available in the UK e.g. Sativex and Nabilone or being assessed for a marketing authorisation and not affected by the new laws on CBPMs.

- Sativex® – (cannabis extracts containing THC and CBD) is the only licensed cannabis based medicinal product that is available in the UK. It has been authorised by the MHRA as a treatment for spasticity in multiple sclerosis since 2010. Sativex is listed under Schedule 4 of the Misuse of Drugs Regulations 2001 at present. However, Sativex® is currently subject to a NICE 'do not do' recommendation: Do not offer Sativex to treat spasticity in people with MS because it is not a cost effective treatment (www.nice.org.uk/donotdo/ do-not-offer-sativex-to-treat-spasticity-in-people-with-ms-because-it-is-not-a-cost-effective-treatment). NICE suggests other medicines that can be used to treat spasticity, instead.

- Nabilone – a synthetic, non-natural cannabinoid, is licenced in the UK for use in treatment resistant nausea and vomiting caused by chemotherapy; and treat severe nausea and vomiting caused by cancer chemotherapy in patients with inadequate response to conventional antiemetic treatments.

- Epidiolex® – (pure cannabidiol (CBD)) is approved by the US Food and Drug Administration (FDA) for Lennox-Gastaut Syndrome or Dravet Syndrome in patients 2 years of age and older. This product does not have a UK marketing authorisation, but this is currently being assessed by the European Medicines Agency. A decision is expected later this year. Meanwhile Epidiolex is available in the UK through the manufacturers Extended Access Scheme and supply as an unlicensed 'special'. If a pharmacy receives a prescription for Epidiolex, the pharmacist will need to contact GW Pharmaceuticals to obtain the medicine as an unlicensed special and a discussion with the prescriber may be helpful to confirm the required process to obtain the medicine from the manufacturer GW Pharmaceuticals.

- Dronabinol, a synthetic nature-identical, version of THC is listed under Schedule 2 of the Misuse of Drugs Regulations 2001, but it does not have a market authorisation from the MHRA in the UK, although it is available internationally. It has been approved by the US Food and Drug Administration (FDA) to treat loss of appetite in people with AIDS, and to treat severe nausea and vomiting caused by cancer chemotherapy in patients with inadequate response to conventional antiemetic treatments.

(See BNF or product SPSCs for more information on the products above.)

3 CANNABIS-BASED PRODUCTS FOR MEDICINAL USE (CBPMS) –

There are three broad requirements that a product should satisfy:

- The product is or contains cannabis, cannabis resin, cannabinol or a cannabinol derivative

- It is produced for medicinal use in humans; and

- It is a product that is regulated as a medicinal product, or an ingredient of a medicinal product.

  The definition is necessarily broad to take account of the range of preparations which are cannabis-based that have been used for therapeutic purposes.

  This area is still evolving following the changes in the legislation. Product choice, suitability for prescribing and supply arrangements are being put in place nationally.

Supplying CBPMs against prescriptions

Currently the only CBPMs are unlicensed medicines. As with prescribing any other unlicensed medicine, it is a clinician who will decide the most appropriate medicine or course of treatment to prescribe for a patient, having taken into account the patient, the clinical condition, the clinical evidence of effectiveness and safety, that cannot be met by a licensed medicine. The decision to commence treatment should be a joint decision between the prescriber and the patient and/carer.

- CBPMs are schedule 2 CDs and staff must follow all the legal and CD requirements for Schedule 2 CDs, including any Trust CD requirements (see section 3.6.7).

- Prescribing is currently restricted to clinicians listed on the Specialist Register of the GMC (www.gmc-uk.org/registration-and-licensing/ the-medical-register/a-guide-to-the-medical-register/specialist-registration). The decision to prescribe must be in line with guidance from the NHS England (or other country specific guidance and consideration given to guidance issued by Royal Colleges, and the Trust's unlicensed medicines and CD policies. Patients and/carers must be involved in the treatment decision.

- Patients should be made aware that the product being prescribed is unlicensed and a note of this should be made in the patient's medical records.

- Private prescriptions for CBPMs must meet legal requirements for Schedule 2 CDs, be on the specially designated forms (**FP10PCD (England), PPCD(1) (Scotland), WP10PCD (Wales)**) and specify the private prescriber's six digit identification number (see section 3.6.7).

- There is limited domestic availability of these products. However, several specialist importers have imported a range of products on a named patient basis. Products currently available via import come in a variety of forms (flos, oils, granules) and variety of CBD/THC ratios. The pharmacy should be able to advise on available products and routes of supply.

- Patients should be informed that there may be a small delay in obtaining the product as there are a limited number of THC containing products that are available in this country and so may have to be imported and the process for the supply of unlicensed medicines followed. Further advice should be sought from specialist importers.

FURTHER READING

Royal Pharmaceutical Society
Support alert: Medicinal cannabis pharmacy alert
www.rpharms.com/publications/pharmacy-alerts/details//Medicinal-Cannabis-Pharmacy-Alert

Royal Pharmaceutical Society
Practical guide on CBD oil
www.rpharms.com

Association of British Neurologists
Interim guidelines on the Use of cannabis-based products in neurological disorders
www.theabn.org/resources/abn/a/abn-guidelines-use-of-cannabis-based-products-in-neurology-december-2018.html

British Paediatric Neurology Association
Interim guidance on the use of cannabis-based products for medicinal (CBPMs) use in children and young people with epilepsy
www.bpna.org.uk/?page=cdmp

Guy's and St Thomas's NHS Foundation Trust
Medicinal cannabis guide
www.rpharms.com/Portals/0/RPS%20document%20library/Open%20access/Support%20alert/Cannabis%20based%20preparations%20%20overview.docx?ver=2019-03-21-150932-177

This provides a brief overview for the prescribing and supply of cannabis-based products for medicinal use. Individual Trusts can use and adapt this guidelines to meet their local needs.

Home Office
Drug Licensing Factsheet – Cannabis, CBD and other cannabinoids
https://assets.publishing.service.gov.uk/government/uploads/system/uploads/attachment_data/file/778357/Factsheet_Cannabis_CBD_and_Cannabinoids_2019.pdf

Medicines and Healthcare products Regulatory Agency
Guidance on the supply, manufacture, importation and distribution of unlicensed cannabis-based products for medicinal (CBPMs) use as a 'special'.
https://assets.publishing.service.gov.uk/government/uploads/system/uploads/attachment_data/file/752796/Cannabis_Guidance__unlicensed_CBPMs__-_Final_311018.pdf

This guidance also contains details about:

- Record keeping
- Labelling
- Packaging requirements
- A flowchart process for prescribing, supplying and importing unlicensed CBPMs
- A supply chain checklist – this contains a prescription validation check and dispensing label checklist

Medicines and Healthcare products Regulatory Agency
Guidance note 8: A guide to what is a medicinal product
https://assets.publishing.service.gov.uk/government/uploads/system/uploads/attachment_data/file/759581/012__GN8_-_final_2018_combined_doc_Oct.pdf
Appendix 10 Guidance on Cannabidiol (CBD) products

NHS England
Guidance to clinicians: Cannabis-based products for medicinal use and an FAQ document.
www.england.nhs.uk/publication/cannabis-based-products-for-medicinal-use-guidance-to-clinicians/

NHS England

Guidance for clinicians: Cannabis-based products for medicinal use
www.england.nhs.uk/publication/additional-guidance-to-clinicians-cannabis-based-products-for-medicinal-use/

This has been endorsed by the Scottish Government, Department of Health Northern Ireland and Welsh Government. The letter clarified the status of the clinical guidance issued so far and provides further details in relation to synthetic cannabinoids for medicinal use.

NHS website

Further information on Medical cannabis (and cannabis oils)
www.nhs.uk/conditions/medical-cannabis/

National Institute for Health and Care Excellence

Developing guidance on the use of cannabis-based products for medicinal use, which is expected to be published in October 2019.

Royal College of Physicians

Recommendations on cannabis-based products for medicinal use (CBPMs)
www.rcplondon.ac.uk/projects/outputs/recommendations-cannabis-based-products-medicinal-use

(This has been jointly produced with the Royal College of Radiologists and in liaison with the Faculty of Pain Medicine of the Royal College of Anaesthetists.)

Scottish Government

Letter for Clinicians: Cannabis-based products for medicinal use
www.sehd.scot.nhs.uk/cmo/CMO(2018)15.pdf

Welsh Government

Letter for Clinicians: Cannabis-based products for medicinal use
https://gweddill.gov.wales/docs/dhss/publications/whc2018-039en.pdf

3.7
Additional legal and professional issues

3.7.1 EXPIRY DATES

3.7.2 WASTE MEDICINES

3.7.3 REQUESTS FOR POISONS AND CHEMICALS

3.7.4 DELIVERY AND POSTING OF MEDICINES TO PATIENTS (INCLUDING ABROAD)

3.7.5 SECURE ENVIRONMENTS

3.7.6 CHILD-RESISTANT PACKAGING

3.7.7 REPORTING ADVERSE EVENTS

3.7.8 EMERGENCY CONNECTION TO EX-DIRECTORY TELEPHONE NUMBERS

3.7.9 HOMEOPATHIC AND HERBAL REMEDIES

3.7.10 CHARITABLE DONATION OF MEDICINES

3.7.11 COLLECTION AND PURCHASE OF MEDICINES BY CHILDREN

3.7.12 PROTECTING CHILDREN AND YOUNG PEOPLE

3.7.13 PROTECTING VULNERABLE ADULTS

3.7.14 MEDICAL DEVICES

3.7.15 ADMINISTRATION OF ADRENALINE IN AN EMERGENCY

3.7.16 MULTI-COMPARTMENT COMPLIANCE AIDS

3.7.17 DRUGS AND DRIVING

3.7.18 RETENTION OF PHARMACY RECORDS

3.7.19 NEW PSYCHOACTIVE SUBSTANCES

3.7.1
EXPIRY DATES

Where a product states 'Use by' or 'Use before', this means that the product should be used before the end of the previous month. For example, 'Use by 06/2019' means that the product should not be used after 31 May 2019.

MHRA's advice to pharmaceutical manufacturers is: the term 'expiry date' should be taken to mean that the product should not be used after the end of the month stated. Therefore, an expiry date of 12/2019 means that the product should not be used after 31 December 2019.

3.7.2
WASTE MEDICINES

Table 17 outlines the arrangements for disposing of pharmaceutical waste in England, Scotland and Wales. For information regarding denaturing of CDs, see section 3.6.10.

TABLE 17: WASTE ARRANGEMENTS IN ENGLAND, SCOTLAND AND WALES

For information regarding denaturing of CDs, see section 3.6.10

	ENGLAND AND WALES	SCOTLAND
ENFORCEMENT BODY	Environment Agency	Scottish Environment Protection Agency (SEPA)
CAN PHARMACIES RECEIVE WASTE MEDICINES?	Yes. Generally, activities relating to waste require a licence. However, there are certain exemptions in place that allow these activities to occur without a licence. Some exemptions need to be registered while others do not Under the Non-Waste Framework Directive (temporary storage at a collection point), pharmacies do not need to register an exemption to receive waste as long as the terms of the exemption are complied with. For further details see the Environment Agency website: www.gov.uk/government/organisations/environment-agency	Yes. The Waste Management Licensing (Scotland) Regulations 2011 allow registered pharmacies to accept returned medicines from patients or individuals and care services.
SOURCES OF ADDITIONAL INFORMATION	Comprehensive information is available in a Department of Health publication entitled Safe management of healthcare waste: www.gov.uk/government/organisations/department-of-health Other sources of information include the Environment Agency website (www.gov.uk/government/organisations/environment-agency) and the PSNC website (www.psnc.org.uk) – information specific to England but of use in Wales.	Comprehensive information is available in a Department of Health publication Safe management of healthcare waste (www.gov.uk/government/organisations/department-of-health) and the Scottish Health Technical Note 3 Part B – NHS Scotland. *Waste Management Guidance: Waste Management Policy Template* www.hfs.scot.nhs.uk Other sources of information include the SEPA website: www.sepa.org.uk

	ENGLAND AND WALES	SCOTLAND
WHERE SHOULD WASTE MEDICINES BE STORED?	Waste medicines must be kept in secure waste containers in a designated area preferably away from medicines that are fit for use. If sharps are accepted, they should be stored in a sharps container.	
DEALING WITH CONFIDENTIAL INFORMATION	Ensure that any patient identifiable information is destroyed or totally obscured.	
TABLETS AND CAPSULES	Blister strips can be removed from their inert outer packaging but tablets and capsules should not be de-blistered. *NB: An exemption applies to CD tablets and capsules, which require denaturing – see section 3.6.10*	
SHARPS	Dispose of syringes and needles in a sharps container	
LIQUIDS	The whole bottle (including empty bottles that may contain residue) should be placed into a pharmaceutical waste container because the mixing of different medicines could be hazardous. *NB: Exceptions apply to CD liquids, which require denaturing – see section 3.6.10*	
ADVICE FOR PATIENTS	Patients should be advised that unused, unwanted medicines should be returned to a pharmacy for safe disposal	

3.7.3
REQUESTS FOR POISONS AND CHEMICALS

Amendments to the Poisons Act 1972 have changed how poisons and some chemicals are classified and regulated. These require pharmacies to report suspicious transactions, significant stock loss and theft to the local police (dial 101) or the anti-terrorism hotline (dial 0800 789321). There is also a requirement for the public to present a valid licence issued by the Home Office before being able to purchase the most dangerous poisons or chemicals which could be used as explosive precursors. Where a licence is required, pharmacy teams will need to check that the licence is valid, unaltered and matches the request. Transaction details must be added to the licence, substances must be suitably labelled and regulated poisons require additional record keeping in a poisons register. Where licences are not required, the

pharmacist should consider whether requests are suspicious and whether commercial alternatives or commercial retailers are appropriate to refer to.

Further information and details, including lists of regulated and reportable poisons and explosive precursors are available from the RPS guidance Poisons and chemicals from pharmacy: www.rpharms.com

Information on REACH (Registration, Evaluation, Authorisation and restriction of CHemicals), the CLP Regulation (Classification, Labelling and Packaging of substances and mixtures) and COSHH Regulations (Control of Substances Hazardous to Health) are available from the Health and Safety Executive: www.hse.gov.uk

3.7.4
DELIVERY AND POSTING OF MEDICINES TO PATIENTS (INCLUDING ABROAD)

The following are professional and practical points to help you decide whether or not to deliver/post medicines (prescribed/sold) to patients (this list is not exhaustive):

- Patient consent for delivery or posting

- Patient confidentiality during the delivery or posting process

- Whether it is necessary for face-to-face contact with the patient to ensure that the medicine can be safely, effectively and appropriately used

- Whether it is necessary to interview the patient

- Whether the patient has been assessed or directly interviewed by the prescriber

- Medicines and medical devices are not ordinary items of commerce and must be handled and supplied to the patient safely. An adequate audit trail must be in place for delivery and receipt from the point at which the medicine leaves the pharmacy and is received by the patient/patient representative or returned to the pharmacy in the event of delivery failure. Wherever possible a signature should be obtained to indicate safe receipt of medicines

- Pharmacies offering medicines for sale via a website are required to be registered with MHRA and display the EU common logo

- It is a requirement of EU common logo registration that medicines supplied have a marketing authorisation for use in the destination EEA country

- Storage requirements during transit

- When posting – will the postal carrier agree to transport the medicinal product (check terms of carriage, prohibited and restricted goods)

- When posting abroad – are there legal restrictions in the destination country which would prevent you from posting? (E.g. guidance produced by the U.S. Food and Drug Administration (FDA) makes it clear that it is illegal for a foreign pharmacy to ship prescription medicines that are not approved by the FDA to the United States)

- When posting abroad – are there UK legal restrictions which would prevent you dispensing in the first instance? (e.g. is the prescriber recognised as an appropriate practitioner (see 3.3.1) for the medicinal product in the UK?).

FURTHER READING

Royal Pharmaceutical Society
Repeat medication management – professional reference guide.
www.rpharms.com

General Pharmaceutical Council
Guidance for registered pharmacies providing pharmacy services at a distance, including on the internet. 2019.
www.pharmacyregulation.org
(see MEP Appendix 10)

International Narcotics Control Board
Lists of narcotic and psychotropic drugs under international control.
www.incb.org

Medicines and Healthcare products Regulatory Agency
Distance selling logo.
www.gov.uk

United States Food and Drug Administration (FDA)
Buying medicines over the internet.
Various resources available.
www.fda.gov

3.7.5
SECURE ENVIRONMENTS

Secure environments include prisons, police custody suites, secure hospitals, immigration removal centres and other places where persons are detained. Medicines and other health legislation may not refer specifically to the particular environment, and where this is the case then consideration should be given to best practice in either primary or secondary care, as appropriate, acting within the confines of the relevant legislation.

When medicines are dispensed from an 'in-house' pharmacy for administration or supply to patients within a prison, the pharmacy does not need to be registered with the GPhC. Nonetheless, general pharmaceutical legal and good practice guidelines should be followed.

If provision of a pharmacy service to another prison is being considered from an in-house pharmacy, advice should be obtained from the GPhC and MHRA to discuss whether the pharmacy premises would require registration or whether a Wholesale Dealer's Licence will be required.

FURTHER READING

Royal Pharmaceutical Society
Professional standards for optimising medicines for people in secure environments.
www.rpharms.com

Royal Pharmaceutical Society
Professional Standards for Hospital Pharmacy.
For providers of pharmacy services in or to acute hospital, mental health, private, community service, prison, hospice and ambulance settings.
www.rpharms.com

3.7.6
CHILD-RESISTANT PACKAGING

Suitable, child-resistant packaging should be used for supplying all solid, all oral and external liquid dose preparations unless there is a good reason for not doing so. Such reasons may include:

- **Specific request**
  The patient, carer or representative requests a packaging that is not child resistant, perhaps due to difficulty in opening it. The request may be met by supplying a non-child-resistant lid

- **Original pack**
  The original pack may not be child resistant and there may be reasons underpinning why the medicine should remain in the original container. It may also be the case that no child-resistant packaging exists for a particular liquid medicine so it is not possible to change the container

Where appropriate, the patient should be counselled to keep medicines away from the reach and sight of children.

3.7.7
REPORTING ADVERSE EVENTS

We encourage, as a matter of best practice, the reporting of suspected adverse drug reactions under the Yellow Card scheme. Following a discussion with the patient, it may also be appropriate to make a record in the patient's notes and to notify the prescriber.

Reporting is possible online at www.yellowcard.mhra.gov.uk Otherwise, a tear-out paper copy is available at the back of the BNF. A Yellow Card mobile app is also available though which side effects to medicines can be reported.
The app also enables users to receive news updates from the MHRA.

The following examples highlight the value of the Yellow Card Scheme and the importance of reporting suspected adverse events in this way. Warnings were added to the product information for varenicline after the MHRA received reports of suicidal ideation via the scheme and the Yellow Card reporting of adverse reactions to rimonabant (which was formerly used to treat obesity) contributed to the drug being withdrawn as new evidence meant the risks were considered to outweigh any benefits.

If a suspected adverse drug reaction (SADR) is related to a veterinary medicine which has affected a human and/or an animal, refer to section 3.5.

3.7.8
EMERGENCY CONNECTION TO EX-DIRECTORY TELEPHONE NUMBERS

Pharmacists can be connected to ex-directory British Telecom (BT) telephone numbers if they need to contact patients in a real emergency. This privilege is also available to doctors, hospitals and emergency authorities. *NB: Connection is made by the BT operator and only if the called party agrees, the ex-directory telephone number will not be divulged under any circumstances.*

Pharmacists must use the privilege appropriately and only exercise their right of access when strictly necessary.

The following guidelines must be adhered to:

- Pharmacists should only consider asking for connection to an ex-directory number in a life or death situation. This can be interpreted as an emergency that is likely to pose a very serious threat to the health of a patient if information cannot be passed on immediately and when the patient's telephone number cannot be found from another source (e.g. the patient's GP surgery)

- A pharmacist needing to contact an ex-directory number should dial 100, explain the situation and request connection to the number

The pharmacist will only be connected when the following criteria are met:

- The pharmacist explains the reason for the emergency connection request and advises the operator that it is a life or death situation (the operator will not judge the nature of the emergency but will accept the word of the pharmacist)

- The pharmacist must give his or her name and the name and telephone number of the pharmacy premises from which he or she is calling

- The call must be made from a fixed line that is in the name of the pharmacy, so the number can be checked and verified. Calls from mobiles or residential lines will not be accepted

- The pharmacist must agree to pay the Operator Connection fee (which will be charged to the number they are calling from)

BT monitors all requests for emergency connection. If the privilege is abused it is likely that this important facility will be withdrawn.

3.7.9
HOMEOPATHIC AND HERBAL REMEDIES

DIFFERENCES BETWEEN HOMEOPATHIC AND HERBAL PRODUCTS

The public can confuse homeopathic with herbal products as homeopathic products are often derived from herbs and are called by their botanical name, e.g. Aloe, and also because a single manufacturer may produce both homeopathic and herbal products.

Pharmacists can help the public understand the difference between homeopathy and herbal products using information in our quick reference guide on *Homeopathic and Herbal remedies* www.rpharms.com

Homeopathy has been defined as a holistic complementary and alternative therapy based on the concept of 'like to treat like' and involves the administration of dilute and ultradilute products prepared according to methods given in homeopathic pharmacopoeias.

Herbal preparations contain plant-derived materials, either as raw or processed ingredients which may be from one or more plants.

EVIDENCE FOR HOMEOPATHY

There is no scientific or clinical evidence to support the efficacy of homeopathic products above the placebo effect, although anecdotal reports of their effectiveness have been published, particularly when used as part of individualised homeopathic treatment by a homeopathic practitioner. There is no evidence to support the clinical efficacy of homeopathic products beyond a placebo effect, and no scientific basis for homeopathy.

Given the lack of clinical and scientific evidence to support homeopathy, the RPS does not endorse homeopathy as a form of treatment because there is no scientific basis for homeopathy nor any evidence to support the clinical efficacy of homeopathic products beyond a placebo effect. The RPS does not support the prescribing of homeopathic products on the NHS.

ADVICE FOR PATIENTS

If a patient requests advice on homeopathy, you should advise on the lack of evidence on the efficacy of homeopathic products, discuss the formulation and composition of the product, and provide advice relevant to the patient's condition. You should also ensure that patients do not stop taking their prescribed medication if they take a homeopathic product.

REFERRAL

Pharmacists will be in a position to identify serious, underlying undiagnosed medical conditions requiring the patients to be referred to another healthcare professional. Homeopathic products should only be used for the treatment of minor, self-limiting conditions, and must never be used for the treatment of serious medical conditions.

LICENSING

For the purpose of licensing, the MHRA does not currently require homeopathic products to demonstrate efficacy, only quality and safety. Further information about regulation of homeopathic products and registration is available on the MHRA website: https://www.gov.uk/government/organisations/medicines-and-healthcare-products-regulatory-agency

Herbal remedies must either have a full marketing authorisation based upon safety, quality and efficacy or a traditional herbal registration (THR) based upon safety, quality and evidence of traditional use. Further information is available on the MHRA website: https://www.gov.uk/government/organisations/medicines-and-healthcare-products-regulatory-agency

FURTHER READING

Royal Pharmaceutical Society
Homeopathic and herbal products comparison table – quick reference guide.
www.rpharms. com

Royal Pharmaceutical Society
Homeopathy – quick reference guide.
www.rpharms. com

Royal Pharmaceutical Society
The Traditional Herbal Medicine Registration Scheme – quick reference guide.
www.rpharms.com

Williamson E, Driver S, et al
Stockley's Herbal Medicines Interactions. 2nd Edition. 2013. London; Pharmaceutical Press.
www.pharmpress.com

3.7.10
CHARITABLE DONATION OF MEDICINES

The World Health Organization (WHO) in co-operation with major international agencies involved with humanitarian and developmental aid (including the International Pharmaceutical Federation (FIP), International Federation of the Red Cross and Red Crescent Societies) has published guidance titled *'Guidelines for medicine donations'* (Revised 2010) that provides clear guidelines for the donation of medicine. We encourage any pharmacist considering donating medicines to read the document and adhere to the guidelines.

Pharmacists should be aware that if a pharmacy, in the course of its business, supplies a medicine to another business who obtains it for further supply, the supplying pharmacy will require a Wholesale Dealer's Licence (WDA(H))*. This is regardless of whether the medicine is stock surplus to the requirements of the pharmacy or general stock that is to be donated for charitable use or in times of conflict. See section 3.4 for further information on Wholesale Dealing.

CONSIDER ALTERNATIVES

WHO encourages, in the acute phase of an emergency, that standardised health kits of medicines are donated. These kits are permanently stocked by major international suppliers such as Médecins Sans Frontières and the United Nations Children's Fund.

After the acute phase, WHO encourages the donation of cash that can be used to purchase essential medicines and is usually more useful than donations of medicines. Pharmacists and patients who want to help should be advised to donate money to charitable organisations to enable them to purchase supplies.

These cash donations may then be used by charitable organisations to obtain reduced price purchases from manufacturers (where available) who are able to supply suitable medicines for the target area, in appropriate quantities and with viable shelf life.

PATIENT RETURNS

The WHO guidelines specifically advise that patient-returned medicines should not be donated and describes these types of donation as an example of a double standard. This is because most countries do not allow the reuse of patient returned medicines within their own country. The WHO guidelines describe how these donations also frustrate management efforts to administer medicine stocks in a rational way and as a result, donation of patient-returned medicines is forbidden in an increasing number of countries. In the past, unsuitable medicines have been donated, leading to situations where stocks could not be used within their remaining shelf life and as a result the receiving country has faced costly and inconvenient destruction procedures. Most charitable organisations supporting the developing world or providing disaster or emergency relief will find it very difficult to use the miscellaneous collection of medicines that is received from the donation of patient-returned medicines.

Pharmacies accept patient returned medicines in the course of their business for destruction. MHRA has advised that if a pharmacy takes in a patient returned medicine and supplies it to another legal entity which then makes a further supply of the medicine, the pharmacy will be wholesale dealing the patient returned medicine. Wholesale dealing medicines requires a WDA(H)*. However, a condition of the licence provides that a medicine can only be obtained from a licensed manufacturer or wholesale dealer, or in the case of import from a non-EEA country for re-export to a non-EEA country, from a person in the non-EEA country who is complying with their local regulations. This condition therefore prevents the activity of taking in patient returned medicines for onward wholesale supply and reuse.

Articles 77(1) and 77(2) of Directive 2001/83/EC require anyone undertaking wholesale dealing activities to hold an authorisation.

FURTHER READING

World Health Organization
Guidelines for medicines donations
(3rd edition). Revised 2010
www.who.int

3.7.11
COLLECTION AND PURCHASE OF MEDICINES BY CHILDREN

Pharmacists may be asked to supply dispensed medicines to a child for themselves, on behalf of another person, such as a parent, other relative or neighbour, or for persons whom they care for.

The decision on whether a supply is appropriate will need to be dealt with on a case by case basis and will involve considering the individual circumstances. The following factors can be considered:

1 **Knowledge of the child**

- Is the child known to the pharmacy?

- What information is known?

2 **Maturity of the child**

- Are you satisfied the child is capable and competent to understand the importance of the medicines they are collecting and there are no further concerns with them delivering the medicines.

- Are you confident the child will not misuse or tamper with the medicine?

3 **Nature of the medicine(s) supplied**

- What are the medicines being collected or supplied?

- Can the medicine be misused? E.g. CDs or laxatives.

4 **Prior arrangement**

- Does the child regularly collect medicines from the pharmacy?

- Is there an arrangement in place for this child to collect medicines for themselves/others, for example has this been previously discussed and agreed with a parent/guardian/representative (and recorded appropriately)?

5 **Reason for collection**

- Is there a good reason why the child is collecting or purchasing the medicine in the circumstances?

- Is the person who the medicine is for housebound or unable to collect for an acceptable reason?

- Is the child/young person a carer for the person that the medicine is for?

- Is the child expected to self-medicate, such as with an inhaler?

6 **Advise on the use of medicines**

- Does the person that the medicine is for require any additional information? How will this be communicated?

- Would the child understand any important information and are you confident these instructions will be passed on to the person the medicine is for?

- Do you need to consider contacting an appropriate adult if special instructions for use are required?

7 **Local policies**

- Is there a local policy in place in your area?

- You could contact your local Primary Care Organisation (CCG, LHB, HB etc.)

- Does your organisation have a policy on children collecting medicines? Is there an SOP in place?

- Consider making appropriate records.

8 **Proof of identity**

- Collecting Schedule 2 CDs require proof of identity which children may not have. You can use your professional judgement on making a supply without ID.

FURTHER READING

Carers Trust
Various resources available to support young carers.
www.carers.org

3.7.12
PROTECTING CHILDREN AND YOUNG PEOPLE

You have a professional, legal and moral duty to protect children from abuse or neglect and to work with other organisations and authorities to safeguard children. The following points may help with recognising signs of abuse or neglect; however, the list is not exhaustive and a series of minor factors could also be indicative of child abuse or neglect:

- **Physical abuse**
  Unusual/unexplained injuries, injuries in inaccessible places, bite marks, scalds, fingertip bruising, fractures, repeated injuries, age of injuries inconsistent with account given by adult, injuries blamed on siblings

- **Neglect**
  Poor growth and weight. Poor hygiene, dirty and messy. Inappropriate food or drink

- **Emotional abuse**
  Evidence of self-harm/self mutilation, behavioural problems, inappropriate verbal abuse, fear of adults or a certain adult

- **Sexual abuse**
  Indication of sexually transmitted disease, evidence of sexual activity or relationship that is inappropriate to the child's age or competence

- **Parent/carer signs**
  Delays seeking medical treatment or advice and/or reluctant to allow treatment, detachment from

DIAGRAM 13: WHAT TO DO IF CHILD ABUSE IS SUSPECTED

the child, lacks concern at the severity or extent of injury, reluctant to give information, aggressive towards child or children

If child abuse is suspected, you should follow local child protection procedures where these are available. If not, the process outlined in Diagram 13 may be useful.

Where you consider the nature of the child abuse to be an emergency then the police should be contacted.

Otherwise make a decision on next steps such as referring to local Social Services where appropriate or taking further advice. You should feel comfortable with sharing concerns and suspicions of abuse, even where these are not proven facts with Social Services.

You should not attempt to investigate suspicions or allegations of abuse directly.

You should make appropriate records of concerns and suspicions, decisions taken and reasons whether or not further action was taken on a particular occasion.

SEXUAL ACTIVITY IN CHILDREN

Children under the age of 13 are legally too young to consent to any sexual activity. Instances should be treated seriously with a presumption that the case should be reported to Social Services, unless there are exceptional circumstances backed by documented reasons for not sharing information.

Sexual activity with children under the age of 16 is also an offence but may be consensual. The law is not intended to prosecute mutually agreed sexual activity between young people of a similar age, unless it involves abuse or exploitation.

You can provide contraception (e.g. on prescription or under PGD) or sexual health advice to a child under 16 and the general duty of patient confidentiality applies, so consent should be sought whenever possible prior to disclosing patient information. This duty is not absolute and information may be shared if you judge on a case-by-case basis that sharing is in the child's best interest (e.g. to prevent harm to the child or where the child's welfare overrides the need to keep information confidential).

Remember that it is possible to seek advice from experts without disclosing identifiable details

of a child and breaking patient confidentiality – and that where there is a decision to share information, this should be proportionate.

FURTHER READING

Royal Pharmaceutical Society
Support alert: Mandatory reporting of female genital mutilation
www.rpharms.com

Royal Pharmaceutical Society
Protecting children and young people – a quick reference guide.
www.rpharms.com

Children's Society
Safeguarding children and young people. Policy, procedure and guidance.
www.childrenssociety.org.uk

General Pharmaceutical Council
Female genital mutilation: mandatory duty for pharmacy professionals to report
www.pharmacyregulation.org

Scottish Government
Protecting children and young people: framework for standards.
www2.gov.scot

3.7.13
PROTECTING VULNERABLE ADULTS

You have a professional, social and moral duty to protect vulnerable adults from abuse or neglect and to work with other organisations and authorities to safeguard vulnerable adults. The vulnerable adult's wishes should be taken into account at all times as a key issue is patient consent. Vulnerable adults are persons who are over the age of 18 and are at a greater risk of abuse or neglect.

They may fall into one of the following groups:

• Suffers from mental or physical disability

• Has learning difficulties

• Is frail or elderly

• Is in an abusive relationship

• Is a substance misuser.

Be aware that any of our patients, including those who do not fall within the groups above, could be a vulnerable adult. There are various types of abuse or neglect and the following lists may be helpful but are not exhaustive. The presence of one or more of these signs may not necessarily be caused by abuse or neglect.

- **Physical abuse**
  Injuries which are unusual or unexplained. Bite marks, scalds, fingertip bruising, fractures. Repeated injury

- **Neglect**
  Failure to thrive – evidence of malnourishment. Poor hygiene, dirty and messy

- **Emotional abuse**
  Evidence of self-harm/selfmutilation. Inappropriate verbal abuse. Fear of certain people

- **Sexual abuse and rape**
  Indication of sexually transmitted disease. Repeated requests for emergency hormonal contraception

- **Financial abuse**
  Sudden changes to their finances, e.g. getting into debt. Inappropriate, exploitative or excessive control over the finances of the vulnerable adult

- **Additional perpetrator signs**
  Delays seeking medical treatment or advice and/or reluctant to allow treatment of the vulnerable adult. Detachment from the vulnerable adult. Lacks concern at the severity or extent of injury or other signs. Is reluctant to give information. Aggressive towards the vulnerable adult.

Local procedures may be available from your employer, the NHS trust, Health Board or local council, and you should follow these procedures where available when abuse or neglect is suspected.

The process outlined in Diagram 14 on the next page may also be useful.

A vulnerable adult's wishes should be taken into account at all times. Obtain consent from the patient before disclosing confidential information about them. However, if there are overriding circumstances requiring you to take immediate action to ensure the safety of the individual or others the need for referral, even if they do not give consent, should be considered. If you are unsure

of someone's mental capacity to provide consent seek additional advice, e.g. from their GP.

You should not attempt to investigate suspicions or allegations of abuse directly or to discuss concerns with the alleged perpetrator of the abuse or neglect.

You should make appropriate records of concerns and suspicions, decisions taken and reasons whether or not further action was taken on a particular occasion.

FURTHER READING

Royal Pharmaceutical Society
Protecting vulnerable adults – quick reference guide.
www.rpharms.com

Care Information Scotland
Adult support and protection.
https://careinfoscotland.scot/topics/your-rights/adult-support-and-protection/

Department of Health and Social Care
Mental Health Act 1983: Code of practice. 2015.
www.gov.uk/government/publications

NHS England
Abuse and neglect of vulnerable adults.
www.nhs.uk

NHS Wales
Mental Health Act 1983: Code of practice for Wales. Revised 2016.
www.wales.nhs.uk

Office of the Public Guardian
Safeguarding policy: protecting vulnerable adults.
www.gov.uk

Public Health Wales
National safeguarding team (NHS Wales): safeguarding adults.
www.wales.nhs.uk

Scottish Government
Mental Health (Care and Treatment) (Scotland) Act 2003: Code of practice.
www.gov.scot

DIAGRAM 14: WHAT TO DO
IF ABUSE OR NEGLECT IS SUSPECTED

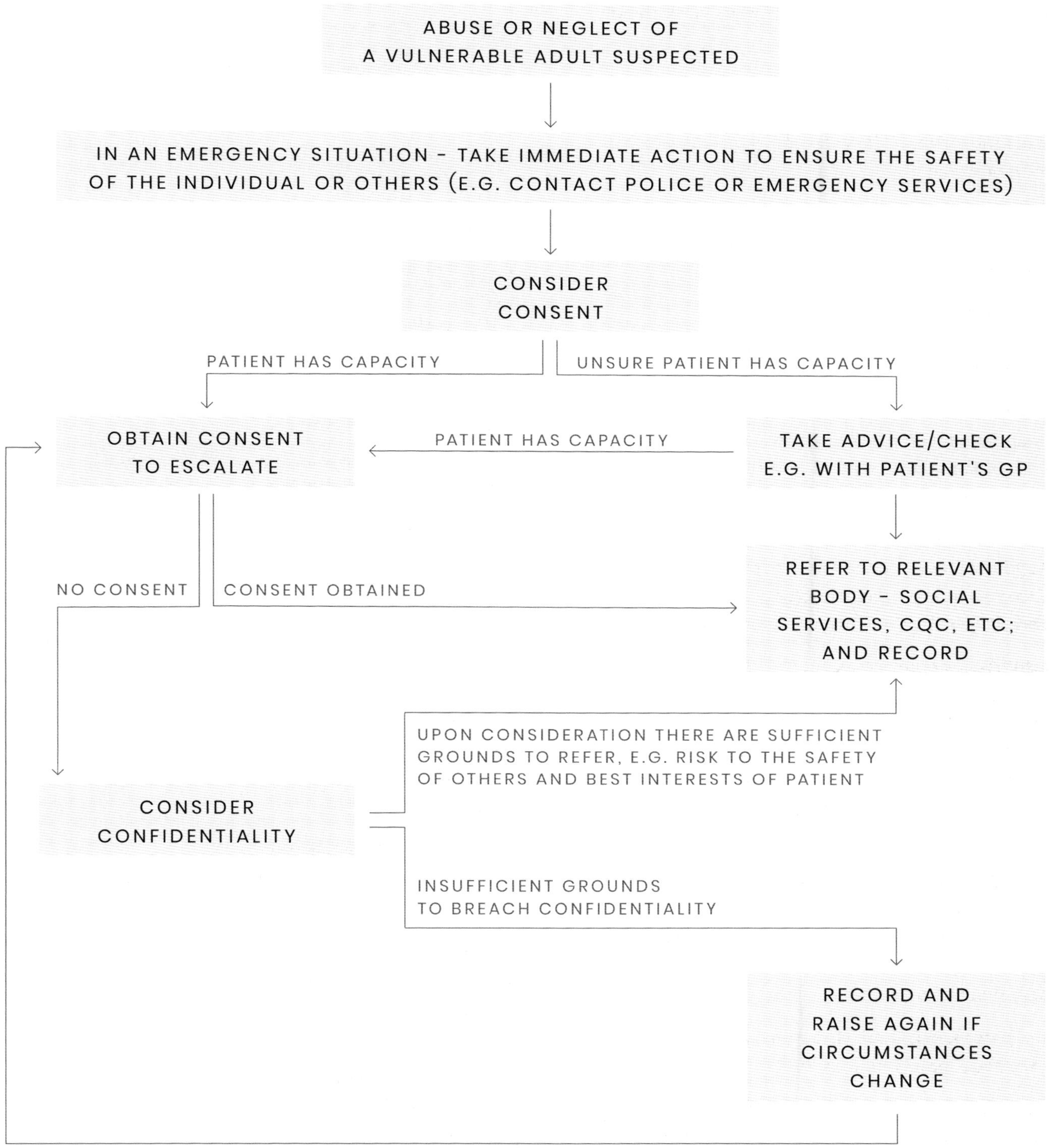

ABUSE OR NEGLECT OF
A VULNERABLE ADULT SUSPECTED

IN AN EMERGENCY SITUATION - TAKE IMMEDIATE ACTION TO ENSURE THE SAFETY
OF THE INDIVIDUAL OR OTHERS (E.G. CONTACT POLICE OR EMERGENCY SERVICES)

CONSIDER
CONSENT

PATIENT HAS CAPACITY

UNSURE PATIENT HAS CAPACITY

OBTAIN CONSENT
TO ESCALATE

PATIENT HAS CAPACITY

TAKE ADVICE/CHECK
E.G. WITH PATIENT'S GP

REFER TO RELEVANT
BODY - SOCIAL
SERVICES, CQC, ETC;
AND RECORD

NO CONSENT

CONSENT OBTAINED

UPON CONSIDERATION THERE ARE SUFFICIENT
GROUNDS TO REFER, E.G. RISK TO THE SAFETY
OF OTHERS AND BEST INTERESTS OF PATIENT

CONSIDER
CONFIDENTIALITY

INSUFFICIENT GROUNDS
TO BREACH CONFIDENTIALITY

RECORD AND
RAISE AGAIN IF
CIRCUMSTANCES
CHANGE

3.7.14
MEDICAL DEVICES

A medical device is defined under European legislation as *any instrument, apparatus, appliance, material or other article, whether used alone or in combination, including the software necessary for its proper application intended by the manufacturer to be used on human beings for the purpose of:*

- *diagnosis, prevention, monitoring, treatment or alleviation of disease*

- *diagnosis, monitoring, treatment, or alleviation of or compensation for an injury or handicap*

- *investigation, replacement or modification of the anatomy or of a physiological process*

- *control of conception*

and which does not achieve its principal intended action in or on the human body by pharmacological, immunological or metabolic means, but which may be assisted in its function by such means.

Examples of medical devices (not exhaustive) available from a pharmacy include dressings, thermometers, needles, syringes, blood pressure monitors, stoma care products, condoms, test kits (e.g. cholesterol test kits, pregnancy test kits, etc.), inhalers, glucose meters and test strips, screening tests, some emollients, some eye drops, etc.

All medical devices are regulated by the MHRA.

All devices are required to carry the CE mark denoting compliance with the medical devices regulations and indicating that the device performs as intended, is fit for purpose with all associated risks reduced as far as possible.

Medical devices which incorporate an active pharmaceutical ingredient (e.g. pre-filled sodium chloride 0.9% syringes) can also be considered, following appropriate risk assessment, within the principles covered in the RPS Safe and secure handling of medicines (see RPS website www.rpharms.com)

FURTHER READING

Royal Pharmaceutical Society
Medical devices – quick reference guide.
www.rpharms.com

Royal Pharmaceutical Society
Professional guidance for the procurement and supply of specials. 2015. (Includes guidance and case study on medical devices.)
www.rpharms.com

General Medical Council
Good practice in prescribing and managing medicines and devices. 2013.
www.gmc-uk.org

Medicines and Healthcare products Regulatory Agency
Medical devices regulation and safety.
www.gov.uk

Medicines and Healthcare products Regulatory Agency
Report a problem with a medicine or medical device.
www.gov.uk/report-problem-medicine-medical-device

NHS England and Medicines and Healthcare products Regulatory Agency
Patient safety alert. Improving medical device incident reporting and learning. 2014.
www.england.nhs.uk

3.7.15
ADMINISTRATION OF ADRENALINE IN AN EMERGENCY

WHAT IS ADRENALINE?

Adrenaline is a POM and is given intramuscularly for the treatment of anaphylaxis. Brands of adrenaline intramuscular injections in your pharmacy may include Epipen®, Emerade® and Jext®.

Where a pharmacist is expected to recognise and treat an anaphylactic reaction as part of their usual clinical role (for example, if they are offering a vaccination service), they must have access to an anaphylaxis pack (as outlined in the Green Book) and have received the required training in the recognition of anaphylaxis and administration of adrenaline. The anaphylaxis pack will include ampoules of adrenaline and syringes and needles or prefilled syringes which should be used in preference to auto injectors such as those listed above.

WHAT IS ANAPHYLAXIS?

Anaphylaxis is a severe, life-threatening, systemic hypersensitivity reaction resulting in rapidly developing airway and/or breathing difficulty and/or hypotension. Other features of an allergic reaction are often present, including skin and mucosal changes such as urticaria and angio-oedema of the face. Anaphylaxis is an emergency which should be treated immediately once identified.

ADMINISTRATION OF ADRENALINE

Regulation 238 of the Human Medicines Regulations 2012 allows adrenaline to be administered by anyone for the purpose of saving life in an emergency (for further information see section 3.3.8).

Therefore pharmacists using their professional and clinical judgement can administer adrenaline in an emergency to persons presenting with symptoms of anaphylaxis.

If a pharmacist administers adrenaline they must also ensure that an ambulance is called by dialling 999 and reporting that there is a case of suspected anaphylaxis.

FURTHER READING

British National Formulary
www.medicinescomplete.com
or www.evidence.nhs.uk

National Institute for Health and Care Excellence
Anaphylaxis: assessment and referral after emergency treatment. Clinical guideline. 2011.
www.nice.org.uk

Public Health England
The Green Book: Immunisation against infectious diseases. (Chapter 8)
www.gov.uk/government/collections/immunisation-against-infectious-disease-the-green-book

Resuscitation Council (UK)
Emergency treatment of anaphylactic reactions: Guidelines for healthcare providers.
www.resus.org.uk/anaphylaxis

3.7.16 MULTI-COMPARTMENT COMPLIANCE AIDS

Although multi-compartment compliance aids (MCA), (also known as monitored dosage systems (MDS)) may be of value to help some patients with problems managing their medicines and maintaining independent healthy living, they are one option following a comprehensive assessment of a patient's ability to safely manage their medicines.They may not be the best intervention for everyone and many alternative interventions are available. Evidence indicates that MCA should not automatically be the intervention of choice for all patients.

Not all medicines are suitable for inclusion in MCA and pharmacists should be aware that the re-packaging of medicines from a manufacturer's original packaging may often be off-licence and involves risks and responsibility for decisions made. The decision to supply a MCA needs to be reviewed and reassessed regularly to ensure its use continues to meet the need and is in the best interest of the user.

With the limited evidence base currently indicating a lack of patient benefit outcomes with the use of MCA, the RPS recommends that the use of original packs of medicines, supported by appropriate pharmaceutical care, should be the preferred intervention for the supply of medicines in the absence of a specific need identified by individual assessment for a MCA in all settings.

We have has published a repository of MCA information where key resources can be accessed including patient assessment tools and our guidance Improving patient outcomes: The better use of multi-compartment compliance aids. This can be viewed on our website at www.rpharms. com.

Pharmacists are encouraged to be aware of the risks associated with MCA use on a population basis without individual assessments, to be aware of the alternatives and to share this knowledge with other health and social care professionals. Alternatives may include:

- medicines administration record (MAR) charts
- labels with pictograms
- large print labels

- information sheets

- reminder alarms

- IT solutions and new technology such as phone apps and telemedicine

All of these interventions have a place in ensuring patients take or receive the correct medicines at the right time. The use of an MCA is just one additional intervention in a range of intervention options.

UK Medicines Information provide some information on the stability of medicines in compliance aids which can be accessed by all pharmacy staff via the Specialist Pharmacy Services website www.sps.nhs.uk.

3.7.17
DRUGS AND DRIVING

BACKGROUND
Section 4 of the Road Traffic Act 1988 includes an offence of driving whilst impaired through drugs, regardless of whether or not the drugs are being used legitimately. This means that if a patient driving is found to be impaired by medicines, even if he or she is taking them as prescribed or as recommended in the product information, he or she may still be prosecuted.

A new additional offence of driving with certain specified drugs in excess of specified levels came into force on 2 March 2015 in England and Wales. The legislation also provides for a statutory 'medical defence' for patients taking their medicines as prescribed or in accordance with product information.

Roadside drug screening devices use saliva to identify if a driver has taken one of the drugs listed in Table 18, or a drug that is metabolised to one of these. The first group are commonly abused drugs for which low limits have been set, the second group consists mainly of licensed medicines that have a significant liability to be abused and the specified limits have been set higher than those or the first group.

To protect patients who may test positive for certain drugs as a result of taking medicines in accordance with advice from a healthcare professional or the patient information leaflet, the new offence has a statutory 'medical defence'.

This may be raised at any point providing that the drug was:

- Lawfully prescribed, supplied or purchased over-the-counter, for medical or dental purposes; and

- Taken in accordance with advice given by the prescriber or supplier, and in accordance with any accompanying written instructions (provided these are consistent with any advice given by the prescriber).

Patient specific advice provided by a healthcare professional may sometimes differ from the general information given in the patient information leaflet of a medicine. In these cases, the advice provided by the healthcare professional may be used as a basis for the patient's statutory 'medical defence'.

Pharmacists should be mindful of any new medicines added to a patient's regime that may interact with their existing therapies, affecting the metabolism of one of the specified drugs. They should also be cautious if there is a developing medical condition that could increase the risk of side effects from a medicine (e.g. during the development of a serious illness with significant weight loss).

TABLE 18: SPECIFIED DRUGS

FIRST GROUP	SECOND GROUP
Cannabis (THC)	Clonazepam
MDMA (ecstasy)	Diazepam
Ketamine	Lorazepam
Methylamfetamine	Oxazepam
Cocaine (and a cocaine metabolite, BZE)	Temazepam
Lysergic acid diethylamide (LSD)	Flunitrazepam
Heroin/diamorphine metabolite (6-MAM)	Methadone
	Morphine
	Amfetamine

DIAGRAM 15: SUMMARY OF HOW THE NEW DRUG DRIVING OFFENCE FITS IN WITH EXISTING LEGISLATION

SPECIFIED DRUG DETECTION AT HIGHER LEVELS THAN THOSE PERMITTED IN THE REGULATIONS

↓   ↓

THERE IS EVIDENCE THAT THE DRUG HAS BEEN TAKEN IN ACCORDANCE WITH INSTRUCTIONS FROM A HEALTHCARE PROFESSIONAL AND/OR THE ACCOMPAGNYING PATIENT INFORMATION LEAFLET

NO EVIDENCE THAT THE DRUG HAS BEEN PRESCRIPED OR PURCHASED LEGIMATELY

↓   ↓   ↓   ↓

| DRIVING IMPAIRED | DRIVING NOT IMPAIRED | DRIVING IMPAIRED | DRIVING NOT IMPAIRED |

↓   ↓   ↓   ↓

| OFFENCE | STATUORY MEDICAL DEFENCE CAN BE RAISED | OFFENCE | OFFENCE |

ADVICE FOR PATIENTS

Reminder of the advice that should be provided to all patients receiving medicines that may impair driving ability:

- You must not drive if you feel sleepy, dizzy, are unable to concentrate or make decisions, have slowed thinking, or if you experience sight problems. If the medicine is one that could affect your driving ability, you should not drive until you know how the medicine affects you as an individual, particularly when starting a new medicine or following a dose change

- If you start a new medicine, even if it is one that does not directly affect your driving you should check with your pharmacist if it could have an effect on any of the medicines you are already taking, that could in turn affect your driving

- Remember that alcohol taken in combination with medicines, even in small amounts can greatly increase the risk of accidents

- An untreated medical condition may itself cause driving impairment and so it is important that you do not stop taking your medicines.

In addition to this, patients who are taking medicines that are affected by the new legislation should also receive the following information and advice:

- There is new legislation in place which places limits on the amounts of certain drugs that you can have in your bloodstream whilst driving. There is a 'medical defence' for those who are taking medicines in line with a healthcare professional's advice, provided that their driving is not impaired

- Keep some suitable evidence with you when driving to show that you are taking your medicine as prescribed or supplied by a healthcare professional. Examples of evidence could include a repeat prescription slip for a prescribed medicine or the patient information leaflet for a P or GSL medicine.

It is important to note that if the individual's driving is impaired, they can still be prosecuted under the existing offence of driving whilst impaired through drugs, for which there is no statutory 'medical defence'. It remains the responsibility of all drivers to consider whether their driving is or could be impaired by their medicines.

We are aware new safety laws for zero tolerance for people caught driving with illegal drugs in their system will be introduced in Scotland during October 2019. Further information can be viewed on the Scottish Government website at www.gov.scot/news/new-drug-driving-laws-and-roadside-testing-to-improve-road-safety/.

MEDICAL CONDITIONS AND DRIVING

In addition to the drugs and driving offences described in this section there are also rules on fitness to drive requirements for patients with certain medical conditions. Further information on medical conditions, disabilities and driving is available on the Driving and Vehicle Licensing (DVLA) website: www.gov.uk/driving-medical-conditions

FURTHER READING

Department for Transport
Guidance for healthcare professionals on drug driving. 2014.
https://assets.publishing.service.gov.uk/government/uploads/system/uploads/attachment_data/file/325275/healthcare-profs-drug-driving.pdf

Electronic Medicines Compendium
Information about whether a medicine is affected by the new legislation is included in its 'Summary of Product Characteristics'.
www.medicines.org.uk

Medicines and Healthcare Products Regulatory Agency
Drug Safety Update – Drugs and driving: blood concentration limits to be set for certain controlled drugs in a new legal offence. 2014.
www.gov.uk

Medicines and Healthcare Products Regulatory Agency
Guidance for healthcare professionals on drug driving. 2014.
www.gov.uk

Perkins K.
Driving after taking drugs and medicines.
The Pharmaceutical Journal, Vol 293, September 27 2014.
www.pharmaceutical-journal.com
(URI: 20066477)

Road Traffic Act
SI 2014/2868 The Drug Driving (Specified Limits) (England and Wales) Regulations. 2014
www.legislation.gov.uk

Road Traffic Act
SI 2015/911 The Drug Driving (Specified Limits) (England and Wales) (Amendment) Regulations. 2015.
www.legislation.gov.uk

Road Traffic Act
SI 2019/83 The Drug Driving (Specified Limits) (Scotland) Regulations. 2019.
www.legislation.gov.uk

3.7.18
RETENTION OF PHARMACY RECORDS

MEP refers to record keeping requirements throughout. In addition, East and South East England Specialist Pharmacy Services has published a document Recommendations for Retention of Pharmacy Records: www.sps.nhs.uk/articles/retention-of-pharmacy-records/. This document includes guidance for all pharmacy settings as well as some sector-specific information.

FURTHER READING

NHS Digital
Records Management Code of Practice for Health and Social Care. 2016.
https://digital.nhs.uk

3.7.19
NEW PSYCHOACTIVE SUBSTANCES

The UK Psychoactive Substances Act (PSA) 2016 has described compounds commonly known as new psychoactive substances (NPS) as 'substances' that are 'capable of producing a psychoactive effect'.

For detailed guidance on NPS see RPS website www.rpharms.com for the 'New Psychoactive Substances quick reference guide' and the summary factsheet.

WHY PHARMACISTS SHOULD KNOW ABOUT NPS?

Pharmacists may encounter NPS products (such as tablets, capsules, powders, oils or herbs/seeds) in a range of settings including urgent and emergency care, secure environments, community pharmacies, pharmacists working in GP practices and in mental health units. In a similar way to the yellow card scheme, pharmacists can report drug reactions related to NPS via a pilot scheme through the following link: https://report-illicit-drug-reaction.phe.gov.uk/ The PSA (2016) has given powers to officers to stop and search people, vehicles and vessels, enter and search premises in accordance with a warrant, and to seize and destroy psychoactive substances.

Although the PSA does not criminalise simple possession of NPSs, it is an offence to possess them within custodial institutions, or anywhere with intent to supply them to another. It is also an offence to import them (e.g. by buying them from a foreign website).

It is important that pharmacists are aware that the labels on NPS are not compliant with legal and professional requirements, as is the case with pharmaceuticals (e.g. requirements of Good Manufacturing Practices (GMP)). Furthermore, NPS products may contain unclaimed Schedule 1 or 2 substances (The Misuse of Drugs Regulations 2001), for which legal requirements apply.

Pharmacists need to be aware of possible NPS/POM interactions, some of which are documented, such as interactions with anti-retrovirals (http://neptune-clinical-guidance.co.uk/wp-content/uploads/2015/03/NEPTUNE-Guidance-March-2015.pdf) In addition, pharmacists need to be aware of interactions arising from unclaimed active ingredients present in NPS. Furthermore, research has shown that NPS have not replaced the current repertoire of traditional drugs of abuse (e.g. amphetamine, cocaine, heroin, ecstasy) but rather have supplemented it, with or without alcohol, resulting upon co-administration in a high risk of synergistic or additive pharmacological effects.

NPS may also have an impact on the enforcement of the drug-driving laws. For example, if a patient takes an NPS that inhibits the metabolism of a prescribed Schedule 2 POM, a road-side test may show greater concentrations of the Schedule 2 drug than that allowed whilst driving, which may result in the arrest of the patient. NPS are not included in the drug-driving lists.

Pharmacists should be aware of the 're-classification' of OTC and P medicines to NPS when used for recreational purposes e.g. the diverted use of OTC and P medicines.

The use of NPS may induce addiction and psychosis, therefore, there are legal (under the Mental Health Act 2007), professional, clinical and cost implications.

FURTHER READING

Royal Pharmaceutical Society (RPS)
New psychoactive substances –
quick reference guide and factsheet.
www.rpharms.com

European Monitoring Centre for Drugs and Drug Addiction
New psychoactive substances in Europe.
An update from the EU Early Warning System. 2015.
www.emcdda.europa.eu/attachements.cfm/
att_235958_EN_TD0415135ENN.pdf

European Monitoring Centre for Drugs and Drug Addiction
Various resources available. These include risk assessment reports on high-risk NPS, which have induced severe harm or fatalities.
www.emcdda.europa.eu/publications

United Nations Office on Drugs and Crime
The challenge of new psychoactive substances. 2013.
https://www.unodc.org/documents/scientific/
NPS_2013_SMART.pdf

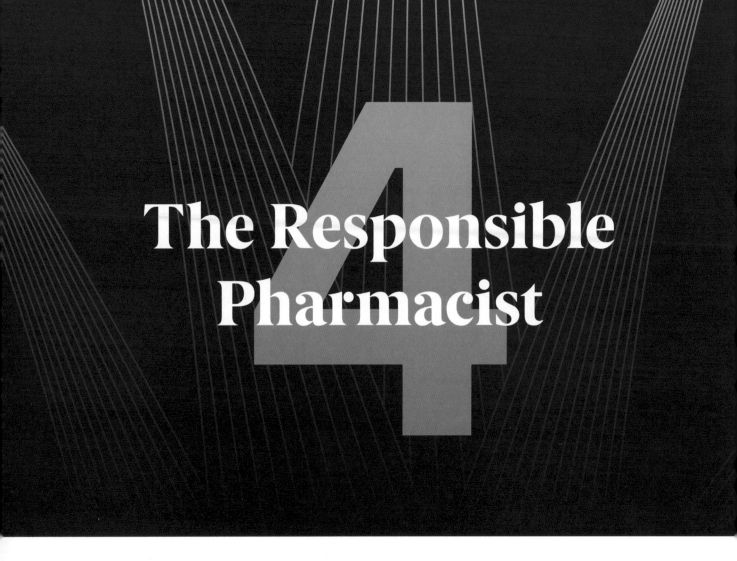

The Responsible Pharmacist

A pharmacist must be in charge of a registered pharmacy as the responsible pharmacist, in order to lawfully conduct a retail pharmacy business.

There can only be one responsible pharmacist in charge at any one time, and the pharmacist can only be in charge of one registered premises at any one time.

Legislation introducing the role and responsibilities of the Responsible Pharmacist are set out in full in the Medicines Act 1968 (as amended by the *Health Act 2006*) and the *Medicines (Pharmacies) (Responsible Pharmacist) Regulations 2008*.

NOTE: AT THE TIME OF WRITING, THE REBALANCING MEDICINES LEGISLATION AND PHARMACY REGULATION PROGRAMME BOARD WERE REVIEWING PHARMACY REGULATION AND CONSIDERING CHANGES TO THE ROLE AND RESPONSIBILITIES OF SUPERINTENDENT AND RESPONSIBLE PHARMACIST. WWW.GOV.UK/GOVERNMENT/GROUPS/ PHARMACY-REGULATION-PROGRAMME-BOARD

WHAT BEING A RESPONSIBLE PHARMACIST INVOLVES

A Responsible Pharmacist will need to:

SECURE THE SAFE AND EFFECTIVE RUNNING OF THE PHARMACY

↓

DISPLAY A NOTICE

↓

COMPLETE THE PHARMACY RECORD

↓

ESTABLISH, MAINTAIN AND REVIEW PHARMACY PROCEDURES

SECURING THE SAFE AND EFFECTIVE RUNNING OF A REGISTERED PHARMACY

The responsible pharmacist is responsible for the safe and effective running of the pharmacy and should establish the scope of the responsibilities before taking on a role. If unsure about anything reasonable measures can be taken to clarify with the pharmacy owner, superintendent pharmacist or other delegated person.

Further material on how a responsible pharmacist can secure the safe and effective running of a registered pharmacy can be found on the RPS Responsible Pharmacist Toolkit on RPS website at www.rpharms.com.

If a responsible pharmacist believes the pharmacy is not safe or patients are at risk then steps should be taken to secure the safe and effective running of the pharmacy. If this is not possible then the pharmacy may need to be closed.

DISPLAYING A NOTICE

A responsible pharmacist is required to display a notice that is clearly visible to patients and the public with the information below for as long as she/he is a responsible pharmacist.

This needs to include:

- The name of the responsible pharmacist

- The GPhC registration number

- The fact that the responsible pharmacist is in charge of the pharmacy at the time

If the responsible pharmacist is temporarily absent from the pharmacy (see below under "Absence") but remains the responsible pharmacist, the notice should not be removed even if there is a second pharmacist in the pharmacy. However, if the responsible pharmacist changes throughout the day, so too should the name and registration number on the notice.

COMPLETING THE PHARMACY RECORD

The pharmacy record is an important legal document. It shows who the responsible pharmacist is at any given date and at any time.

The pharmacy record may be kept in the following formats:

- In writing

- Electronically

- Or in both forms

THE RECORD SHOULD:

- Be recorded accurately and reflects who the responsible pharmacist is and was at any given date and time (including any absences).

- Should be made contemporaneously personally by the responsible pharmacist. An entry may be made remotely as long as the record complies with all the relevant and professional requirements.

- Any alterations or amendments made for both paper-based and electronic pharmacy records need to identify when and by whom the alteration/amendment was made.

- For electronic records appropriate measures should be made to back up the record and be kept on the pharmacy premises, available for GPhC inspection if required.

THE FOLLOWING DETAILS MUST BE RECORDED IN THE PHARMACY RECORD:

- The responsible pharmacist's name

- The responsible pharmacist's registration number

- The date and time at which the pharmacist became the responsible pharmacist

- The date and time at which the responsible pharmacist stopped being the responsible pharmacist

- If you are absent from the premises:

  - The date of absence

  - The time which the responsible pharmacist left the pharmacy premises

  - The time at which the responsible pharmacist returned to the pharmacy premises

The pharmacy owner or superintendent pharmacist must keep the pharmacy record for a period of FIVE years. The record must be available at the pharmacy to which it relates to.

PHARMACY PROCEDURES

A responsible pharmacist must establish, maintain and review the pharmacy procedures in the pharmacy she/he is working in.

Regulation 4 of The Medicines (Pharmacies) (Responsible Pharmacist) Regulations 2008 outlines the pharmacy procedures must cover the following:

1   The arrangements to secure that medicinal products are:

- ordered

- stored

- prepared

- sold by retail

- supplied in circumstances corresponding to retail sale

- delivered outside the pharmacy and

- disposed of in a safe and effective manner

2   The circumstances in which a member of pharmacy staff who is not a pharmacist may give advice about medicinal products

3   The identification of members of pharmacy staff who are, in the view of the Responsible Pharmacist, competent to perform certain tasks relating to the pharmacy business

4   The keeping of records about the arrangements

5   The arrangements which are to apply during the absence of the Responsible Pharmacist from the premises

6   The steps to be taken when there is a change of Responsible Pharmacist at the premises

7   The procedure which is to be followed if a complaint is made about the pharmacy business

8   The procedure which is to be followed if an incident occurs which may indicate that the pharmacy business is not running in a safe and effective manner and

9   The manner in which changes to the pharmacy procedures are to be notified to pharmacy staff

THE PHARMACY PROCEDURES CAN BE KEPT IN THE PHARMACY IN THE FOLLOWING FORMATS:

- In writing

- Electronically (consider any backups required)

- Or in both forms

Adequate back-ups of the contents of the procedures should be made.

THE PHARMACY PROCEDURE SHOULD:

- Be available for inspection by the person who owns the pharmacy business, the superintendent pharmacist, the responsible pharmacist, the pharmacy staff and GPhC inspectorate.

- Be reviewed regularly. They can be reviewed once every two years or following an incident which may indicate that the pharmacy may not be running safely and effectively (such as a dispensing error).

  - Identify the responsible pharmacist who reviewed the procedure

  - Identify which procedures are in place

  - Identify which procedures were previously in place

A responsible pharmacist can use her/his professional judgement to make a temporary amendment to the pharmacy procedures if the circumstances in the pharmacy change (for example a key member of staff if off sick, etc).

If temporary amendments are made the responsible pharmacist should maintain an audit trail to identify:

- Which procedures are in place

- Which procedures were previously in place

- The responsible pharmacist who amended the procedure

- The date on which the amendment was made

The responsible pharmacist needs to be satisfied the pharmacy staff are aware of and understand the pharmacy procedures which are in place.

ABSENCE

Legislation allows the responsible pharmacist to be absent for up to a maximum period of two hours during the pharmacy's business hours between midnight and midnight.

If there is more than one responsible pharmacist in charge of the pharmacy during the pharmacy's business hours, the total period of absence for all the responsible pharmacists must not exceed two hours.

If the responsible pharmacist is absent, the following arrangements must be in place:

- Only be absent if the pharmacy can continue to run safely and effectively

- Remain contactable with the pharmacy staff, where this reasonably practical and be able to return with reasonable promptness.

- If the responsible pharmacist cannot remain contactable and return with reasonable promptness, she/he must arrange for another pharmacist to be contactable and available to provide advice (this does not need to be another responsible pharmacist).

WHAT TO DO IF A RESPONSIBLE PHARMACIST DECIDES TO BE ABSENT?

If a responsible pharmacist is absent from the premises as a minimum she/he must record:

- The date of absence

- The time which the responsible pharmacist left the pharmacy premises

- The time at which the responsible pharmacist returned to the pharmacy premises

Further information on how a responsible pharmacist can deal with an absence can be found on the RPS Responsible Pharmacist Toolkit at www.rpharms.com.

WHICH ACTIVITIES REQUIRE A RESPONSIBLE PHARMACIST?

The operational activities that may take place in the registered pharmacy when a responsible pharmacist is in charge of the pharmacy depend on the level of supervision provided and whether or not she/he is absent from the registered pharmacy. Examples of operational activities and the level of supervision required can be found in tables below

TABLE 19 : ACTIVITIES THAT CAN TAKE PLACE WITH A RESPONSIBLE PHARMACIST IN CHARGE OF THE PHARMACY UNDER THE SUPERVISION OF A PHARMACIST AND THE SUPERVISING PHARMACIST WILL NEED TO BE PHYSICALLY PRESENT AT THE PHARMACY

ACTIVITY	OTHER POINTS TO CONSIDER
Professional check (clinical and legal check) of a prescription	This check is required under the NHS pharmaceutical legislation www.legislation.gov.uk/uksi/2013/349/contents/made
Sale/supply of P medicines	'Supervision' in this context requires physical presence and pharmacist being able to advise and intervene
Sale/supply of POMs (e.g. handing dispensed medicines to patient, patient representative or a delivery person)	'Supervision' in this context requires physical presence and pharmacist being able to advise and intervene
Supply of medicines under a patient group direction (PGD)	'Supervision' in this context requires physical presence
Wholesale of medicines	'Supervision' in this context requires physical presence and pharmacist being able to advise and intervene
Emergency supply of a medicine(s) at the request of a patient or healthcare professional	'Supervision' in this context requires physical presence and pharmacist being able to advise and intervene

ACTIVITY	OTHER POINTS TO CONSIDER
The assembly process (including assembly of compliance aids (monitored dosage systems): • Generating a dispensing label • Taking medicines off the dispensary shelves • Assembly of the item (e.g. counting tablets) • Labelling of containers with the dispensing label • Accuracy checking	'Supervision' in this context may not require the physical presence of a pharmacist. The level of supervision required of the suitable trained staff who undertake this work will depend on what is regarded as good practice within the pharmacy profession.

EXPLANATION OF 'ASSEMBLY'

The assembly of medicines against a prescription is controlled by Section 10 of the Medicines Act 1968 defining medicinal product 'assembly'.

Section 10 of the Medicines Act 1968 requires that the assembly process takes place under the 'supervision' of a pharmacist.

Supervision is not defined in the Act, and since the time the legislation was written the nature of assembly has changed in many instances such as the introduction of patient packs.

The courts have considered the issue of the nature of 'supervision' required for the purposes of sale or supply of medicines and have concluded that, where supervision by a pharmacist is required, the actual transaction cannot take place without the physical presence of a pharmacist who is able to advise and intervene, even though s/he will not need to carry out the transaction themselves. However, the level of supervision required for assembly activities is less clear, and so for these activities, reference has to be made to more general case law of what 'supervision' means in the context of professional supervision. The general position (derived from the Court of Appeal's judgement in Summers v Congreve Horner and Co [1992] 2 EGLR 152) is that supervision, in the context of professional supervision, means the degree of supervision required by what is regarded as good practice within the profession, having regard to the qualifications and experience of the person being supervised, but actual physical presence may not be necessary.

Applying that to the present context, it means that if the pharmacist responsible for supervising assembly of a medicinal product is absent, pharmacy support staff may continue to carry out activities which are considered to be 'assembling' activities for the purposes of the definition set out above, without breaching the legislation, provided it is recognised good practice within the pharmacy profession that they be allowed to do so. The RPS publishes good practice guidance, but it is important to emphasise that no single solution fits all circumstances. What may be good practice for one type of assembling activity may not be good practice for other types of assembling activities, and all such activities must be 'supervised' at an appropriate level. It is also important to emphasise that this does not affect the position that the supply of assembled medicines against a prescription is prohibited unless the pharmacist is physically present in the registered pharmacy and in a position to advise and intervene. However, 'supervision' is not a 'one size fits all circumstances' legal concept, and the courts have recognised this.

ACTIVITY	OTHER POINTS TO CONSIDER
Processing of prescription forms that have been dispensed (eg. Counting number of items dispensed, sorting prior submission for reimbursement)	Undertaken by suitable trained staff and operating within an agreed documented operating procedure. NHS reimbursement covered under NHS legislation.
Delivery person conveying medicines to patient	Undertaken by suitable trained staff and operating within an agreed documented operating procedure. Responsible Pharmacists and Superintendents should give consideration to what will happen to undelivered medicines especially relating to CDs.
Receiving patient returned medicines (excluding CDs)	Undertaken by suitable trained staff and operating within an agreed documented operating procedure. Responsible Pharmacists and Superintendents should give consideration to how the pharmacy handles receipt of patient returned medicines which are CDs in accordance with the Misuse of Drugs Regulations 2001. Also see MEP 43 , section 3.6 for further guidance on CDs.

FURTHER READING

Royal Pharmaceutical Society
Responsible pharmacist – toolkit.
www.rpharms.com

General Pharmaceutical Council
Information for employers: Responsible pharmacist.
www.pharmacyregulation.org/
responsible-pharmacist

Pharmaceutical Services Negotiating Committee
Responsible pharmacist. Includes a series of FAQs.
www.psnc.org.uk/contract-it/pharmacy-regulation/
responsible-pharmacist

SEE ALSO
Rebalancing Medicines Legislation and Pharmacy Regulation Programme Board
www.gov.uk/government/groups/pharmacy-
regulation-programme-board#minutes-and-
associated-papers

Other resources published by the Royal Pharmaceutical Society

Apart from the MEP guide, we publish a wide variety of resources to support members across all sectors and career stages.

These include:

- Professional standards and guidance

- Professional development resources and competency frameworks

- Pharmacy practice and public health resources

- Science and research resources

- Policy and thought-leadership papers

- Resources to support mentoring, tutoring and leadership

  The full range of RPS resource is available from the RPS website.

  www.rpharms.com/resources

6 Professional standards

The RPS develops professionals standards together with the profession to describe good practice, good systems of care, and good ways of working. Our standards are not regulatory, and can be used to improve patient care by challenging the profession to improve the way that work. They can provide a framework to support pharmacists and their teams to improve services and deliver high quality patient care across all settings and sectors, and can also be used to benchmark services.

They sit between legislation and regulation on one side, and local policies and procedures on the other and are widely accepted by the healthcare and regulatory system as having a valuable role to play in supporting healthcare professionals to deliver high quality care.[1, 2]

The GPhC and RPS published a joint statement *Using standards to help provide safe and effective care for members of the public – February 2019* www.rpharms.com/Portals/0/RPS%20document%20library/Open%20access/Policy%20statements/RPS%20GPhC%20Joint%20statement.pdf?ver=2019-02-07-095714-967

This aims to highlight the importance of regulatory and professional standards and guidance as a way to create frameworks which protect the health, safety and wellbeing of the public by upholding standards and public trust in pharmacy.

HOW WE DEVELOP STANDARDS, GUIDANCE AND FRAMEWORKS

NICE has accredited our process to produce professional standards, competency frameworks and guidance. Accreditation is valid for 5 years from 17 February 2017.

More information on accreditation can be viewed at www.nice.org.uk/accreditation

We intend to develop future professional standards using this process manual which is available at

---

1 Quality in the new Health System – Maintaining and improving quality from April 2013 www.gov.uk

2 GPhC Standards of conduct, ethics and performance – standard 6.6. www.pharmacyregulation.org

(www.rpharms.com/Portals/0/RPS%20document%
20library/Open%20access/Manuals/How%20the%
20RPS%20develops%20standards%20and%20
guidance.pdf)

**Professional standards, guidance and frameworks
developed under our NICE accredited process
include:**

- RPS single competency framework for
  all prescribers

- Professional standards for Hospital
  Pharmacy Services

- Safe and secure handling of medicines

- Polypharmacy

**Professional standards and guidance developed
under other processes include:**

- Best practice standards for managing medicines
  shortages in Secondary Care in England

- Best practice standards for managing medicines
  shortages in Secondary Care in Scotland

- Medicines optimisation principles (England)

- Professional guidance on the administration
  of medicines in healthcare settings

- Professional standards for error reporting

- Professional standards for Homecare services

- Professional standards for optimising medicines
  in secure environments

- Professional standards for Public Health

- Professional standards for quality assurance
  of aseptic services

- Transfer of care principles

**Professional standards, guidance and frameworks
under development:**

- Professional standards for Community
  pharmacy services

- Prescribing supervisor competency framework

Our professional standards and tools for
implementation are available on our website
www.rpharms.com

Royal pharmaceutical society code of conduct

The Code of Conduct for members of the RPS has been reproduced below and is available online in appendix A of the RPS regulations (www.rpharms.com/Portals/0/RPS%20document%20library/Open%20access/Governance%20documents/NEW%20REGULATIONS%20final%20version%20APPROVED%20BY%20ASSEMBLY.pdf?ver=2018-06-20-114508-663).

CODE OF CONDUCT

Assembly may create, and from time to time amend or rescind, a Code of Conduct to be observed by all members of the Society. Breaches of the Code may, upon proper investigation under the process set out in the appropriate Regulations, lead to a Disciplinary Panel hearing which may, in turn, depending on the nature of the breach, ultimately lead to expulsion from the Society.

All Members

Being a member of the RPS is a mark of professionalism and members, as ambassadors of the Society, should do nothing that might detract from the high standing of the profession. This includes any aspect of a member's personal conduct which could have a negative impact upon the profession. On admission to, and annually on renewal of membership, all members must therefore:

- be in good standing professionally, including with the Society and any other professional body or regulator of which they are a member or registrant

- conduct themselves in a manner that upholds and enhances the reputation of the Society

- further the interests of and maintain the dignity and welfare of the Society and the profession

- exercise their professional skills and judgement to the best of their ability, discharge their professional responsibilities with integrity and do all in their power to ensure that their professional activities do not put the health and safety of others at risk

- when called upon to give a professional opinion, do so with objectivity and reliability

- be truthful and honest in dealings with clients, colleagues, other professionals and all they come into contact with in the course of their duties

- never engage in any activity that will impair the dignity, reputation or welfare of the Society, fellow members or their profession

- never knowingly engage in any corrupt or unethical practice

- not implicate the Society, through direct reference or use of membership status, in any statement that may be construed as defamatory, discriminatory, libellous, offensive, slanderous, subversive or otherwise damaging to the Society

- if convicted of a criminal or civil offence anywhere in the world inform the Society promptly, and provide such information concerning the conviction as the Institution may require. *NB this does not included Fixed Penalty Notice offences.*

- observe the Policies of the Society

Conduct

If a member generally becomes aware of, or has reasonable grounds for believing, that another member is engaged in or has engaged in conduct which is in breach of the Regulations and/or Code of Conduct of the Society, they shall inform the Society in writing of that belief, but shall not maliciously or recklessly injure or attempt to injure, directly or indirectly, the reputation, practice, employment or livelihood of another member.

Complaints about the professional practice, performance or conduct of a member should be referred to the General Pharmaceutical Council, and any action by the Society shall be postponed until the outcome of the Council's proceedings is known.

If the complaint is summarily dismissed by the General Pharmaceutical Council, the procedures set out in the Conduct Scheme for Members will be followed.

If the complaint is the subject of proceedings before a court or other regulatory authority, any action by the Society shall be postponed until the outcome of those proceedings is known.

In exceptional circumstances, the Society may take action in advance of a decision of a court or regulatory authority, in which case the complaint shall be referred to the Chairman of the Membership Committee, and the procedures set out in the Conduct Scheme for Members will be followed.

Working with partners, affiliates and other organisations

We work in partnership with organisations in and outside of the profession, across Great Britain and internationally, to ensure the purpose and vision of the Society is accomplished for the benefit of the profession, patient care and public health.

We do this by:

- Co-producing, where appropriate, and endorsing information which both parties can distribute as appropriate to their stakeholder bodies

- Supporting each other to achieve shared goals

- Channelling expertise and practice across defined areas of pharmacy practice

- Communicating regularly to ensure effective relations and common partnership purpose.

   Details of our partners, affiliates and other organisations we work with are available on our website: www.rpharms.com/about-us/working-with-other-organisations

Pharmacist support

Pharmacist Support is an independent charity providing a range of free and confidential support services to pharmacists and their families, former pharmacists, pre-registration trainees and MPharm students in times of need. Services include:

Information and enquiry service

- Wardley wellbeing service – workshops and resources to help manage wellbeing

- Listening Friends – a confidential helpline staffed by trained volunteer pharmacists

- Financial assistance – provided to assist with a range of situations for those experiencing financial difficulty

- Specialist advice in the areas of debt, benefits and employment law

- Addiction support to assist pharmacists experiencing problems with alcohol, drugs, or other types of dependency.

  To discuss your situation and the support available to you in more detail call: 0808 168 2233.

Alternatively you can email the support team on info@pharmacistsupport.org

- To speak with a Listening Friend call: 0808 168 5133

- To speak with an addiction specialist call: 0808 168 5132.

All enquiries will be dealt with in confidence.

Further information can be found on the Pharmacist Support website at www.pharmacistsupport.org

Appendices

The appendices are key regulatory standards and guidance that have been reproduced with the permission of the GPhC. These documents are subject to change and review by the GPhC and the latest versions can be obtained from the GPhC website www.pharmacyregulation.org

Additional standards and guidance have not been reproduced in the appendices and can be obtained from the GPhC website www.pharmacyregulation.org

The GPhC Standards Team can be contacted at:

STANDARDS TEAM

General Pharmaceutical Council
25 Canada Square
London E14 5LQ
Tel: 020 3713 8000
Email: standards@pharmacyregulation.org

Appendix 1:
GPhC standards for pharmacy professionals

MAY 2017

INTRODUCTION

1   Pharmacy professionals' (pharmacists and pharmacy technicians) play a vital role in delivering care and helping people to maintain and improve their health, safety and wellbeing. The professionalism they demonstrate is central to maintaining trust and confidence in pharmacy.

2   Patients and the public have a right to expect safe and effective care from pharmacy professionals. We believe it is the attitudes and behaviours of pharmacy professionals in their day-to-day work which make the most significant contributions to the quality of care, of which safety is a vital part.

3   The standards for pharmacy professionals describe how safe and effective care is delivered through 'person-centred' professionalism. The standards are a statement of what people expect from pharmacy professionals and also reflect what pharmacy professionals have told us they expect of themselves and their colleagues.

4   At the heart of the standards is the principle that every person must be treated as an individual. Pharmacy professionals have an important role in involving, supporting and enabling people to make decisions about their health, safety and wellbeing. For example, what is important to one person managing their short or long-term condition may not be important to another.

THE STANDARDS FOR PHARMACY PROFESSIONALS

5   There are nine standards that every pharmacy professional is accountable for meeting. The standards apply to all pharmacists and pharmacy technicians. We know that pharmacy professionals practise in a number of sectors and settings and may use different ways to communicate with the people they provide care to. The standards apply whatever their form of practice. And even when pharmacy professionals do not provide care directly to patients and the public, their practice can indirectly have an impact on the safe and effective care that patients and the public receive, and on the confidence of members of the public in pharmacy as a whole.

6   The standards need to be met at all times, not only during working hours. This is because the attitudes and behaviours of professionals outside of work can affect the trust and confidence of patients and the public in pharmacy professionals.

7   The meaning of each of the standards is explained, and there are examples of the types of attitudes and behaviours that pharmacy professionals should demonstrate. The examples may not apply in all situations.

8   The standards include the term 'person centred care' and refer to a 'person' throughout. This means 'the person receiving care'. The term may also apply to carers or patients' representatives depending on the situation.

THE STANDARDS AND PHARMACY STUDENTS AND TRAINEES

9   The standards for pharmacy professionals are relevant to all pharmacy students and trainees while they are on their journey towards registration and practice. The standards explain the knowledge, attitudes and behaviours that will be expected of students and trainees if they apply to join the register.

10   They should be interpreted in the context of education and training and used as a tool to prepare students and trainees for registration as a pharmacy professional.

11   Pharmacy students and trainees should consider the standards as they move closer to registration and professional practice, and should read them alongside other relevant documents that are provided by initial education and training providers.

12 The standards are designed to reflect what it means to be a pharmacy professional. They are also at the heart of initial education and training, registration and renewal as a pharmacy professional, and continuing fitness to remain registered.

APPLYING THE STANDARDS

13 Pharmacy professionals are personally accountable for meeting the standards and must be able to justify the decisions they make.

14 We expect pharmacy professionals to consider these standards, their legal duties and any relevant guidance when making decisions.

15 The standards and supporting explanations do not list the legal duties pharmacy professionals have, as all pharmacy professionals must keep to the relevant laws. Relevant guidance is published by a number of organisations, including professional leadership bodies, other regulators, the NHS, National Institute for Health and Care Excellence and Scottish Intercollegiate Guidelines Network, as well as by the GPhC.

16 There will be times when pharmacy professionals are faced with conflicting legal and professional responsibilities. Or they may be faced with complex situations that mean they have to balance competing priorities. The standards provide a framework to help them when making professional judgements. Pharmacy professionals must work in partnership with everyone involved, and make sure the person they are providing care to is their first priority.

STANDARDS FOR PHARMACY PROFESSIONALS

All pharmacy professionals contribute to delivering and improving the health, safety and wellbeing of patients and the public. Professionalism and safe and effective practice are central to that role. Pharmacy professionals must:

1 Provide person-centred care

2 Work in partnership with others

3 Communicate effectively

4 Maintain, develop and use their professional knowledge and skills

5 Use professional judgement

6 Behave in a professional manner

7 Respect and maintain the person's confidentiality and privacy

8 Speak up when they have concerns or when things go wrong

9 Demonstrate leadership

APPLYING STANDARD 1
PHARMACY PROFESSIONALS MUST PROVIDE PERSON-CENTRED CARE

People receive safe and effective care when pharmacy professionals:

- Obtain consent to provide care and pharmacy services

- Involve, support and enable every person when making decisions about their health, care and wellbeing

- Listen to the person and understand their needs and what matters to them

- Give the person all relevant information in a way they can understand, so they can make informed decisions and choices

- Consider the impact of their practice whether or not they provide care directly

- Respect and safeguard the person's dignity

- Recognise and value diversity, and respect cultural differences – making sure that every person is treated fairly whatever their values and beliefs

- Recognise their own values and beliefs but do not impose them on other people

- Take responsibility for ensuring that person-centred care is not compromised because of personal values and beliefs

- Make the best use of the resources available

PHARMACY PROFESSIONALS MUST WORK IN PARTNERSHIP WITH OTHERS

People receive safe and effective care when pharmacy professionals:

- Work with the person receiving care

- Identify and work with the individuals and teams who are involved in the person's care

- Contact, involve and work with the relevant local and national organisations

- Demonstrate effective team working

- Adapt their communication to bring about effective partnership working

- Take action to safeguard people, particularly children and vulnerable adults

- Make and use records of the care provided

- Work with others to make sure there is continuity of care for the person concerned

PHARMACY PROFESSIONALS MUST COMMUNICATE EFFECTIVELY

People receive safe and effective care when pharmacy professionals:

Adapt their communication to meet the needs of the person they are communicating with

- Overcome barriers to communication

- Ask questions and listen carefully to the responses, to understand the person's needs and come to a shared decision about the care they provide

- Listen actively and respond to the information they receive in a timely manner

- Check the person has understood the information they have been given

- Communicate effectively with others involved in the care of the person.

PHARMACY PROFESSIONALS MUST MAINTAIN, DEVELOP AND USE THEIR PROFESSIONAL KNOWLEDGE AND SKILLS

People receive safe and effective care when pharmacy professionals:

- Recognise and work within the limits of their knowledge and skills, and refer to others when needed

- Use their skills and knowledge, including up-to-date evidence, to deliver care and improve the quality of care they provide

- Carry out a range of continuing professional development (CPD) activities relevant to their practice

- Record their development activities to demonstrate that their knowledge and skills are up to date

- Use a variety of methods to regularly monitor and reflect on their practice, skills and knowledge

PHARMACY PROFESSIONALS MUST USE THEIR PROFESSIONAL JUDGEMENT

People receive safe and effective care when pharmacy professionals:

- Make the care of the person their first concern and act in their best interests

- Use their judgement to make clinical and professional decisions with the person or others

- Have the information they need to provide appropriate care

- Declare any personal or professional interests and manage these professionally

- Practise only when fit to do so

- Recognise the limits of their competence

- Consider and manage appropriately any personal or organisational goals, incentives or targets and make sure the care they provide reflects the needs of the person

APPLYING STANDARD 6
PHARMACY PROFESSIONALS MUST BEHAVE IN A PROFESSIONAL MANNER

People receive safe and effective care when pharmacy professionals:

- Are polite and considerate

- Are trustworthy and act with honesty and integrity

- Show empathy and compassion

- Treat people with respect and safeguard their dignity

- Maintain appropriate personal and professional boundaries with the people they provide care to and with others

APPLYING STANDARD 7
PHARMACY PROFESSIONALS MUST RESPECT AND MAINTAIN A PERSON'S CONFIDENTIALITY AND PRIVACY

People receive safe and effective care when pharmacy professionals:

- Understand the importance of managing information responsibly and securely, and apply this to their practice

- Reflect on their environment and take steps to maintain the person's privacy and confidentiality

- Do not discuss information that can identify the person when the discussions can be overheard or seen by others not involved in their care

- Ensure that everyone in the team understands the need to maintain a person's privacy and confidentiality

- Work in partnership with the person when considering whether to share their information, except where this would not be appropriate

APPLYING STANDARD 8
PHARMACY PROFESSIONALS MUST SPEAK UP WHEN THEY HAVE CONCERNS OR WHEN THINGS GO WRONG

People receive safe and effective care when pharmacy professionals:

- Promote and encourage a culture of learning and improvement

- Challenge poor practice and behaviours

- Raise a concern, even when it is not easy to do so

- Promptly tell their employer and all relevant authorities (including the GPhC) about concerns they may have

- Support people who raise concerns and provide feedback

- Are open and honest when things go wrong

- Say sorry, provide an explanation and put things right when things go wrong

- Reflect on feedback or concerns, taking action as appropriate and thinking about what can be done to prevent the same thing happening again

- Improve the quality of care and pharmacy practice by learning from feedback and when things go wrong

APPLYING STANDARD 9
PHARMACY PROFESSIONALS MUST DEMONSTRATE LEADERSHIP

People receive safe and effective care when pharmacy professionals:

- Take responsibility for their practice and demonstrate leadership to the people they work with

- Assess the risks in the care they provide and do everything they can to keep these risks as low as possible

- Contribute to the education, training and development of the team or of others

- Delegate tasks only to people who are competent and appropriately trained or are in training, and exercise proper oversight

- Do not abuse their position or set out to influence others to abuse theirs

- Lead by example, in particular to those who are working towards registration as a pharmacy professional

Appendix 2:
GPhC standards for registered pharmacies

REVISED JUNE 2018

The purpose of these standards is to create and maintain the right environment, both organisational and physical, for the safe and effective practice of pharmacy. The standards apply to all pharmacies registered with the General Pharmaceutical Council.

We recognise that for anyone operating a registered pharmacy there will always be competing demands. These may be professional, managerial, legal or commercial. However, medicines are not ordinary items of commerce. Along with pharmacy services, the supply of medicines is a fundamental healthcare service. Pharmacy owners must take account of this when applying these standards.

Although registered pharmacies may have different ownership structures, it is important that the culture and processes within the pharmacy deliver safe and effective care to patients and the public.

In a limited, or public limited company, the board of directors has a significant role in making sure people receive safe and effective care from registered pharmacies. The Companies Act, and other relevant legislation, sets out the legal responsibilities for directors. In a pharmacy where healthcare is being delivered to the public, there is further guidance[1] for directors about their extra responsibilities in delivering a public service. This applies whether they are in a private or a voluntary organisation.

As a pharmacy owner you should consider the context of each individual pharmacy. This includes:

- the range of services provided

- the skill mix and number of staff in the pharmacy team

- most importantly, the needs of patients and people who use pharmacy services

As well as meeting our standards, the pharmacy owner must make sure they comply with all legal requirements including those covering medicines legislation, health and safety, employment, data protection and equalities legislation.

Pharmacy owners must make sure that all staff, including non-pharmacists, involved in the management of pharmacy services are familiar with the standards and understand the importance of their being met. All registered professionals working in a registered pharmacy should also be familiar with these standards; and pharmacists and pharmacy technicians must understand that they have a professional responsibility to raise concerns if they believe the standards are not being met.

The standards can also be used by patients and the public so that they know what they should expect when they receive pharmacy services from registered pharmacies. Throughout this document we use the term 'pharmacy services'. This covers all pharmacy-related services provided by a registered pharmacy including the management of medicines, provision of advice and referral, clinical services such as vaccination services, and services provided to care homes.

Throughout this document we use the term 'staff '. This includes agency and contract workers, as well as employees and other people who are involved in the provision of pharmacy services by a registered pharmacy. Where we use the term 'you,' this means the pharmacy owner.

In some limited circumstances (for example, following death or bankruptcy), a representative can take the role of the pharmacy owner. In these cases, the appointed representative will be responsible for making sure these standards are met.

STANDARDS FOR REGISTERED PHARMACIES

We have grouped the standards under five principles. The principles are the backbone of our regulatory approach and are all equally important.

---

[1] https://assets.publishing.service.gov.uk/government/uploads/system/uploads/attachment_data/file/481535/6.1291_CO_LAL_Ethical_standards_of_public_life_report_Interactive__2_.pdf

THE PRINCIPLES

Principle 1 The governance arrangements safeguard the health, safety and wellbeing of patients and the public.

Principle 2 Staff are empowered and competent to safeguard the health, safety and wellbeing of patients and the public.

Principle 3 The environment and condition of the premises from which pharmacy services are provided, and any associated premises, safeguard the health, safety and wellbeing of patients and the public.

Principle 4 The way in which pharmacy services, including the management of medicines and medical devices, are delivered safeguards the health, safety and wellbeing of patients and the public.

Principle 5 The equipment and facilities used in the provision of pharmacy services safeguard the health, safety and wellbeing of patients and the public.

THE STANDARDS

The standards under each principle are requirements that must be met when you operate a registered pharmacy.

Responsibility for meeting the standards lies with the pharmacy owner. If the registered pharmacy is owned by a 'body corporate' the directors must assure themselves that the standards for registered pharmacies are being met.

APPLYING THE STANDARDS

The principles for registered pharmacies, and the standards that must be met, are all equally important. Therefore you should read all the standards in their entirety. Pharmacy owners and other pharmacy professionals should also be familiar with the standards for pharmacy professionals.

We know that a pharmacy owner may be accountable for one, a few or a large number of registered pharmacies. We expect the pharmacy owner to make sure that these standards are met whatever the number of pharmacies they are accountable for.

PRINCIPLE 1

The governance arrangements safeguard the health, safety and wellbeing of patients and the public. 'Governance arrangements' includes having clear definitions of the roles and accountabilities of the people involved in providing and managing pharmacy services. It also includes the arrangements for managing risks, and the way the registered pharmacy is managed and operated.

STANDARDS

1.1   The risks associated with providing pharmacy services are identified and managed.

1.2   The safety and quality of pharmacy services are reviewed and monitored.

1.3   Pharmacy services are provided by staff with clearly defined roles and clear lines of accountability.

1.4   Feedback and concerns about the pharmacy, services and staff can be raised by individuals and organisations, and these are taken into account and action taken where appropriate.

1.5   Appropriate indemnity or insurance arrangements are in place for the pharmacy services provided.

1.6   All necessary records for the safe provision of pharmacy services are kept and maintained.

1.7   Information is managed to protect the privacy, dignity and confidentiality of patients and the public who receive pharmacy services.

1.8   Children and vulnerable adults are safeguarded.

PRINCIPLE 2

Staff are empowered and competent to safeguard the health, safety and wellbeing of patients and the public.

The staff you employ and the people you work with are key to the safe and effective practice of pharmacy. Staff members, and anyone involved in providing pharmacy services, must be competent and empowered to safeguard the health, safety and wellbeing of patients and the public in all that they do.

STANDARDS

2.1 There are enough staff, suitably qualified and skilled, for the safe and effective provision of the pharmacy services provided.

2.2 Staff have the appropriate skills, qualifications and competence for their role and the tasks they carry out, or are working under the supervision of another person while they are in training.

2.3 Staff can comply with their own professional and legal obligations and are empowered to exercise their professional judgement in the interests of patients and the public.

2.4 There is a culture of openness, honesty and learning.

2.5 Staff are empowered to provide feedback and raise concerns about meeting these standards and other aspects of pharmacy services.

2.6 Incentives or targets do not compromise the health, safety or wellbeing of patients and the public, or the professional judgement of staff.

PRINCIPLE 3

The environment and condition of the premises from which pharmacy services are provided, and any associated premises, safeguard the health, safety and wellbeing of patients and the public.

It is important that patients and the public receive pharmacy services from premises that are suitable for the services being provided and which protect and maintain their health, safety and wellbeing. To achieve this you must make sure that all premises where pharmacy services are provided are safe and suitable. Any associated premises, for example non-registered premises used to store medicines, must also comply with these standards where applicable.

STANDARDS

3.1 Premises are safe, clean, properly maintained and suitable for the pharmacy services provided.

3.2 Premises protect the privacy, dignity and confidentiality of patients and the public who receive pharmacy services.

3.3 Premises are maintained to a level of hygiene appropriate to the pharmacy services provided.

3.4 Premises are secure and safeguarded from unauthorised access.

3.5 Pharmacy services are provided in an environment that is appropriate for the provision of healthcare.

PRINCIPLE 4

The way in which pharmacy services, including the management of medicines and medical devices, are delivered safeguards the health, safety and wellbeing of patients and the public. 'Pharmacy services' covers all pharmacy-related services provided by a registered pharmacy including the management of medicines, advice and referral, and the wide range of clinical services pharmacies provide. The management of medicines includes arrangements for obtaining, keeping, handling, using and supplying medicinal products and medical devices, as well as security and waste management.

Medicines and medical devices are not ordinary commercial items. The way they are managed is fundamental to ensuring the health, safety and wellbeing of patients and the public who receive pharmacy services.

STANDARDS

4.1 The pharmacy services provided are accessible to patients and the public.

4.2 Pharmacy services are managed and delivered safely and effectively.

4.3 Medicines and medical devices are:

- Obtained from a reputable source
- Safe and fit for purpose
- Stored securely
- Safeguarded from unauthorised access
- Supplied to the patient safely
- Disposed of safely and securely.

4.4 Concerns are raised when it is suspected that medicines or medical devices are not fit for purpose.

PRINCIPLE 5

The equipment and facilities used in the provision of pharmacy services safeguard the health, safety and wellbeing of patients and the public.

The availability of safe and suitable equipment and facilities is fundamental to the provision of pharmacy services and is essential if staff are to safeguard the health, safety and wellbeing of patients and the public when providing effective pharmacy services.

STANDARDS

5.1 Equipment and facilities needed to provide pharmacy services are readily available.

5.2 Equipment and facilities are:

- Obtained from a reputable source

- Safe to use and fit for purpose

- Stored securely

- Safeguarded from unauthorised access

- Appropriately maintained.

5.3 Equipment and facilities are used in a way that protects the privacy and dignity of the patients and the public who receive pharmacy services.

Appendix 3:
GPhC in practice: guidance on confidentiality

REVISED JUNE 2018

ABOUT THIS GUIDANCE

This guidance explains to pharmacy professionals (pharmacists and pharmacy technicians) the importance of maintaining confidentiality, and their relevant responsibilities. Pharmacy professionals should use their professional judgement in applying this guidance.

Pharmacy professionals should satisfy themselves that all members of the team are familiar with the issues raised within this guidance and understand their own responsibilities in relation to confidentiality.

If a pharmacy professional is not sure about what they should do in a specific situation, they should always ask for advice from their employer, professional indemnity insurance provider, union, professional body or other pharmacy organisation, or get independent legal advice.

This guidance should be read alongside the standards for pharmacy professionals which all pharmacy professionals must meet. This guidance covers standard 7 of the standards for pharmacy professionals, which says:

Pharmacy professionals must respect and maintain a person's confidentiality and privacy

APPLYING THE STANDARD

People trust that their confidentiality and privacy will be maintained by pharmacy professionals, whether in a healthcare setting – such as a hospital, primary care or community pharmacy setting – in person, or online. Maintaining confidentiality is a vital part of the relationship between a pharmacy professional and the person seeking care. People may be reluctant to ask for care if they believe their information may not be kept confidential. The principles of confidentiality still apply after a person's death. There are a number of ways to meet this standard and below are examples of the attitudes and behaviours expected.

People receive safe and effective care when pharmacy professionals:

- understand the importance of managing information responsibly and securely, apply this to their practice

- reflect on their environment and take steps to maintain the person's privacy and confidentiality

- do not discuss information that can identify the person, when the discussions can be overheard or seen by others not involved in their care

- ensure that everyone in the team understands the need to maintain a person's privacy and confidentiality

- work in partnership with the person when considering whether to share their information, except where this would not be appropriate

This guidance is not intended to cover every aspect of confidentiality and it does not give detailed legal advice. However, it reflects the law in Great Britain at the time of publication.

Pharmacy professionals must make sure that they keep up to date and comply with data protection legislation, for example: UK domestic data protection legislation, the **General Data Protection Regulation ((EU) 2016/679) (GDPR)** https://eur-lex. europa.eu/eli/reg/2016/679/oj and the **Human Rights Act 1998 (HRA)** https://www.equalityhumanrights. com/en/human-rights/human-rights-act. The common law duty of confidentiality also applies, as do any NHS or employment policies on confidentiality that apply to their particular area of work.

UK data protection legislation covers personal information, including data about the physical or mental health or condition of a person (called a 'data subject' in data protection legislation). The **Information Commissioner's Office (ICO)** https://ico.org.uk/for-organisations/ enforces data protection legislation and produces advice and guidance on it.

The HRA incorporates the European Convention on Human Rights (ECHR) into UK law. This, and the Charter of Fundamental Rights of the European Union, gives individuals a right to respect for their private life.

The charter also gives them a right to the protection of their personal data[1]. These issues can be complex and pharmacy professionals should get legal advice, if they need it.

Pharmacy professionals providing NHS services must also follow NHS codes of practice, and the guidance on handling information in health and care.

We have a range of guidance on our website to help pharmacy professionals apply our standards. In particular, when reading this guidance, please also see our *In practice: Guidance on consent*.

1
THE IMPORTANCE OF MAINTAINING CONFIDENTIALITY

1.1 Maintaining confidentiality is a vital part of the relationship between a pharmacy professional and a person under their care. A person may be reluctant to ask for advice, or give a pharmacy professional the information they need to provide proper care, if they believe that the pharmacy professional may not keep the information confidential. When pharmacy professionals do not handle confidential information appropriately it can damage public trust and confidence in the pharmacy professions and other healthcare professions.

2
DUTY OF CONFIDENTIALITY

2.1 Pharmacy professionals have a professional and legal duty to keep confidential the information they obtain during the course of their professional practice. The duty of confidentiality applies to information about any person, whatever their age (see our *In practice: Guidance on consent*), and continues to apply after a person's death.

2.2 A duty of confidentiality arises when one person discloses information to another in circumstances where it is reasonable to expect that the information will be held in confidence. This duty applies to all information that pharmacy professionals obtain during the course of their professional practice.

2.3 Confidential information includes:

- Electronic and hard copy data

- Personal details

- Information about a person's medication (prescribed and non-prescribed)

- Other information about a person's medical history, treatment or care that could identify them, and

---

1 The rights under Article 8 of the HRA are complicated and there are conditons and exceptions. For more information on Article 8 see: https://www.equalityhumanrights.com/en/human-rights-act/article-8-respect-your-private-and-family-life

- Information that people share that is not strictly medical in nature, but that the person disclosing it would expect to be kept confidential

2.4 Confidential information does not include:

- Anonymous information - information from which individuals cannot reasonably be identified

- Pseudonymised information - information from which individuals cannot reasonably be identified, but which allows information about different people receiving care to be distinguished (for example, to identify drug side effects)

- Information that is already legitimately in the public domain

3
PROTECTING INFORMATION

3.1 It is essential that pharmacy professionals take steps to protect the confidential information they are given either in the course of their professional practice or because they are a pharmacy professional

They must:

- Take all reasonable steps to protect the confidentiality and security of information they receive, access, store, send or destroy, including protection against unauthorised or unlawful processing and against intrusion, destruction or damage

- Take steps to make sure that, when processing personal data, it is accurate and, where necessary, kept up to date

- Take steps to prevent accidental disclosure of confidential information

- Access confidential information and records only as part of providing treatment and care for a person, or for another permitted purpose that meets one of the conditions for lawfully processing personal data set out in legislation

- Make sure that everyone they work with in their pharmacy, hospital, practice

or other setting knows about their responsibility to maintain confidentiality

- Raise concerns with the person who is responsible for data control (the data controller) where they work, or with any other appropriate authority, if they find that the security of personal information there is not appropriate

- Continue to protect a person's confidentiality after they have died, subject to disclosures required by law or when it is in the public interest (see below)

- Store hard copy and electronic documents, records, registers, prescriptions and other sources of confidential information securely for no longer than is necessary for the purposes for which the personal data are processed

- Not leave confidential information where it may be seen or accessed by people receiving care, the public or anyone else who should not have access to it

- Not discuss information that can identify people receiving care if the discussions can be overheard or seen by others not involved in their care

- Not disclose information on any websites, internet chat forums or social media that could identify a person (see our guidance on demonstrating professionalism online).

4
DISCLOSING CONFIDENTIAL INFORMATION

4.1 Decisions about disclosing confidential information can be complex. In most situations pharmacy professionals will not have to disclose information immediately. However, there will be limited situations where to delay is not practical, for example if this may cause a risk to another person. Pharmacy professionals should take the necessary steps to satisfy themselves that any disclosure being asked for is appropriate and meets the legal requirements covering confidentiality, and the conditions for lawfully processing personal data in data protection legislation. If it is practicable, pharmacy professionals may find it useful to get advice on what to do from appropriate sources (without identifying the person under their care).

4.2 Maintaining confidentiality is an important duty, but there are circumstances when it may be appropriate to disclose confidential information. These are when a pharmacy professional:

- Has the consent of the person under their care

- Has to disclose by law

- Should do so in the public interest, and/or

- Must do so in the vital interests of a person receiving treatment or care, for example if a patient needs immediate urgent medical attention

4.3 In the course of their professional practice pharmacy professionals may receive requests for confidential information about people under their care from a variety of people (for example a person's relative, partner or carer) or organisations (for example the police or a healthcare regulator). Decisions about disclosing information should be made on a case-by-case basis and after fully considering all relevant factors.

4.4 If a person with capacity (see our *In practice: Guidance on consent* for more information on capacity) refuses to give consent for information to be shared with other healthcare professionals involved in providing their care, it may mean that the care they can be provided with is limited. Pharmacy professionals must respect that decision, but tell the person receiving care about the potential implications for their care or treatment.

4.5 Pharmacy professionals must respect the wishes of a person with capacity under their care who does not consent to information

about them being shared with others, unless the law says they must disclose the information or it is in the public interest to make such a disclosure.

4.6 If a pharmacy professional decides to disclose confidential information about a person, they should:

- Pseudonymise information or make it anonymous, if they do not need to identify the person receiving care

- Get the person's consent to share their information. But they do not need to do this if:

  - Disclosure is required by law, or

  - the disclosure can be justified in the public interest[1], or

  - To do so is impracticable, would put the pharmacy professional or others (including the person receiving treatment or care) at risk of serious harm, or would prejudice the purpose of the disclosure, for example to prevent a crime

- Disclose only the information needed for the particular purpose

- Make sure that, if they disclose confidential information, the people receiving the information know that it is confidential and is to be treated as such

- Make appropriate records to show:

  - Who the request came from

  - Whether they obtained the consent of the person under their care, or their reasons for not doing so

  - Whether consent was given or refused

  - What they disclosed

  - How it was ensured that the disclosure was made securely, and

  - What the lawful authority or provision was under which the request and/or disclosure was made

[1] When considering whether disclosing confidential information without consent may be justified in the public interest, pharmacy professionals must be satisfied that the disclosure would comply with data protection legislation. Please see the ICO's website for more information.

- Be prepared to justify the decisions and any actions they take

- Release the information promptly once they are satisfied what information should be disclosed and have taken all necessary steps to protect confidentiality

- Retain a copy of the disclosure made

5 DISCLOSING INFORMATION WITH CONSENT

5.1 Pharmacy professionals should get the person's consent to share their information unless that would undermine the purpose of disclosure (see 4.6 above).

5.2 They should make sure the person in their care understands:

- What information will be disclosed

- Why information will be disclosed

- Who it will be disclosed to

- The likely consequences of disclosing and of not disclosing the information.

5.3 When the reason for sharing confidential information is one that the person receiving care would not reasonably expect, pharmacy professionals must get their explicit consent before disclosure.

5.4 If a pharmacy professional is unsure whether they have the person's consent to share their information, they should contact them and obtain their consent.

5.5 Pharmacy professionals should also take data protection legislation into account in these circumstances, as those requirements also need to be followed. Under data protection legislation, information can be shared when express consent (specific permission to do something) is given. Consent to share information under the duty of confidentiality may not be valid for the purposes of data protection legislation.

6 DISCLOSING INFORMATION WITHOUT CONSENT

6.1 Pharmacy professionals should make every effort to get consent to disclose confidential information. However, if that would undermine the purpose of disclosure (for example, when there is a risk to others) or is not practicable, then they should use the guidance in this section.

6.2 Before disclosing information without the consent of the person receiving care, a pharmacy professional should:

- Be satisfied that the law says they have to disclose the information, or that disclosure can be justified as being in the public interest and also meets the requirements of data protection legislation. (This would be through an exemption or condition that would apply for the information to be processed and disclosed.)

- If they are unsure about the basis for the request, ask for clarification from the person making the request

- Ask for the request in writing.

6.3 If necessary, pharmacy professionals should get advice from a relevant body, for example their indemnity insurance provider, union, professional body or other pharmacy organisation, or an independent legal adviser. The ICO can give advice, and has issued guidance, on the requirements of data protection legislation.

7 DISCLOSURES REQUIRED BY LAW

7.1 There are circumstances when the law says a pharmacy professional must disclose information that they hold. These circumstances include when a person or body is using their powers under the law to ask for the information, for example:

- The police or another enforcement, prosecuting or regulatory authority

- A healthcare regulator, such as the GPhC or the GMC

- An NHS counter-fraud investigation officer

- A coroner, procurator fiscal, judge or relevant court which orders that the information should be disclosed

7.2 These individuals and organisations do not have an automatic right to access all confidential information about people receiving care. Pharmacy professionals must be satisfied they have a legitimate reason for requesting the information.

7.3 If necessary, pharmacy professionals should get advice from a relevant body, for example their indemnity insurance provider, union, professional body or other pharmacy organisation, the ICO, or an independent legal adviser.

8
DISCLOSURES MADE IN THE PUBLIC INTEREST

8.1 These decisions are complex and must take account of both the person receiving care and public interest in either maintaining or breaching confidentiality.

8.2 A pharmacy professional may disclose confidential information when they consider it to be in the public interest to do so, for example if the information is required to prevent:

- A serious crime

- Serious harm to a person receiving care or to a third party, or

- Serious risk to public health

8.3 Pharmacy professionals must carefully balance the competing interests of maintaining the confidentiality of the information and the public interest benefit in disclosing the information.

8.4 Pharmacy professionals must consider the possible harm that may be caused by not disclosing the information against the potential consequences of disclosing the information. This includes considering how disclosing the information may affect the care of the person and the trust that they have in pharmacy professionals.

8.5 When considering whether disclosing confidential information without consent may be justified in the public interest, pharmacy professionals must be satisfied that the disclosure would comply with the requirements of data protection law.

8.6 If necessary, pharmacy professionals should get advice from a relevant body, for example their indemnity insurance provider, union, professional body or other pharmacy organisation, the ICO, or an independent legal adviser.

Appendix 4:
GPhC in practice: guidance on consent

REVISED JUNE 2018

ABOUT THIS GUIDANCE

This guidance explains to pharmacy professionals (pharmacists and pharmacy technicians) the importance of consent and their relevant responsibilities. Pharmacy professionals should use their professional judgement in applying this guidance.

Pharmacy professionals should satisfy themselves that all members of the team are familiar with the issues raised within this guidance and understand their own responsibilities in relation to consent. If a pharmacy professional is not sure about what they should do in a specific situation, they should always ask for advice from their employer, professional indemnity insurance provider, union, professional body or other pharmacy organisation, or get independent legal advice.

This guidance should be read alongside the standards for pharmacy professionals which all pharmacy professionals must meet. This guidance covers standard 1 of the standards for pharmacy professionals, which says:

Pharmacy professionals must provide person-centred care

APPLYING THE STANDARD

Every person is an individual with their own values, needs and concerns. Person-centred care is delivered when pharmacy professionals understand what is important to the individual and then adapt the care to meet their needs – making the care of the person their first priority. All pharmacy professionals can demonstrate 'person-centredness' – whether or not they provide care directly – by thinking about the impact their decisions have on people.

There are a number of ways to meet this standard, and below are examples of the attitudes and behaviours expected.

People receive safe and effective care when pharmacy professionals:

- obtain consent to provide care and pharmacy services

- involve, support and enable every person when making decisions about their health, care and wellbeing

- listen to the person and understand their needs and what matters to them

- give the person all relevant information in a way they can understand, so they can make informed decisions and choices

- consider the impact of their practice – whether or not they provide care directly

- respect and safeguard the person's dignity

- recognise and value diversity, and respect cultural differences – making sure that every person is treated fairly whatever their values and beliefs

- recognise their own values and beliefs but do not impose them on other people

- take responsibility for ensuring that person centred care is not compromised because of personal values and beliefs

- make the best use of the resources available

This guidance is not intended to cover every aspect of consent, and it does not give legal advice. However, it reflects the law in Great Britain at the time of publication.

Pharmacy professionals must make sure that they keep up to date and comply with the law, and with any NHS or employment policies on consent that apply to their particular area of work.

Pharmacy professionals work in many different settings. So how relevant this guidance is to a pharmacy professional, and how consent is obtained, may vary depending on their role and the type of contact they have with people receiving care.

We have a range of guidance on our website to help pharmacy professionals apply our standards. In particular, when reading this guidance please also see our *In practice: Guidance on confidentiality*.

1 WHAT IS CONSENT?

1.1 The Oxford English Dictionary defines 'to consent' as 'to express willingness, give permission, agree'.

1.2 People have a basic right to be involved in decisions about their healthcare. Obtaining consent is a fundamental part of respecting a person's rights.

1.3 Obtaining consent is also essential in forming and maintaining effective partnerships between pharmacy professionals and the people receiving care.

1.4 Pharmacy professionals have a professional and legal duty to get a person's consent for the professional services, treatment or care they provide, and for using a person's information.

1.5 Pharmacy professionals must know and comply with the law and the good practice requirements about consent which apply to them in their day-today practice.

2 TYPES OF CONSENT

2.1 There are two types of consent:

- Explicit (or 'express') consent: when a person gives a pharmacy professional specific permission, either spoken or written, to do something

- Implied consent: when a person gives their consent indirectly, for example by bringing their prescription to a pharmacy professional to be dispensed. This is not a lesser form of consent but it is only valid if the person knows and understands what they are consenting to. If a pharmacy professional is not sure whether they have implied consent, they should get explicit consent.

2.2 Pharmacy professionals must use their professional judgement to decide what type of consent to get. Pharmacy professionals should take into account legal requirements and NHS service requirements, and the policies where they work that may set this out.

2.3 When appropriate, pharmacy professionals should record the fact that the person receiving care has given explicit consent and what they have consented to.

2.4 Consent may be used as a condition for processing a person's information under data protection legislation, including: UK domestic data protection legislation, the General Data Protection Regulation ((EU) 2016/679) (GDPR) and the Human Rights Act 1998 (HRA) . Consent would be required to allow a person's information to be shared with third parties if there was no other legal basis for doing so. When consent is used as a condition for processing, a person needs to have taken positive action and shown that they agreed to their personal data being processed. This cannot be inferred or taken as understood from a lack of action – such as a failure to object or to tick an 'opt-out' box. Please also see our *In practice: Guidance on confidentiality* for more information. For more guidance on data protection and on consent in the context of GDPR see the Information Commissioner's Office (ICO) website.

3
OBTAINING CONSENT

3.1 For consent to be valid the person must:

- Have the capacity to give consent (see section 4 for an explanation of 'capacity')

- Be acting voluntarily – they must not be under any undue pressure from a pharmacy professional or anyone else to make a decision

- Have sufficient, balanced information to allow them to make an informed decision. This includes making sure the person receiving care knows about any material risks involved in the recommended treatment, and about any reasonable alternative treatments. Material risks are those a reasonable person would think are significant in the circumstances, but also those the particular person would find significant. Material risks must be disclosed unless to do so would be seriously detrimental to the person's health[1] (See also Section 16 – Emergencies, for when it may be allowable not to obtain consent)

- Be capable of using and weighing up the information provided.

- Understand the consequences of not giving consent

3.2 The information a pharmacy professional provides to the person must be clear, accurate and presented in a way that the person can understand. For example, pharmacy professionals must consider any disabilities, and literacy or language barriers.

3.3 Pharmacy professionals should not make assumptions about the person's level of knowledge and they should give them the opportunity to ask questions.

3.4 Pharmacy professionals are responsible for making sure that a person has given valid consent. Pharmacy professionals must use their professional judgement to decide whether they themselves should get consent from the person, or whether this task can properly be delegated. If the pharmacy professional does delegate the task of obtaining consent they must make sure they delegate it to a competent and appropriately trained member of staff.

3.5 Getting consent is an ongoing process between a pharmacy professional and the

---

1 Montgomery v Lanarkshire Health Board. [2015] UKSC 11. www.supremecourt.uk/cases/docs/uksc-2013-0136-judgment.pdf

person receiving care. Consent cannot be presumed just because it was given on a previous occasion. Pharmacy professionals must get a person's consent on each occasion that it is needed, for example when there is a change in treatment or service options. Consent must be recorded.

3.6 People with capacity are entitled to withdraw their consent at any time. (See section 7 – When a competent adult refuses to give consent.)

4
WHAT IS CAPACITY?

4.1 In England and Wales, under the Mental Capacity Act 2005, a person lacks capacity if at the time the decision needs to be made, they are unable to make or communicate the decision because of an impairment or disturbance that affects the way their mind or brain works.

4.2 In Scotland, under the Adults with Incapacity (Scotland) Act 2000, a person lacks capacity if they cannot act, make decisions or communicate them, or understand or remember their decisions because of a mental disorder or physical inability to communicate in any form.

5
ASSESSING CAPACITY

5.1 A pharmacy professional must base an assessment of capacity on the person's ability to make a specific decision at the time it needs to be made. A person receiving care may be capable of making some decisions but not others.

5.2 In general, to make an informed decision the person should be able to:

- Understand the information provided
- Remember the information provided
- Use and weigh up the information provided, and
- Communicate their decision to the pharmacy professional (by any means).

5.3 Pharmacy professionals must not assume that because a person lacks capacity on one occasion, or in relation to one type of service, that they lack capacity to make all decisions.

5.4 A person's capacity to consent may be temporarily affected by other factors, for example: fatigue, panic, or the effects of drugs or alcohol. This should not lead to an automatic assumption that the person does not have the capacity to consent. Instead, pharmacy professionals should use their professional judgement to make a decision based on the individual circumstances.

5.5 Pharmacy professionals must not assume that a person lacks capacity based just upon their age, disability, beliefs, condition or behaviour, or because they make a decision that the pharmacy professional disagrees with.

5.6 Pharmacy professionals must take all reasonable steps to help and support people to make their own decisions, or to be as involved as they can be in a decision. They should, for example:

- Time the discussion for when the person's understanding may be better
- Use appropriate types of communication, simple language or visual aids
- Get someone else to help with communication such as a family member, support worker or interpreter.

5.7 If a pharmacy professional is unsure about a person's capacity they must get advice from other healthcare professionals or from people involved in their care.

5.8 If a pharmacy professional is still unsure they must get legal advice.

5.9 Any advice they get or assessments carried out should be properly recorded, along with the outcome.

5.10 Pharmacy professionals can find more guidance on how people should be helped to make their own decisions, and how to assess capacity, in the Codes of Practice that accompany the Mental Capacity Act 2005 and Adults with Incapacity (Scotland) Act 2000.

6
ADULTS WITH CAPACITY

6.1 Every adult is presumed to have the capacity to make their own decisions (that is, that they are competent) and to give consent for a service or treatment unless there is enough evidence to suggest otherwise.

7
WHEN A COMPETENT ADULT REFUSES TO GIVE CONSENT

7.1 If an adult with capacity makes a voluntary, informed decision to refuse a service or treatment, pharmacy professionals must respect their decision – even when they think that their decision is wrong or may cause the person harm. This does not apply when the law says otherwise, such as when compulsory treatment is authorised by mental health legislation.[2]

7.2 Pharmacy professionals should clearly explain the consequences of the decision, but must make sure that they do not pressure the person to accept their advice.

7.3 Pharmacy professionals should make a detailed record if a person refuses to give consent. This should include the discussions that have taken place and the advice given.

7.4 If a pharmacy professional believes that the person is at risk of serious harm because of their decision to refuse a service or treatment, they must raise this issue with relevant healthcare or pharmacy colleagues or with people involved in the person's care, and with their own employer (if they have one). They should also consider getting legal advice if necessary.

8
ADULTS WITHOUT CAPACITY

8.1 If the person is not able to make decisions for themselves, pharmacy professionals must work with people close to the person receiving care and with other members of the healthcare team.

8.2 The Mental Capacity Act 2005 and Adults with Incapacity (Scotland) Act 2000 set out the criteria and the processes to be followed in making decisions and providing care services when a person lacks the capacity to make some or all decisions for themselves. They also give legal authority to certain people to make decisions on behalf of people receiving care who lack capacity.

8.3 If pharmacy professionals believe that a person lacks capacity to make decisions for themselves, they should consult the Codes of Practice that accompany the Mental Capacity Act 2005 or Adults with Incapacity (Scotland) Act (2000). These set out who can make decisions on the person's behalf, in which situations, and how they should go about this.

9
YOUNG PEOPLE AND CHILDREN

9.1 The capacity to consent depends more on the person's ability to understand and consider their decision than on their age.

9.2 In this guidance 'a young person' means anyone aged 16 or 17, and 'a child' means anyone aged under 16. However, people gain full legal capacity in relation to medical treatment at a different age in Scotland than in England and Wales.

9.3 As with any person receiving care, a young person or child may have the capacity to consent to some services or treatments but not to others. Therefore it is important that pharmacy professionals assess the maturity and understanding of each person individually, and keep in mind the complexity and importance of the decision to be made.

9.4 If a person with parental responsibility has to give consent, pharmacy professionals may need to get legal advice if: they are in any doubt about who has parental responsibility for the person, or those that have parental responsibility cannot agree whether or not to give consent.

---

2 Mental Health Act 1983 (as amended by the Mental Health Act 2007), and the Mental Health (Care and Treatment) (Scotland) Act 2003

9.5 Young people and children should be involved as much as possible in decisions about their care, even when they are not able to make decisions on their own.

10
YOUNG PEOPLE WITH CAPACITY

10.1 Young people are presumed to have the capacity to make their own decisions and give consent for a service or treatment, unless there is enough evidence to suggest otherwise.

10.2 To decide whether a young person has the capacity to consent to a service or treatment, pharmacy professionals should use the same criteria as for adults (see section 5 – Assessing capacity).

10.3 Pharmacy professionals should encourage young people to involve their parents in making important decisions. However, pharmacy professionals should respect a competent young person's request for confidentiality.

11
CHILDREN WITH CAPACITY

11.1 Children are not presumed to have the capacity to consent. They must demonstrate their competence.

11.2 A child can give consent if the pharmacy professional is satisfied that the treatment is in their best interests, and that they have the maturity and ability to fully understand the information given and what they are consenting to. In this case pharmacy professionals do not also need consent from a person with parental responsibility.

12
WHEN COMPETENT YOUNG PEOPLE AND CHILDREN REFUSE TO GIVE CONSENT

ENGLAND AND WALES
12.1 In some circumstances, the courts can override the refusal of consent of a young person or child. Pharmacy

professionals should get legal advice on this issue if needed.

12.2 The law is complex when a competent young person or child refuses to give consent for a treatment or service and someone with parental responsibility wants to override their decision. Pharmacy professionals should get legal advice if they are faced with this situation.

SCOTLAND
12.3 When a young person or child has capacity to make a decision, then their decision should be respected. This applies even if the decision differs from the pharmacy professional's view, or from the views of those with parental responsibility.

12.4 However, this position has not yet been fully tested in the Scottish courts. Nor has the issue of whether a court can override a young person's or child's decision. Pharmacy professionals should therefore get legal advice if they are faced with this situation.

13
YOUNG PEOPLE WITHOUT CAPACITY

ENGLAND AND WALES
13.1 A person with parental responsibility for a young person without capacity can give consent on behalf of that young person to investigations and treatment that are in the young person's best interests.

SCOTLAND
13.2 The rights of a person with parental responsibility to make decisions on behalf of a child end when the child reaches the age of 16.

13.3 Young people who do not have the capacity to consent should be treated as though they are adults and in line with the Adults with Incapacity (Scotland) Act 2000.

14
CHILDREN WITHOUT CAPACITY

14.1 When a child lacks capacity to give consent,

any person with parental responsibility for that child, or the court, can give consent on their behalf.

15
ADVANCE DECISIONS

15.1 People who understand the implications of their choices can say in advance how they want to be treated if they later suffer loss of mental capacity.

15.2 An unambiguous advance refusal for a treatment, procedure or intervention which is voluntarily made by a competent, informed adult is likely to have legal force.

15.3 An advance refusal of treatment cannot override the legal authority to give compulsory treatment under the mental health laws.

15.4 Any advance decision is superseded by a competent decision by the person concerned, made at the time consent is sought.

ENGLAND AND WALES

15.5 Advance decisions are covered by the Mental Capacity Act 2005. For an advance refusal of treatment to be legally valid, it must meet certain criteria set out in the Mental Capacity Act 2005.

15.6 If an advance decision does not meet these criteria, it is not legally binding but can still be used in deciding the person's best interests.

15.7 Pharmacy professionals must follow an advance decision if it is valid and applicable to current circumstances.

SCOTLAND

15.8 The Adults with Incapacity (Scotland) Act 2000 does not specifically cover advance decisions. However, it says that health professionals must take account of the person receiving care's past and present wishes, however they were communicated.

15.9 It is likely that pharmacy professionals would be bound by a valid and applicable advance decision. However, there have been no specific cases yet considered by the Scottish courts. If in any doubt, pharmacy professionals should get legal advice.

16
EMERGENCIES

16.1 In an emergency, when a person needs urgent treatment, if a pharmacy professional cannot get consent (for example, if the person is unconscious and unable to make a decision) they can provide treatment that is in the person's best interests and is needed to save their life or prevent deterioration in their condition. This applies to children, young people and adults.

16.2 There is an exception to 16.1 above if a pharmacy professional knows that there is a valid and applicable advance decision to refuse a particular treatment. For more information pharmacy professionals should see the relevant incapacity legislation and its code of practice, or ask their professional indemnity insurance provider or a legal adviser.

Appendix 5:
GPhC in practice: guidance on raising concerns

MAY 2017

1
THE IMPORTANCE OF RAISING CONCERNS

1.1 Every pharmacy professional has a duty to raise any concerns about individuals, actions or circumstances that may be unacceptable and that could result in risks to people receiving care and public safety.

1.2 Pharmacy professionals have a professional responsibility to take action to protect the wellbeing of people receiving care and the public. Raising concerns about individual pharmacy professionals, the members of the pharmacy team they work with (including trainees), employers and the environment they work in is a key part of this.

1.3 This includes raising and reporting any concerns pharmacy professionals have about the people they come into contact with during the course of their work, including pharmacists, pharmacy technicians, pharmacy owners, managers and employers, other healthcare professionals or people responsible for providing care and treatment for others, such as carers, care home staff or key workers. It includes concerns about behaviours, competency, the working environment and any action that may compromise an individual's safety.

1.4 We recognise that pharmacy professionals may be reluctant to raise a concern for a variety of reasons. For example, they may be worried that:

- They will cause trouble for their colleagues

- There may be a negative impact on their career

- It may lead to difficult working relationships with their colleagues

- They could face reprisals

- Nothing will be done as a result of the concern being raised.

1.5 Raising concerns at an early stage can help to identity areas of practice that can be improved. It allows employers, regulators and other authorities to take correct action as quickly as possible and before any direct harm comes to people receiving care and the public.

1.6 Pharmacy professionals must remember that:

- Their professional duty to safeguard the people they are providing care for and public safety must come before any other loyalties or considerations

- Failing to raise concerns about poor practice could result in harm to people receiving care

- The Public Interest Disclosure Act 1998 (PIDA) protects employees who

raise genuine concerns and expose 'malpractice' in the workplace

- If they do not report any concerns they may have about a colleague or others it may be out of line with our standards for pharmacy professionals, and this may call into question their own fitness to practise.

2
HOW TO RAISE A CONCERN

2.1 Pharmacy professionals have a professional responsibility to raise genuine concerns. They have this responsibility whether they are an employer, employee, a locum or temporary staff. Pharmacy professionals should normally raise their concern with their employer first, before taking it to a regulator or other organisations. If they are not sure whether or how to raise their concern they should get advice from one of the organisations listed in the other sources of information section. How pharmacy professionals raise a concern will vary, depending on:

- The nature of their concern

- Who or what they are concerned about, and

- Whether they consider there is a direct or immediate risk of harm to people receiving care or the public.

2.2 FIND OUT THE ORGANISATION'S POLICY
Pharmacy professionals should find out their employer's policy on raising concerns or 'whistle blowing' and follow this whenever possible.

2.3 REPORT WITHOUT DELAY
If pharmacy professionals believe that people receiving care are, or may be, at risk of death or serious harm they should report their concern without delay.

2.4 REPORT TO THE IMMEDIATE SUPERVISOR
The person pharmacy professionals report their concerns to will vary depending on the nature of the concern. In most situations they will be able to raise their concerns with their line manager.

2.5 REPORT TO ANOTHER SUITABLE PERSON IN AUTHORITY OR AN OUTSIDE BODY

There may be some situations when it isn't possible for pharmacy professionals to raise their concerns with their line manager. For example, they may be the cause of the concern or may have strong loyalties to those who are the cause of the concern. In these situations pharmacy professionals may need to speak to:

- A person who has been named as responsible for handling concerns

- A senior manager in the organisation for example a chief pharmacist, pharmacy owner or superintendent pharmacist or non-pharmacist manager

- The primary care organisation (including the accountable officer if the concern is about controlled drugs)

- The health or social care profession regulator [1]

- The relevant systems regulator for the organisation. [2]

2.6 KEEP A RECORD

Pharmacy professionals should keep a record of the concerns they have, who they have raised them with and the response or action that has been taken as a result of their action.

2.7 MAINTAIN CONFIDENTIALITY

If a concern raised by a pharmacy professional is about a specific person, for example a person receiving care or colleague, they should, where possible, maintain confidentiality and not disclose information without consent.

3
THE LAW

3.1 The PIDA sets out a step-by-step approach to raising and escalating concerns. It aims to protect employees from unfair treatment or victimisation from their employer if they have made certain disclosures of information in the public interest.

3.2 Under the PIDA pharmacy professionals should raise a concern about issues which have happened, or which they reasonably believe are likely to happen, and involve:

- A danger to the health or safety of an individual (for example, irresponsible or illegal prescribing, abuse of a person receiving care, or a professional whose health or fitness to practise may be impaired)

- A crime, or a civil offence (for example, fraud, theft or the illegal diversion of drugs)

- A miscarriage of justice

- Damage to the environment

- A cover-up of information about any of the above

3.3 This is not a full list. The other sources of information section gives contact details for other sources of information if pharmacy professionals have a concern and are unsure about whether or how they should raise it.

4
EXTRA GUIDANCE FOR EMPLOYERS

4.1 It is important that employees know about the procedures to follow if they have a concern about a colleague or the organisation they work in. There should

---

[1] The healthcare regulators are: General Chiropractic Council; General Dental Council; General Medical Council; General Optical Council; General Osteopathic Council; Health and Care Professions Council; Nursing and Midwifery Council; General Pharmaceutical Council and Pharmaceutical Society of Northern Ireland. The social care regulators are the Care Council in Wales; Health and Care Professions Council in England; Northern Ireland Social Care Council and the Scottish Social Services Council.

[2] These include, within the hospital setting, the Care Quality Commission in England, the Health Inspectorate Wales, Healthcare Improvement Scotland and the General Pharmaceutical Council if the concern is about registered pharmacy premises.

also be procedures to identity concerns that should be referred to a regulatory body such as ourselves. Creating an open working environment where employees feel comfortable raising concerns will safeguard people's safety by helping to identify and therefore improve poor practice.

4.2 Employers should:

- Make sure they have fair and robust policies and procedures to manage concerns that are raised with them. These policies and procedures need to be accessible to all staff

- Encourage all staff, including temporary staff and locums, to raise concerns about the safety of people receiving care, including risks posed by colleagues

- Make sure that all concerns raised with them are taken seriously and the person who has raised them is not victimised

- Make sure that all concerns are properly investigated and that all staff, including temporary staff and locums, are kept informed of the progress

- Have systems in place to give adequate support to pharmacy professionals who have raised concerns, and treat any information they are given in confidence

- Take appropriate steps to deal with concerns that have been raised because of a failure to maintain standards

- Have systems in place to support pharmacy professionals who are the subject of the concern, whether it is due to their poor performance, health or behaviour

- Keep appropriate records of any concerns raised and the action taken to deal with them

- Pass records of concerns raised to the manager or superintendent pharmacist so that they can consider an overall assessment of the concerns

- Not stop anyone from raising a concern

5
WHERE TO GO FOR MORE ADVICE

5.1 For more information on the PIDA and how to raise concerns under this employment legislation pharmacy professionals may want to contact the charity Public Concern at Work (PCaW). This is an independent charity that gives free, confidential legal advice to people who are not sure whether or how to raise concerns about 'malpractice' at work. If pharmacy professionals are not sure whether or how to raise their concern they should get advice from:

- Senior members of staff in their organisation

- The accountable officer, if the concern is about controlled drugs

- Their professional indemnity insurance provider, professional body or other pharmacy organisation

- The General Pharmaceutical Council or, if their concern is about a colleague in another healthcare profession, the appropriate regulatory body

- The charity Pharmacist Support

- Their union

Appendix 6:
GPhC in practice: guidance on maintaining clear sexual boundaries

MAY 2017

1
THE IMPORTANCE OF MAINTAINING CLEAR SEXUAL BOUNDARIES

1.1 When healthcare professionals cross personal and professional boundaries the result for people under their care can be serious and can cause harm. Crossing these boundaries can damage public trust and confidence in the pharmacy profession and other healthcare professions.

1.2 People receiving care must be able to trust that pharmacy professionals will act in their best interests. If pharmacy professionals are sexually, or inappropriately involved with a person under their care their professional judgement can be affected. This involvement may affect the decisions that they make about a person's healthcare.

2
POWER IMBALANCE

2.1 People receiving care are in a vulnerable position. In the relationship between a healthcare professional and a person under their care, there is often a power imbalance. This may be because personal information is shared with the pharmacy professional or because they have information and resources (such as medicines) that are needed. The person receiving care may not know what is appropriate professional behaviour. They may not be able to judge whether the relationship, or what happens to them, is appropriate. It is the pharmacy professional's responsibility to be aware of the imbalance of power and to maintain clear personal and professional boundaries at all times.

2.2 Pharmacy professionals should always be clear with the person receiving care about the reason for an examination or why they want them to come into the consultation room. The person receiving care should be given all the information they need and the opportunity to ask questions, and they should give their consent before the pharmacy professional goes with them into a consultation room.

3
SEXUALISED BEHAVIOUR AND BREACHES OF SEXUAL BOUNDARIES

3.1 The Professional Standards Authority (PSA) provides its own guidance on the

responsibilities that healthcare professionals have on maintaining clear sexual boundaries between healthcare professionals and patients. The PSA document defines sexualised behaviour as 'acts, words or behaviour designed to arouse or gratify sexual impulses or desires'.

3.2 A breach of sexual boundaries is not limited to criminal acts, such as rape or sexual assault. For example, carrying out an unnecessary physical examination or asking for details of sexual orientation when it is not necessary or relevant, would both be a breach.

4
AVOIDING BREACHES OF SEXUAL BOUNDARIES

4.1 There are a number of behaviours that may be signs of showing sexualised behaviour towards people receiving care or carers. These include:

- When the healthcare professional reveals intimate personal details about themselves to a person under their care during a consultation

- When the reason behind the following actions is sexual:

- Giving or accepting social invitations (dates and meetings)

- Visiting a home of a person under their care without an appointment

- Meeting people under their care outside of normal practice, for example arranging appointments for a time when no other staff are in the pharmacy, or

- Asking questions unrelated to a person's health

4.2 If a pharmacy professional finds themselves in a situation where they are attracted to a person under their care, they must not act on these feelings. If they have concerns that this may affect their professional judgement, or if they are not sure whether they are abusing their professional position, they may find it helpful to discuss this with someone else. They might discuss this with an impartial colleague, a pharmacy organisation that represents them, a professional leadership body or their professional indemnity insurance provider.

4.3 If pharmacy professionals cannot continue to care for the person and be objective, they should find other care for the person. They must make sure there is a proper handover to another pharmacy professional and that the person receiving care does not feel that they are in the wrong as a result of these actions.

4.4 There may be situations when people receiving care or their carers are attracted to a pharmacy professional. If a person receiving care shows sexualised behaviour towards a pharmacy professional, the pharmacy professional should think about whether they should discuss the person's feelings in a constructive way and try to re-establish a professional relationship. If this is not possible, they should transfer the person's care to another pharmacy professional. A pharmacy professional may find it helpful to discuss the matter with a colleague, a pharmacy organisation that represents them, a professional leadership body or their professional indemnity insurance provider.

5
CULTURAL AND OTHER DIFFERENCES

5.1 Cultural differences can affect a person's view of their personal boundaries and what is appropriate. Pharmacy professionals need to be sensitive to this, and always treat people receiving care as individuals in a way that respects their views and maintains their dignity. For example, an individual may prefer to talk to or be examined by a pharmacy professional of the same gender, or have another person present. (See 6 Chaperones).

6
CHAPERONES

6.1 A chaperone is a person (usually the same sex as the patient) who is present as

a safeguard for the person receiving care and the healthcare professional. They are also a witness to the person's continuing consent for the procedure. Their role may vary depending on the needs of the person, the pharmacy professional and the examination or procedure being carried out.

6.2 The pharmacy professional should ask the person receiving care whether they would like a chaperone to be with them in the consultation room, and for any examination that they might consider to be intimate. The pharmacy professional should discuss the need for a chaperone with the person receiving care and should not guess what their wishes are.

6.3 Pharmacy professionals should record any discussion that they have with a person receiving care about chaperones, including when they do not want to have a chaperone present.

6.4 If no chaperone is available, the pharmacy professional should offer to delay and rearrange the consultation or examination until one is available (unless a delay is not making the care of the person their first priority).

7
PEOPLE WHO HAVE PREVIOUSLY RECEIVED CARE

7.1 The same principles apply to carers or people who have received care from pharmacy professionals in the past. The previous professional relationship may also have involved an imbalance of power, and so would affect any personal relationship. If this type of relationship develops, the consequences should be considered and any harm this may cause to the person. The impact on the professional standing of the pharmacy professional should also be considered. We advise pharmacy professionals to consider the following:

- How long the professional relationship lasted and when it ended

- The nature of the previous professional

relationship and whether it involved a significant imbalance of power

- Whether the former person under their care or carer was, or is, vulnerable

- Whether the knowledge or influence that was gained through the professional relationship is being used to develop or continue the personal relationship, and

- Whether they are already treating, or are likely to treat, any other members of the former person under their care or carer's family.

7.2 It is the pharmacy professional's responsibility to act appropriately and professionally, even if the relationship is agreed by everyone involved. They must consider all the issues above and, if necessary, get appropriate advice.

8
RAISING CONCERNS

8.1 Pharmacy professionals have a professional duty to raise concerns if they believe the actions of other individuals are putting patients at risk. This would include when they are concerned that clear sexual boundaries have not been maintained by colleagues or other healthcare professionals. They must also take appropriate action if others report concerns to them.

8.2 See our *In practice: Guidance on raising concerns* for more information.

Appendix 7:
GPhC in practice: Guidance on religion, personal values and beliefs

JUNE 2017

ABOUT THE GUIDANCE

This guidance should be read alongside the GPhC standards for pharmacy professionals which all pharmacy professionals must meet.

It gives further guidance to pharmacy professionals on applying standard 1, when their religion, personal values or beliefs might impact on their willingness to provide certain services.

Pharmacy professionals should use their professional judgement in applying this guidance in practice and be able to justify their decisions. This guidance cannot cover every situation and does not give legal advice on equalities-related issues. However, it sets out the key factors for pharmacy professionals to consider when applying the standards in this context.

Pharmacy professionals should satisfy themselves that all members of the team are familiar with the issues raised within this guidance and understand their own responsibilities in relation to religion, personal values and beliefs in pharmacy.

Standard 1 says:

Pharmacy professionals must provide person-centred care.

APPLYING THE STANDARD

Every person is an individual with their own values, needs and concerns. Person-centred care is delivered when pharmacy professionals understand what is important to the individual and then adapt the care to meet their needs – making the care of the person their first priority. All pharmacy professionals can demonstrate 'person-centredness', whether or not they provide care directly, by thinking about the impact their decisions have on people. There are a number of ways to meet this standard, and below are examples of the attitudes and behaviours expected.

People receive safe and effective care when pharmacy professionals:

- Obtain consent to provide care and pharmacy services

- Involve, support and enable every person when making decisions about their health, care and wellbeing

- Listen to the person and understand their needs and what matters to them

- Give the person all relevant information in a way they can understand, so they can make informed decisions and choices

- Consider the impact of their practice whether or not they provide care directly

- Respect and safeguard the person's dignity

- Recognise and value diversity, and respect cultural differences – making sure that every person is treated fairly whatever their values and beliefs

- **Recognise their own values and beliefs but do not impose them on other people**

- **Take responsibility for ensuring that person-centred care is not compromised because of personal values and beliefs**

- Make the best use of the resources available

  This guidance is intended to:

- Reflect the broad range of situations when a pharmacy professional's religion, personal values or beliefs might impact on their willingness to provide certain services

- Help pharmacy professionals understand what it means to take responsibility for ensuring that person-centred care is not compromised

- Outline the key factors that pharmacy professionals should consider, to make sure people receive the care they need as a priority

- Apply whether pharmacy professionals are working in a healthcare setting (such as a hospital, secure accommodation, care home, primary care or community pharmacy setting), another setting, or providing services in person or online

  We have a range of guidance on our website to help pharmacy professionals apply our standards. As well as considering this guidance, all pharmacy professionals and pharmacy owners should read our guidance on confidentiality.

THE LEGAL FRAMEWORK

Pharmacy professionals must make sure that they keep up to date and comply with the law, and with any NHS or employment policies and contractual responsibilities of their employer that apply to their particular area of work.

In the context of religion, personal values and beliefs in pharmacy, it is important that pharmacy professionals understand and keep to the relevant framework of equalities and human rights legislation.

For example, the Equality Act 2010 protects individuals from direct and indirect discrimination, and harassment, because of nine 'protected characteristics'[1] including religion or belief. Protection applies in the workplace, the provision of services and other contexts, and is subject to defined exceptions.

We recognise that all protected characteristics have equal status. This guidance deals specifically with religion and belief as well as personal values, as these can particularly impact on professionals' decision-making in practice. It is also important to note that within equality law, religion means any religion, including a lack of religion. Belief means any religious or philosophical belief, and includes a lack of belief.

Also, the Human Rights Act 1998 incorporates the European Convention on Human Rights into UK law. Article 9 protects the right to freedom of thought, conscience and religion. This right is subject to qualification and cannot be used to support an action that disproportionately infringes the rights and freedoms of others.

The legislation in this area is complex, and there is significant and developing case law on equalities and human rights issues. It is not for our standards or supporting guidance to set out the law in detail or give legal advice. This means that pharmacy professionals need to understand how the law applies to them and get legal advice when they need it.

Employers must also keep to the relevant employment, human rights and equalities law, and must not discriminate against pharmacy professionals because of their stated or perceived personal values or beliefs, including religion.

---

1 The 'protected characteristics' are: age; disability; gender reassignment; marriage and civil partnership; pregnancy and maternity; race; religion or belief; sex; and sexual orientation.

1

RELIGION, PERSONAL VALUES AND BELIEFS IN PHARMACY

We recognise and respect that a pharmacy professional's religion, personal values and beliefs are often central to their lives and can make a positive contribution to their providing safe and effective care to a diverse population. It is important that pharmacy professionals take their own – and others – religion, personal values and beliefs into account when dealing with colleagues and people using pharmacy services, and understand how these have the potential to interact with and impact on the delivery of care.

In some cases, a pharmacy professional's religion, personal values or beliefs may influence their day-to-day practice, particularly whether they feel able to provide certain services.

This might include, for example, services related to:

- contraception (routine or emergency)
- fertility medicines
- hormonal therapies
- mental health and wellbeing
- substance misuse
- sexual health

Pharmacy professionals have the right to practise in line with their religion, personal values or beliefs as long as they act in accordance with equalities and human rights law and make sure that person-centred care is not compromised.

Pharmacy professionals must not discriminate against a person based on their own – or the person's – religion, personal values or beliefs, or lack of religion or belief. They should be sensitive to cultural, social, religious and clinical factors, and recognise that these can guide a person's choices.

It is important that pharmacy professionals work in partnership with their employers and colleagues to consider how they can practise in line with their religion, personal values and beliefs without compromising care. This includes thinking in advance about the areas of their practice which may be affected and making the necessary arrangements, so they do not find themselves in the position where a person's care could be compromised.

If a pharmacy professional is unwilling to provide a certain service, they should take steps to make sure the person asking for care is at the centre of their decision-making, so they can access the service they need in a timely manner and without hindrance. For example, this might include considering any time limits or other barriers to accessing medicines or other services, as well as any adverse impact on the person.

Pharmacy professionals should use their professional judgement when making decisions about what is clinically appropriate for the individual person, and discuss alternative options with the person, if necessary. Pharmacy professionals should keep in mind the difference between religion, personal values or beliefs, and a professional clinical judgement.

1.1

TAKING RESPONSIBILITY

People receive safe and effective care when pharmacy professionals take responsibility for ensuring that person-centred care is not compromised by personal values or beliefs. The way this can be done will depend on the individual situation, and the specific needs and circumstances of the person asking for care.

We want to be clear that referral to another health professional may be an appropriate option, and this can include handover to another pharmacist at the same, or another, pharmacy or service provider.

Pharmacy professionals should use their professional judgement to decide whether a referral is appropriate in each individual situation, and take responsibility for the outcome of the person's care. This includes considering the impact of their decision on the person asking for care, and meeting their legal responsibilities.

There are a number of factors for pharmacy professionals to consider when deciding whether a referral is appropriate in the circumstances. In particular, pharmacy professionals should make sure:

- people receive the care they need as a priority
- people are provided with all the relevant information to help them access the care they need, and

people are treated as individuals, fairly and with respect

A referral may not be appropriate in every situation: for example, if a service is not accessible or readily available elsewhere for the person, or if, due to the person's vulnerability, a referral would effectively obstruct timely access to the service. Again, pharmacy professionals should use their professional judgement to decide what is appropriate in individual cases, and keep a record of these decisions, including any discussions with the person asking for care.

2
FACTORS TO CONSIDER

Below are some of the key factors that pharmacy professionals should think about when providing person-centred care. This includes situations when religion, personal values and beliefs might have an impact on their willingness to provide certain services.

2.1
WORK LOCATION AND RANGE SERVICES

Pharmacy professionals should use their professional judgement to make sure the person asking for care is able to receive or access the services they need. Pharmacy professionals should think in advance about the range of services they can provide, the roles they feel able to carry out, and how to handle requests for services sensitively.

Pharmacy professionals should not knowingly put themselves in a position where they are unwilling to deliver or arrange timely care for a person. They should consider whether this means that, in some cases, certain professional roles will not be appropriate for them.

Pharmacy professionals should also consider:

- the suitability of the location, environment and working hours of the role they choose to work in: for example, an isolated pharmacy in a rural area, or on an out-of-hours rota

- the full range and type of services which their pharmacy is contracted to provide, including whether these are provided regularly or occasionally, and

- whether they will be working on their own and are aware of other local pharmacy professionals who

will be willing and able to provide the service if they feel unable to do so, and what the other service providers' opening hours are

2.2
OPENNESS BETWEEN THE PHARMACY PROFESSIONAL AND THEIR EMPLOYER

Pharmacy professionals should work in partnership with their employers and colleagues to create open and honest work environments. They should be open with their employer about any ways in which their religion, personal values or beliefs might impact on their willingness to provide certain pharmacy services.

Pharmacy professionals should also:

- tell their employer, as soon as possible, if their religion, personal values or beliefs might prevent them from providing certain pharmacy services, and

- work in partnership with their employer to make sure adequate and appropriate arrangements are put in place

2.3
MAKING THE CARE OF THE PERSON THE PRIORITY

Pharmacy professionals have an important role in treating every person as an individual, adapting the care to meet their needs, and putting the person at the centre of their decision-making. They should:

- work with the person asking for care, and others that may need to be involved, so the person can come to an informed decision about how they can access the care and services they need

- understand the needs of the person and any specific barriers they may face

- identify the options available for the person, and not assume that the person knows about these

- check the person understands the full range of information, including any significant risks which may be associated with the care they are seeking or the pharmacy professional's recommendations, to make it as easy as possible for the person to receive care

- be open to having discussions about how the person's religion, personal values or beliefs might relate to their care: for example, by giving advice on taking medicines during periods of fasting or giving advice about supplying non-animal-based medicines, and

- recognise when a person may need extra care or advice – for example, a distressed or vulnerable person or in a matter involving safeguarding – and act when necessary

2.4
HANDLING REQUESTS SENSITIVELY

Pharmacy professionals should be sensitive in the way that they communicate with people asking for care and not imply or express disapproval or judgement. In handling requests, they should:

- make sure the person is treated sensitively by using appropriate facilities or arrangements, such as a consultation room if available

- communicate professionally and with respect

- adapt their communication to meet the needs of the person they are communicating with

- consider the appropriateness of their body language, tone of voice and words

- safeguard, respect and maintain the privacy, dignity and confidentiality of people asking for care, and make sure the person is not made to feel uncomfortable, embarrassed or distressed

3
QUESTIONS TO ASK YOURSELF

Below are some key questions that pharmacy professionals should ask themselves when thinking about how they can ensure and demonstrate that they have provided person-centred care in this context:

- Have I considered the range of services I feel able to provide?

- Is the work location and environment suitable for me?

- Have I made the care of the person my priority?

- Have I considered the impact of my actions on the person?

- Have I been open with my employer about the service I feel able to provide?

- Are the right arrangements in place to make sure people come first?

- If a person has raised their religion, personal values or beliefs, have I considered how it might relate to their care?

- Have I made record of any decisions relating to referral including discussions with the person asking for care?

- How do I handle requests sensitively, without embarrassing the person?

4
EMPLOYERS AND PHARMACY PROFESSIONALS WORKING TOGETHER

Employers have important responsibilities for creating and maintaining a person-centred environment, and ensuring the safe and effective delivery of pharmacy services. This includes considering the needs of the people in their area and how the pharmacy can best meet their expectations and needs as a priority.

Also, employers have responsibilities towards pharmacy professionals and the wider pharmacy team. Everyone has the right to be treated with dignity and respect in the workplace, and employers should be sensitive to the religion, personal values and beliefs of pharmacy professionals, and create and maintain fair working environments. Employers must keep to the relevant employment, human rights and equalities law. They must not unlawfully discriminate against pharmacy professionals because of their stated or perceived religion, personal values or beliefs.

Employers must have governance and staff management processes in place so they can support and enable pharmacy professionals to provide continuous care in a non-discriminatory way for the people using their pharmacy services, throughout the opening hours of the pharmacy. They should consider and review these workplace processes to make sure that these are appropriate, and in line with the law.

Pharmacy professionals who are employed or seeking employment should have open and honest conversations with their employers about any ways in which their religion, personal values or beliefs might impact on their willingness to provide certain pharmacy services. This will enable employers to put in place ways of working to ensure the consistent provision of services and compliance with their NHS contract. Pharmacy professionals should discuss with their employer any necessary arrangements that may be needed, so that the pharmacy services provided are not adversely affected by their personal values and beliefs.

The pharmacy team is often the first point of contact so employers should make sure that the team is aware of this guidance. Employers should also make sure the team understands the importance of treating people sensitively when they request a pharmacy service or care which may not be in line with their religion, personal values or beliefs, so that the person's care is not compromised.

There is a significant amount of advice and guidance available from other professional sources to help employers understand and apply the law in this area. This includes detailed information for employers on their responsibilities in the workplace, the rights of employees (including job applicants) and the rights of people who use pharmacy services.

OTHER SOURCES OF INFORMATION

You can get more information and guidance from professional bodies, indemnity insurance providers, and from other independent bodies such as those listed below:

- ACAS – Religion or belief and the workplace

- Association of Pharmacy Technicians, UK

- Citizens Advice

- Equalities and Human Rights Commission

- Equalities and Human Rights Commission Religion or belief guidance for employers

- Equalities and Human Rights Commission Scotland

- Equalities and Human Rights Commission Wales

- European Convention on Human Rights

- Guild of Healthcare Pharmacists

- National Pharmacy Association

- Royal Pharmaceutical Society

Relevant legislation

- The Equality Act 2010

- The Human Rights Act 1998

Appendix 8:
GPhC guidance on responding to complaints and concerns

SEPTEMBER 2010

The General Pharmaceutical Council is the regulator for pharmacists, pharmacy technicians and registered pharmacy premises in England, Scotland and Wales.

This document provides guidance on dealing with complaints and concerns raised by patients, the public and other healthcare professionals.

We are providing this guidance to assist pharmacy professionals on how to best meet the responsibilities that a pharmacy owner or pharmacy professional has in relation to handling and managing complaints and concerns.

As dispensing errors are frequently the basis for complaints, we will also provide guidance on:

- How to minimise the risk of a dispensing error occurring

- What to do in the event of a dispensing error

- How to review dispensing errors.

1
INTRODUCTION

The standards of conduct, ethics and performance must be followed by pharmacists and registered pharmacy technicians. Principle 1 of these standards is to 'make patients your first concern'. A requirement under this principle is to 'organise regular reviews, audits and risk assessments to protect patient and public safety and to improve your professional service'.

The standards also require you to have standard operating procedures (SOPs) in place which must be followed at all times. The standards for pharmacy owners and superintendent pharmacists of retail pharmacy businesses require pharmacy owners and superintendent pharmacists to ensure the safe and effective running of the pharmacy. To allow this there must be appropriate policies, procedures and records in place that are maintained and reviewed regularly. There must also be an appropriate mechanism in place to respond to and investigate all complaints and concerns raised.

2
WHY COMPLAINTS ARISE

There are numerous reasons for why a complaint or concern may arise. The majority of complaints or concerns are due to:

- Human error

- System failure, for example when a pharmacy doesn't have adequate SOPs in place

- How a complaint or concern is handled in the pharmacy.

The way in which a complaint or concern is handled in the pharmacy can determine whether or not it is then referred to an independent body such as the General Pharmaceutical Council (GPhC) or the primary care organisation (PCO).

3
HOW TO DEAL WITH A COMPLAINT OR CONCERN THAT HAS BEEN RAISED

When something goes wrong or someone reports a concern to you, you should make sure you deal with it appropriately.

There should be an effective complaints procedure where you work and you must follow it at all times. You should make a record of the complaint, concern or incident and the action taken. You should review your records and findings and audit them regularly.

DISPENSING ERRORS

The investigating committee considered 732 cases between April 2009 and March 2010. Approximately 32% of these cases concerned dispensing errors. The Disciplinary Committee considered 396 cases during the same period of which 15% concerned dispensing errors.

4
HOW TO MINIMISE THE RISK OF MAKING A DISPENSING ERROR

DISPENSARY LAYOUT:
- The dispensary should be organised to keep distractions to a minimum

- The atmosphere of the dispensary should encourage good concentration

- Alert staff to the dangers of stock being placed in the wrong location. Dispensary stock should only be put away by a competent member of staff

- Keep a segregated area of the dispensary workbench for the dispensing process

- Segregate prescriptions on the workbench to avoid patients receiving someone else's medicines. You may use baskets/trays if appropriate.

DISPENSING PROCESS:
- Produce dispensing labels before any product is selected from the shelf

- Do not select stock using dispensing labels or patient medication records (PMR). Refer to the prescritption when selecting stock for dispensing

- Dispense items from the prescription and not the generated label

- You should have systems in place to identify who was involved in the dispensing and checking process of each prescription item (e.g. dispensed by/checked by boxes)

- Two people should be involved in the dispensing process where this is possible. A second competent person should carry out an accuracy check and ideally should not have been involved in the assembly process

- If you are a pharmacist working alone, once you have assembled the medicines, try to create a short mental break between the assembly and final check to avoid carrying over any recollection of preconceived errors from the assembly process

- All accuracy checks should be made against the original prescription re-reading the prescription first

- Dispense balances of medication owed by reference only to the original prescription or a good quality copy. Do not rely solely on the information in the PMR or an owing note or label. This will prevent you making the same error that may have previously been made by another pharmacist. The National Patient Safety Agency (NPSA) (www.npsa.nhs.uk) has published a document entitled A guide to the design of dispensed medicines, which looks at the key aspects of labelling and presentation of a dispensed medicine.

Another publication, entitled A guide to the design of dispensing environments, provides guidance on how the design of a dispensary can improve patient safety. Whilst the physical design of the dispensary can inevitably improve the working environment and therefore patient safety other things should also be considered. For example, the workflow and how the dispensary area is utilised can improve the efficiency and improve safety.

5
WHAT TO DO IN THE EVENT OF A DISPENSING ERROR

Pharmacists should carry out a root cause analysis in the event of a patient safety incident. This is a retrospective technique for looking for the underlying causes of a patient safety incident, behind the immediate and obvious cause. For example, one individual's human error might be the immediate cause, but several factors could have contributed to the error such as fatigue, an inadequate checking system or poor standard operating procedures.

The NPSA is promoting root cause analysis and is encouraging organisations to identify the circumstances in which it should be used. This should take into account the severity of the incident and the scope for learning from it. Further information on root cause analysis can be found on the NPSA website at www.npsa.nhs.uk

You may wish to consider all the points below when dealing with an error or handling a complaint. In addition, locum pharmacists may also wish to keep their own records in case they are contacted later.

When the patient first comes in or indicates that there has been an error:

- **ESTABLISH IF THE PATIENT HAS TAKEN ANY OF THE INCORRECT MEDICINE**
If the patient has taken any of the incorrect medicine, establish whether the patient has been harmed. If they have been harmed, provide the complainant and the patient's GP with the advice they need immediately. Contact the local drug information centre, if appropriate, for advice on the possible effects on the patient (giving details of concurrent medication). Where no harm appears to have been caused, the GP should still be informed.

- **ASK TO INSPECT THE INCORRECT MEDICINE**
Make it clear that you do not wish to retain the medication, and that inspecting the medicine can give valuable clues about what went wrong.

If the patient does not want to hand the medicine over to you, suggest that they retain it until they can hand it over to an appropriate representative of the GPhC or their local PCO. Incorrect medicines should not routinely be posted to these organisations. If the patient does hand over and leave the incorrect medication with you, retain it and keep it segregated from stock and other medicines to be supplied to patients.

Never dispose of any medicine unless the patient has given consent. Before doing so it should be retained carefully, for a reasonable period, in case of further developments.

- **APOLOGISE**
In the case of a dispensing error, an apology should not be confused with an admission of liability.

- **NEVER TRY TO MINIMISE THE SERIOUSNESS OF AN ERROR**
A balance must be struck that reassures the patient, if no harm is likely, but without suggesting that the error is insignificant.

- **MAKE A SUPPLY OF THE CORRECT MEDICINE ORDERED ON THE PRESCRIPTION, IF APPROPRIATE**
You can lawfully make a supply of the correct medicine as this was authorised on the original prescription, even in the case of a Controlled Drug. Where the patient has not taken any of the incorrect medication it is your professional judgement about whether the patient's GP needs to be informed.

It is important to establish what the complainant would like you to do about their complaint

Supply the complainant with the name and address of the Fitness to Practise Department of the GPhC if the complainant feels that the only way forward is to complain to an 'official body'. Explain that a Professional Standards Inspector from the GPhC may visit the pharmacy to undertake a review. You may also provide the details of the PCO so that the matter can be dealt with under the NHS complaints procedure.

You may need to make your own inquiries into any possible causes of the alleged error for preventative purposes unless it is clear from the facts known to you, how the error is likely to have occurred. You may need to speak to the person who presented or collected the prescription about the prevailing conditions in the pharmacy. Contact the complainant and inform them of your findings.

Where you are an employee pharmacist, you should follow the procedures laid down by your employer/Superintendent for who you should notify in the event of a dispensing error. If you are working within a company, you may have to report any errors to your line manager and/or a Superintendent office. You must follow company procedures for such reporting and may wish to consult the superintendent pharmacist and other line managers for advice.

See section on reviewing errors.

You may use the Responsible Pharmacist record to ascertain who was on duty at the time.

In all cases of dispensing errors, the over-riding responsibility is for the health and wellbeing of the patient. Whilst keeping this in mind, you should inform your professional indemnity insurers as soon as possible, in case a claim is later made against you.

6
REVIEWING ERRORS

Make a written record of your findings when you carry out your review to establish what went wrong. You can record your findings using the mnemonic 'CHAPS' to cover the various areas of the supply. CHAPS covers the following points:

C
CONDITIONS IN THE PHARMACY AT THE TIME

This can be established from the:

Complainant

Records – records would help to identify the name of the responsible pharmacist and whether they had been working without a break

Computer – computer records may help to identify the number of prescriptions dispensed that day and the exact time the prescription was dispensed.

Interestingly, most errors do not occur during busy periods of dispensing. You may wish to review the layout of the dispensary and the availability of bench space. You may use baskets or similar to hold dispensed items before checking and handing to the patient with counselling. It has been reported that pharmacists who use this type of system help prevent medicines being crossed from one patient to another, and also to keep the bench space tidy.

H
HEALTH OF THE PHARMACIST AND OTHER MEMBERS OF THE TEAM

Was the pharmacist or other person(s) involved in the dispensing process ill at the time?

A
ASSISTANCE

Was the pharmacist working alone or was s/he assisted? Identify the person who assisted.

Make a judgement about the qualifications and competence of the assistant.

P

PRESCRIPTION SHOULD BE RECOVERED FROM THE FILE OR GET A COPY OF IT FROM THE RELEVANT PRESCRIPTION PRICING AUTHORITY

- Was the error caused by the legibility of the prescription?

- Was the prescription handwritten or computer generated?

- Check endorsements for what was supplied.

S

SYSTEMS USED FOR DISPENSING AND CHECKING MUST BE REVIEWED

Depending upon whether the pharmacist was working alone or with someone assisting, this covers every part of the dispensing process. The type of error may direct your attention to one area of dispensing practice.

Usually errors fall into categories:

- Misreading the prescription

- Incorrect picking of the medicines

- Transposing the label or labelling the medicine incorrectly

- Giving the wrong prescription to the wrong patient (for example, where the error involves placing the medicine in the wrong bag or where the patient's address is not checked properly when handing out the dispensed medicine)

- Selection of the wrong strength (or wrong preparation) from the PMRs when using the repeats facility, then checking the stock against the label, not the original prescription

- Incorrect compounding

- Supplying contaminated or out-of-date stock

- Dispensing against an incorrectly written owing slip, rather than the prescription.

Whatever weaknesses there are in the system, the final accuracy check must overcome them. It is most important to review these critically.

The mnemonic 'HELP' can be used when making the final check on the dispensed medicine, to ensure that all the necessary checks have been made. HELP stands for the following:

H

'HOW MUCH' HAS BEEN DISPENSED

Open all unsealed cartons and sealed cartons, if appropriate, to check that the contents are correct and match the quantity requested on the prescription. Check that the correct patient information leaflet has been included.

E

'EXPIRY DATE' CHECK

Ensure this is sufficient to cover the treatment period.

L

'LABEL' CHECK

Check the patient's name, product name, form, strength and dose are the same as on the prescription. Check that the correct and appropriate warning(s) are included on the label.

P

'PRODUCT' CHECK

Check that the correct medication and strength which has been requested on the prescription has been supplied.

Handing out of dispensed medicines must be carried out by trained staff. To avoid handing medicines to the wrong person, prescription receipts may provide useful safeguards, although even these are not foolproof. The person collecting the dispensed medicine should be asked for the address or date of birth of the patient, which should be checked against the prescription.

When reviewing dispensing errors which have resulted in a serious patient safety incident, the NPSA incident decision tree helps to identify why individuals acted in a certain way, and this may be a very useful tool for pharmacists, managers and organisations to consider using. Information on the incident decision tree can be found at www.npsa.nhs.uk

Appendix 9:
GPhC guidance for registered pharmacies preparing unlicensed medicines

REVISED AUGUST 2018

ABOUT THIS GUIDANCE

This guidance should be followed if an unlicensed medicine is prepared in a registered pharmacy. The preparation of an unlicensed medicine (for example unlicensed methadone, or menthol in aqueous cream) in a pharmacy is often called 'extemporaneous preparation'.

The guidance should be read alongside the standards for registered pharmacies.[1] These aim to create and maintain the right environment, both organisational and physical, for the safe and effective practice of pharmacy. By following this guidance the pharmacy will:

· Demonstrate that it meets our standards, and

· Provide assurances that the health, safety and wellbeing of patients and the public are safeguarded.

Responsibility for making sure this guidance is followed lies with the pharmacy owner. If the registered pharmacy is owned by a 'body corporate' the directors have responsibility. Those responsible for the overall safe running of the pharmacy need to take into account the nature of the pharmacy and the range of services already provided and, most importantly, the needs of patients and members of the public.

As well as meeting our standards, the pharmacy owner must make sure they keep to all legal requirements, including medicines legislation, and health and safety, data protection and equalities legislation.

Pharmacy owners should make sure that all staff, including non-pharmacists, involved in preparing unlicensed medicines are familiar with this guidance.

Individual pharmacy professionals are key to ensuring the safe preparation and supply of unlicensed medicines. Pharmacists and pharmacy technicians involved in preparing unlicensed medicines have a responsibility[2] to provide medicines safely to patients, maintain the quality of their practice, keep their knowledge and skills up to date, and work within their professional competence.

We expect this guidance to be followed. However, we also recognise that there can be a number of ways to meet our standards and achieve the same outcomes for patients – that is, to provide safe treatment, care and services. If you do not follow this guidance, you should be able to show how your alternative ways of working safeguard patients, identify and manage any risks, and meet our standards.

In this document, when we use the term 'you' this means the pharmacy owner.

In some limited circumstances (for example following death or bankruptcy), a representative can take the role of the pharmacy owner. In these cases, the appointed representative will be responsible for making sure these standards are met.

THE SCOPE OF THIS GUIDANCE

This guidance applies only to the process of preparing[3] an unlicensed medicine by (or under the supervision of) a pharmacist in a registered pharmacy in Great Britain, under the exemptions and circumstances described in the law.[4] It applies whether this happens rarely, occasionally or is part of the core business of the registered pharmacy.

---

1 Standards for registered pharmacies.

2 Standards of conduct, ethics and performance.

3 This guidance does not apply to unlicensed medicines that registered pharmacies have not prepared themselves, but have

obtained from elsewhere such as (MS) licensed manufacturers, importers or distributors.

4 Section 10 of the Medicines Act 1968 and Regulation 4 of the Human Medicines Regulations 2012.

This guidance applies to all the following:

- The one-off preparation of an unlicensed medicine in accordance with a prescription for an individual patient

- The preparation of a stock[5] of unlicensed medicines, (in anticipation of a prescription), which will later be supplied from the pharmacy, by or under the supervision of a pharmacist, against a prescription for an individual patient

- The preparation of methadone for supply in accordance with a prescription (either for immediate supply in accordance with the prescription, or initially as stock[5] to be supplied from the pharmacy, by or under the supervision of a pharmacist, against a prescription at a later time)

- The preparation of an unlicensed medicine based upon the pharmacist's judgement[6]

- The preparation of an unlicensed medicine by, or under the supervision of, a pharmacist based on the specification of the patient

If the activity is not covered by the exemptions set out in the law, you will need a Manufacturer's Specials (MS) licence from the Medicines and Healthcare products Regulatory Agency (MHRA).

If the medicines are being prepared for animal use, the exemptions that allow this, and the parts of the law that apply, are found in the Veterinary Medicines Regulations 2013. The body that regulates animal medicines and issues authorisations to manufacturers of special veterinary medicinal products is the Veterinary Medicines Directorate (VMD).

Throughout this document we use the terms 'preparing' and 'preparation' which refer to making a medicine from ingredients or starting materials. These terms are not intended to include the process of simply diluting or dissolving a product in a vehicle designed for that purpose as part of its marketing authorisation – for example, adding a set amount of water to reconstitute an antibiotic powder.

INTRODUCTION

The law[7] sets out the restrictions on how human medicines are licensed, manufactured, advertised, administered, sold and supplied.

Most of the medicines supplied from registered pharmacies are licensed medicines. Licensed medicines are those that have a valid Marketing Authorisation (MA) in the UK, and which are covered by an approval process overseen by the MHRA or the European Medicines Agency (EMA).

The manufacturers who make these medicines or import these are also regulated and licensed by the MHRA for compliance with EU Good Manufacturing Practice (GMP) standards and the strict conditions of their licence. You can find more information about the approval and inspection of manufacturers on the MHRA's website.[8]

These arrangements mean that licensed manufacturers are making medicines to a regulated standard that is consistent throughout the industry. It also means that when medicines are used in line with their licence, they are:

- Assured to a certain level of efficacy, quality and safety, and

- Only available if they are effective.

Overall this means that the public, and patients, can have a high degree of confidence that appropriately prescribed licensed medicines are effective and meet the clinical needs of patients.

As a rule, the law requires that only authorised (licensed) medicines should be made available and supplied ('placed on the market'). There are exemptions in the law which allow unlicensed medicines to be prescribed and supplied to individual patients.

In general, when a prescriber issues a prescription they will prescribe a medicine that is licensed and indicated for the condition to be treated. European and UK law sets out the circumstances under which prescribers can prescribe an unlicensed medicine for supply to a patient. You can find

---

5 Preparation for stock at a pharmacy is acceptable as long as it is subsequently supplied by retail from that pharmacy or another pharmacy which is part of the same legal entity.

6 An unlicensed medicine that is prepared with the intention of

selling it over the counter (one that is not a prescription-only medicine) is often called a 'Chemist's Nostrum'.

7 Medicines Act 1968 and the Human Medicines Regulations 2012.

8 www.mhra.gov.uk

more information on the prescribing of an unlicensed medicine by reading the General Medical Council's (GMC's) Good practice in prescribing and managing medicines and devices on their website.[9]

Under the law, unlicensed medicines ('special products') must be manufactured by the holders of MS ('specials') licences who are regulated by the MHRA and who follow GMP standards and the conditions of their licences.

In general, the law also requires the medicine itself be licensed.[10] However, the law[11] allows a pharmacist to prepare and supply medicines in a registered pharmacy without the need for the product to be licensed. A pharmacist should have acquired the necessary knowledge and skill during their initial education and training leading to registration.

A patient has every right to expect that when an unlicensed medicine is prepared by, or under the supervision of, a pharmacist in a registered pharmacy, it is of an equivalent quality to any licensed medicine they will receive (such as those produced by a regulated and licensed manufacturer). As certain high-profile past cases[12] have shown, preparing an unlicensed medicine in a pharmacy is an activity that can pose a significant risk to patients and have potentially serious consequences when risks and processes are not managed properly.

When a patient is supplied with an unlicensed medicine, it is important that the unlicensed medicine is safe and appropriate. Pharmacists making supplies must also consider their individual professional standards and their responsibilities to the patient. There is also a general legal duty that all medicines supplied to patients are of the nature and quality requested or prescribed.

The law also allows a pharmacist in a registered pharmacy to prepare medicines for animal use in line with a prescription, prescribed under the cascade,[13] from a veterinary practitioner.

The authorised specials manufacturers of veterinary medicines are inspected by the VMD for their compliance with the principles of GMP. If they manufacture human medicines they would also be regulated by the MHRA.

If you choose to prepare unlicensed medicines in your pharmacy under the exemptions in the law, you should follow the guidance set out in this document.

The owner is responsible for making sure that there are systems in place to safeguard the health, safety and wellbeing of patients and the public who use their services. This guidance covers the areas we believe may present an increased risk when medicines are prepared in a registered pharmacy. It will help the owner, and superintendent pharmacist, to meet our standards for registered pharmacies.

GUIDANCE FOR REGISTERED PHARMACIES PREPARING UNLICENSED MEDICINES

The standards for registered pharmacies are grouped under five principles, and this guidance is set out under each of those five principles.

PRINCIPLE 1

The governance arrangements safeguard the health, safety and wellbeing of patients and the public. The following areas relate to this principle in the standards for registered pharmacies.

1.1
RISK ASSESSMENT

A risk assessment is a careful and thorough look at what, in your work, could cause harm to patients and what you need to do to prevent this. Risk assessments should be specific to the individual pharmacy, the staff working in it, and to each unlicensed medicine to be prepared.

You should consider the risks before deciding whether your pharmacy should prepare unlicensed medicines in general, or whether you might consider other options for supplying particular medicines.

---

9 www.gmc-uk.org

10 Regulations 17 and 46 of the Human Medicines Regulations 2012.

11 Section 10 of the Medicines Act 1968 and Regulation 4 of the Human Medicines Regulations 2012.

12 Peppermint water case.

13 Veterinary Medicines Regulations 2013.

You should carry out a risk assessment if an unlicensed medicine is prepared in your pharmacy, and carry out the necessary checks to satisfy yourself that any arrangements you have in place to manage the risks involved meet the requirements of principle 1. If your intention is that your pharmacy will prepare medicines, you will need to be able to produce evidence for the arrangements you have in place to manage the risks identified.

The risk assessment should be reviewed regularly (see section 1.2) and should also be reviewed when circumstances change (see section 1.3).
The risk assessment should state what the risks are, and may include finding out whether equivalent relevant licensed products exist and are available.

While this is not a full list of issues that need to be taken into account, the assessment should, if applicable, look at:

- A formula from a recognised source, for example from an official Pharmacopoeia

- A verification of the preparation method (e.g. the Pharmacopoeia method)

- A calculation verification

- The use of specialist equipment

- Consideration of contamination

- Hygiene measures

- Product-specific risks

- Assurances around ingredients and starting materials

- The suitability of premises

- Relevant staff skills

- Training and competence

- The circumstances that would trigger a new risk assessment.

1.2
REGULAR AUDIT
You should have robust systems in place so that you can demonstrate that your pharmacy:

- Continues to be a safe place in which to prepare unlicensed medicines for patients, and

- Can produce medicines which are safe, effective and of a suitable quality.

You should carry out a regular audit, at an interval that you can show to be appropriate, on the process of preparing unlicensed medicines.
The audit should form part of the evidence which provides assurance and shows that the pharmacy continues to be safe and appropriate to carry out this activity.

While this is not a full list of issues that need to be taken into account, the audit should, if applicable, look at:

- The premises (including temperature, light and moisture controls and where applicable – for example in aseptic preparation – air quality and other environmental requirements)

- The equipment and facilities

- The preparation process and quality control

- The hygiene issues that might have an adverse impact on the product and therefore the patient (including avoiding cross-contamination and microbial contamination)

- Staff training and skills

- The records (including the method of preparation, traceability of ingredients used, labelling applied and how the records themselves are kept).
You should learn from any incidents, complaints or other forms of relevant information and use the learning to make appropriate changes.

1.3
REACTIVE REVIEW
A review should take place when any of the following happens:

- Changes in key staff (those who have specialist training, knowledge and experience and are involved in preparing medicines)

- The introduction of new staff

- A change in the equipment

- A change in the form, or source, of ingredients

- Any incidents

- The environment or facilities available are no longer fit for the task

- Concerns or feedback received

- A review of near misses and error logs indicates concerns about this activity.

This reactive review, which should be documented, should say when a new risk assessment is needed. It can form part of that new risk assessment, when one needs to be carried out.

1.4
RECALL PROCEDURES

It is important that if there is a problem with an unlicensed medicine that has been prepared in your pharmacy, you have the systems in place to contact members of the public and recall unlicensed medicines that have been made in your pharmacy.

These procedures should say who is responsible for taking action, and what action to take. They should also include details of the other bodies or authorities that need to be told about the medicines' recall.

Under the standards you must have arrangements in place that allow all staff to raise concerns when they suspect that medicines are not fit for purpose

1.5
ACCOUNTABILITY – STAFF

It should be clear which pharmacist is accountable and responsible for the preparation of an unlicensed medicine. It should also be clear which pharmacy technician and other staff are involved in preparing an unlicensed medicine.

1.6
RECORD KEEPING

You should keep detailed records of the preparation of the unlicensed medicine to safeguard patients. This is so that if there is a recall, or an incident affecting a patient's safety, the method of preparation can be clearly reconstructed. You should keep records for as long as you consider, and can show, to be appropriate, taking into account any consumer protection laws which apply. If the medicine being prepared is for animal use there are specific requirements in the law for record keeping that also apply. Ask the pharmacy's professional indemnity insurance provider for advice about how long you should keep records for.

The records should include information on the following:

THE PROCESS

- Description of the key preparation steps used
- Calculations: working shown and double checked (detailed)
- The name of the person who prepared the worksheet
- The date that the worksheet was prepared
- The name of the supervising pharmacist (and the name of the pharmacist signing off the final product as ready to be supplied to the patient, if different)
- The name of the pharmacy technician involved (if applicable)

THE FORMULA

- The complete formula
- The source of the formula: Pharmacopoeia formula or other source
- Validation of the formula

THE INGREDIENTS
(FOR EACH INGREDIENT OR
STARTING MATERIAL USED)

- The source: manufacturer, brand and the wholesaler or distributor
- Certificate of conformity[14] (if applicable)
- Certificate of analysis[15] (if applicable)
- Batch number
- Expiry date (if available)
- Quantity used and details of the person measuring, and person double-checking, quantities
- TSE guidance[16] should be followed (if applicable, that is, where an ingredient or product contact material is of animal origin)
- Description of the container and closure used (for example, whether they were glass or plastic)

THE PRODUCT

- Date prepared
- A reference number or identification (batch number)
- Expiry date (give reasons or validation in support)
- Date supplied to the patient or customer

THE PATIENT OR CUSTOMER

- The patient or customer's name
- The patient or customer's address
- The patient or customer's contact details (for example, phone number, email address)
- A sample of the label that has been put on the medicine
- The name of the person who produced the label

(ALSO, IF SUPPLIED
AGAINST A PRESCRIPTION)

- The patient's doctor (name, address and phone number)
- The patient's age (if it is on the prescription)
- Other prescription details (date and type)

INCIDENTS

- Suspected adverse reactions reported
- Complaints and concerns

14 Certificate of conformity provides confirmation that the product supplied complies with a specified set of requirements or specifications, but does not contain any test results.

15 Certificate of analysis provides a summary of testing results on samples of products or materials together with the evaluation for compliance to a stated specification.

16 The TSE guidance is the MHRA guidance: 'Minimising the Risk of Transmission of Transmissible Spongiform Encephalopathies via Unlicensed Medicines for Human Use'. See the Other sources of information section at the end of this document for more information.

PRINCIPLE 2

Staff are empowered and competent to safeguard the health, safety and wellbeing of patients and the public. The following areas relate to this principle in the standards for registered pharmacies.

2.1
TRAINED AND COMPETENT STAFF

Staff should complete recognised training courses before they can be involved in this activity. However, staff may also be involved in this activity if they are still doing such a training course, but their work in this area must be closely supervised until their training is complete.

To prepare an unlicensed medicine from ingredients, staff need expertise and skill over and above that needed to dispense a licensed medicine. Many pharmacists and pharmacy technicians should have acquired this knowledge and skill during their initial education and training leading to registration. If they do not have the necessary knowledge, skills or competence to safely carry out the task, you should consider how you ensure that they obtain (or if they have previously been trained in this area, refresh) the necessary specialist skills.

It is important that training is regularly repeated to make sure that all staff remain up to date and competent. This is particularly important when the activity is only carried out from time to time. Staff working with potentially hazardous substances (such as cytotoxic products), or in areas that require more stringent precautions (such as aseptic preparation), should have done specific, recognised and relevant training.

2.2
TRAINING RECORDS

You should document and keep evidence of the training done for as long as you consider, and can show, to be appropriate. These records should be made available to the relevant authorities if they ask for them. You should ask the pharmacy's professional indemnity insurance provider for advice on how long you should keep records for.

PRINCIPLE 3

The environment and condition of the premises from which pharmacy services are provided, and any associated premises, safeguard the health, safety and wellbeing of patients and the public.

You should assess the risks and consider whether your pharmacy premises are suited to, and capable of, providing this service. You should get specialist advice when you are considering preparing sterile (aseptic) or hazardous medicines (for example cytotoxics, hormones or immunosuppressants).

There are highly specialised requirements for the safe preparation of aseptic medicines, and there are potentially significant adverse consequences to patients if there is an error with, or contamination of, these medicines. You should get specialist advice from a body such as the MHRA or regional NHS Quality Assurance staff (some of which also operate on a consultancy basis and can provide services across Great Britain and to non-NHS organisations too).

See the Other sources of information section at the end of this document for more information on this subject. The following areas relate to this principle in the standards for registered pharmacies.

3.1
MEASURES TO MINIMISE CONTAMINATION

There should be enough space, and segregation where required, to provide this service safely, and the environment of the premises should be suitable for the preparation of medicines.

Specific steps should be taken to make sure that the risk of cross-contamination and microbial contamination is eliminated or minimised within the pharmacy.

These factors should be considered as part of the initial risk assessment.

See the Other sources of information section at the end of this document for links to information provided by governmental infection control agencies.

3.2
HYGIENE CONTROL RECORDS

You should make records of the steps taken to make sure that the environment, conditions and equipment are clean enough for the preparation of medicines. These will form part of the evidence that the pharmacy is suitable for the preparation of unlicensed medicines.

You should keep the records for as long as you consider, and can show, to be appropriate. You should ask the pharmacy's professional indemnity insurance provider for advice on how long you should keep records for.

PRINCIPLE 4

The way in which pharmacy services, including the management of medicines and medical devices, are delivered safeguards the health, safety and wellbeing of patients and the public. This includes the management of medicines and medical devices. The following areas relate to this principle in the standards for registered pharmacies.

4.1
INGREDIENTS

The ingredients and starting materials used in the preparation of the unlicensed medicine will affect the quality of the final product. Therefore you should make sure that any ingredients or starting materials your staff use are obtained from a reputable source: for example, a licensed manufacturer or distributor.

4.2
QUALITY ASSURANCE

Quality assurance, in this context, is the procedures, processes and arrangements in place that make sure a finished medicine is of the quality needed for its intended use. To have a robust system of quality assurance that provides the necessary safeguards, you need to have a range of systems in place, such as those described in this guidance. These include:

- Using worksheets and official formulas

- Confirmation of quantities and identities of ingredients

- Staff whose training is suitable and up-to-date, and

- Appropriately maintained equipment.

You should have procedures in place which include a specific method, process, or system that is used consistently to assure yourself that the unlicensed medicine produced is of suitable quality to be supplied to the patient. When more than a single one-off preparation is made, this quality assurance should be robust enough to safeguard all the patients who may be supplied from a single batch of medicines.

4.3
PATIENT INFORMATION

At the outset, you should make sure that there is a system in place so that the Responsible Pharmacist (or other staff competent to be delegated this task) tells the patient that the pharmacy will be preparing an unlicensed medicine.

They should explain to the patient what this means (including what this means in relation to the amount of information and evidence available about the medicine).

When a pharmacy supplies an unlicensed medicine there is no legal requirement to give a package leaflet, or similar detailed written information. Therefore the patient will rely on the information that your pharmacy staff give them. You should give appropriate advice and information (in writing if possible). This applies equally when there is limited, or no, direct contact with the patient when the medicine is supplied.

You should make sure that the pharmacy staff give the patient any important information they might need so that they can use the medicine safely. The information should include advice on the use of any dosing device that needs explanation to deliver the correct dose. You should also make sure that pharmacy staff consider what extra information they should give the patient about the medicine: for example, the expiry date or any special storage instructions. If the medicine is prepared in line with a British Pharmacopoeia (BP) formula or a general monograph in the BP for the dosage form, there are particular labelling requirements for unlicensed medicines. There are also specific labelling requirements when the prepared medicine is for animal use, which has been prescribed by a veterinary practitioner under the cascade

PRINCIPLE 5

The equipment and facilities used in the provision of pharmacy services safeguard the health, safety and wellbeing of patients and the public. The following areas relate to this principle in the standards for registered pharmacies.

5.1

SPECIALIST EQUIPMENT AND FACILITIES

You should make sure that the pharmacy has equipment and facilities which are specially designed for the intended purpose that staff will use them for. They should be of sufficiently high specification, and accuracy where applicable, to produce a high-quality, safe product. Examples of specialist equipment include, but are not limited to, the following:

· Accurate measuring devices for weight (measuring scales)

· Accurate measuring devices for volume (for example, cylinders)

· Production and mixing equipment

· Cleaning equipment (including suitable detergent)

· Contamination-minimising clothing (for example, masks, gloves, aprons, coats, hats)

· Sterilising equipment (including suitable chemical agents, autoclaves and filtration equipment)

· Fume cupboards, isolators and laminar flow cabinets

5.2

MAINTENANCE LOGS

You should keep maintenance logs, including validation and calibration records, for each type of specialist equipment for as long as you consider, and can show, to be appropriate. These logs will form part of the evidence that the pharmacy is suitable for the preparation of medicines.

You should ask the pharmacy's professional indemnity insurance provider for advice on how long you should keep records for.

OTHER SOURCES OF INFORMATION

Rules and Guidance for Pharmaceutical Manufacturers and Distributors 2017 'The Orange Guide' (or any subsequent revision). You can find more information on the MHRA's website.

European Commission's *Notes for guidance on minimising the risk of transmitting animal spongiform encephalopathy agents via human and veterinary medicinal products*

Veterinary Medicines Guidance Note No. 13 Guidance on the Use of Cascade contains information on the extemporaneous preparation of medicines

The following agencies are a source of information on infection control: **Health Protection Scotland; Public Health England; Health Protection Agency** (for Wales)

Other references that may be useful and of interest include:

Ed. Jackson and Lowey on behalf of the NHS *Handbook of Extemporaneous Preparation*, Pharmaceutical Quality Assurance Committee, Pharmaceutical Press, 2010

Ed. A.M. Beaney on behalf of the NHS *Quality Assurance of Aseptic Preparation Services Edition 5* Pharmaceutical Quality Assurance Committee, Pharmaceutical Press, 2006

PIC/S Guide to Good Practices for the Preparation of Medicinal Products in Healthcare Establishments PE 010-4 2014

Resolution CM/ResAP(2016)1. The European Directorate for the Quality of Medicines and Healthcare has passed a resolution on quality and safety assurance requirements for medicinal products prepared in pharmacies for the special needs of patients.

Appendix 10:
GPhC guidance for registered pharmacies providing pharmacy services at a distance, including on the internet

APRIL 2019

ABOUT THIS GUIDANCE

This guidance explains what pharmacy owners should consider before deciding whether any parts of their pharmacy service can be provided safely and effectively 'at a distance' (including on the internet), rather than in the 'traditional' face-to-face way.

As the pharmacy owner, you are responsible for making sure this guidance is followed. Everyone in the pharmacy team, including managers with delegated responsibility and the responsible pharmacist, should understand the guidance and be aware of their responsibilities to follow it. If the registered pharmacy is owned by a 'body corporate' (for example a company or an NHS organisation) you should make sure the superintendent pharmacist understands it should be followed.

You should read this guidance alongside the standards for registered pharmacies, which pharmacy owners must meet, and our Inspection decision making framework. The standards for registered pharmacies are about creating and maintaining the right environment, both organisational and physical, for the safe and effective practice of pharmacy.

Our standards for pharmacy professionals describe how safe and effective care is delivered through 'person centred' professionalism. Therefore, you must be familiar with those standards, and also the guidance we have published on our website to help pharmacy professionals apply our standards and meet their professional obligations.

Pharmacy owners must also make sure they keep to all the laws that apply to pharmacies. This includes the law on supplying and advertising medicines, new consumer information for online sales, and data protection.

Following this guidance is an important part of making sure you meet our standards for registered pharmacies. These are grouped under five principles, which we refer to throughout this guidance. We therefore expect this guidance to be followed.

Not following this guidance, or not taking the appropriate steps to achieve a desired outcome under our standards, could mean that you fail to meet one or more of the standards for registered pharmacies. This could result in our taking enforcement action.

In this document, when we use the term 'staff' this includes:

- employees (registrants and non-registrants)

- agency and contract workers, and

- any third party who helps the pharmacy provide any part of the pharmacy service, and deals on behalf of the pharmacy owner with people who use pharmacy services

In this document, the term 'you' means the pharmacy owner.

In some limited circumstances (for example following death or bankruptcy), a representative may take the role of the pharmacy owner. In these cases, the representative will be responsible for making sure these standards are met.

Examples of the pharmacy services covered by this guidance include:

1   a pharmacy service where prescriptions are not handed in by people using pharmacy services but are collected by pharmacy staff, or received by post or electronically

2   a delivery service from the registered pharmacy to people in their own home, a care home or a nursing home

3   a collection and delivery service

4   a 'click and collect' service

5   a mail-order service from a registered
     pharmacy

6   an internet pharmacy service, including one
     linked to an online prescribing service, whether
     or not the prescribing service is owned and
     operated by you or by a third party business

7   a 'hub and spoke' pharmacy service –
     where medicines are prepared, assembled,
     dispensed and labelled for individuals
     against prescriptions at a central 'hub'
     registered pharmacy

TYPES OF PHARMACY SERVICES

Collection and delivery
A collection and delivery service is defined
in Regulation 248 of the Human Medicines
Regulations 2012.

Click and collect
This usually refers to the service where a customer
can buy or order goods from a store's website and
collect them from a local branch.

Hub and spoke
The dispensed medicines are supplied by the 'hub'
to 'spokes' or delivered direct to patients in their
homes or to care homes.

The 'spokes' may be other registered pharmacies;
or non-registered premises, where patients drop off
their prescriptions and from where they collect their
dispensed medicines.

INTRODUCTION

Because of changes in society and advances in
technology, different ways of providing pharmacy
services are becoming more common. Pharmacy
services will continue to adapt and change,
bringing opportunities to deliver pharmacy and
other healthcare services in new ways. We support
and encourage responsible innovation as long as
people using these services receive safe, effective
and person-centred care.

But providing pharmacy services at a distance,
especially online, carries particular risks which need
to be managed. We want this guidance to support
appropriate provision of medicines, medical
devices and pharmaceutical care, which keeps
to the law and meets our standards.

The same laws apply whether you provide
pharmacy services in a traditional face-to-face
way, at a distance, or on the internet. For example:
if you offer a delivery service, the handover to the
delivery agent of a pharmacy (P) or prescription-
only (POM) medicine must take place at a
registered pharmacy under the supervision
of a pharmacist.

If you sell or supply medicines to people in
other countries you must keep to any other
laws that apply. Countries have different
restrictions and some do not allow the online
supply of medicines at all. It is your responsibility
to make sure the medicine you supply has the
marketing authorisation needed for it in the
country of destination[1].

If you sell or supply medicines for animal use, the
parts of the law that apply – and the exemptions
that allow this – are covered elsewhere[2]. The
Veterinary Medicines Directorate (VMD) licenses
and approves animal medicines and issues
guidance on supplying medicines for animals.
The VMD also operates a voluntary accredited
internet retailer scheme (AIRS) for online retailers
of veterinary medicinal products. The aim of the
scheme is to provide assurance to the public that
they are buying veterinary medicinal products from
a reputable UK-based retailer.

The NHS Regulations in England[3] include a number
of specific situations that allow distance-selling
pharmacies to open and operate. In Scotland[4] and
Wales[5] the regulations are not the same. However,
they do not prevent pharmacies that are already
open from providing pharmacy services at a
distance or on the internet.

---

1   Regulation 28 of the Human Medicines (Amendment)
    Regulations 2013

2   Veterinary Medicines Regulations 2013

3   The National Health Service (Pharmaceutical and Local
    Pharmaceutical Services) Regulations 2013

4   The National Health Service (Pharmaceutical Services) (Scotland)
    Regulations 2009

5   The NHS (Wales) Act 2006

GUIDANCE FOR REGISTERED PHARMACIES PROVIDING PHARMACY SERVICES AT A DISTANCE, INCLUDING ON THE INTERNET

The standards for registered pharmacies are grouped under five principles, and this guidance is set out under each of the five principles.

PRINCIPLE 1

The governance arrangements safeguard the health, safety and wellbeing of patients and the public.

1.1

RISK ASSESSMENT

The provision of pharmacy services at a distance, particularly online, carries particular risks by its nature.

A risk assessment will help you identify and manage risks. It is a careful and thorough look at what in your work could cause harm to people who use pharmacy services, and what you need to do to keep the risk as low as reasonably practicable.

Risk assessments may apply across whole organisations but still need to take into account the circumstances of each individual pharmacy. This includes the staff working in it; the activities of third parties, agents or contractors; and each individual part of the pharmacy service you intend to provide. It should cover the whole service.

You should review your risk assessment regularly and whenever circumstances change – for example, when you make significant business or operational changes (also see section 1.2).

To meet the standards under Principle 1 we expect you as the pharmacy owner to make sure:

1   you gather evidence about the risks for each individual service, medicine and medical device that you provide at a distance, including on the internet, before you start providing the service

2   your risk assessment includes considering:

- the risks you have identified and how these will be managed

- how staff tell people about the pharmacy services they will receive, and how they get their consent

- how staff communicate between different locations

- how medicines are supplied, including counselling and delivery (see section 4)

- your business's capacity to provide the proposed services

- business continuity plans, including for your website, data security, and equipment

- what records you will keep, depending on the nature of the pharmacy services you provide

- the behaviour of people using pharmacy services or of staff

- different technologies operating together, and

- changes in the number or scale of services

3   your staff know the outcome of any risk assessment and contribute to it appropriately

4   any risk register you keep is kept up to date, and any actions you have taken are recorded

5   if parts of your pharmacy service are the responsibility of several different pharmacies and staff – or the responsibility of a third party, agent or contractor – you have considered how the systems you use to provide your pharmacy service work together. This includes IT systems for exchanging information between different locations. You should also consider how you monitor the accuracy of these systems and manage any potential failures

6   We expect you to make sure you do not work with online providers who are trying to circumvent the regulatory oversight put in place within the UK to ensure patient safety throughout the healthcare system. Working with prescribers who are not appropriately registered with the relevant UK professional regulator, and with prescribing services not based in the UK, could create significant extra risks for patients and the public. If your service lawfully involves working with prescribers or prescribing services operating outside the UK, you should make sure that:

- you successfully manage the extra risks that this may create

- you have sufficient indemnity insurance in place to cover:

  - your service that uses prescribers or prescribing services based outside the UK, and

  - pharmacy staff supplying medicines against prescriptions issued by these prescribers or prescribing services

- the prescriber is registered in their home country where the prescription is issued and can lawfully issue prescriptions online to people in the UK

- the prescriber is working within national prescribing guidelines for the UK

7   We expect you to make sure that any cross-border arrangements in your service design are lawful under UK law.

1.2
REGULAR AUDIT

The safety and quality of pharmacy services must be reviewed and monitored. You should carry out a regular audit, at an interval that you can show to be appropriate for your pharmacy services. The audit should be part of the evidence which gives assurance to people who use your pharmacy that it continues to provide safe pharmacy services. Regular audits may be corporate wide, but still need to be relevant to the circumstances of each individual pharmacy.

If you identify any issues, you should take action to put them right. This may lead to you carrying out a 'reactive' review. You should record this reactive review and say clearly when a new risk assessment needs to be carried out.

To meet the standards under Principle 1 we expect you as the pharmacy owner to make sure:

1   your regular audit includes:

- staffing levels, the training and skills within the team, and any additional training needed so that all staff have the appropriate skills and competence for the tasks they carry out

- suitability of communication methods with people using pharmacy services, and between staff and other healthcare providers, including between hubs and spokes and with collection and delivery points

- systems and processes for receiving prescriptions, including the electronic prescription service (EPS)

- records of decisions to make or refuse a sale

- systems and processes for secure delivery to people receiving care

- any information about your pharmacy services on your website

- how you keep to your information security policy, to the Payment Card Industry Data Security Standard (PCI DSS) and to data protection law

- feedback from people who use pharmacy services

- concerns or complaints received

- activities of third parties, agents or contractors

2   you show how your staff are involved in the audit

3   a reactive review is carried out when any of the following happens:

- you identify any issues during your regular audit

- there is a change in the law affecting any part of your pharmacy service

- there is a significant change in any part of the pharmacy service you provide, such as an increase in the number of people you provide services to; or an increase in the range of services you intend to provide; or a change in a third party, agent or contractor you use

- there is a data security breach

- there is a change in the technology you use

- concerns or negative feedback are received from people who use pharmacy services

- a review of near misses and error logs identifies a concern about an activity

4   your information security practices are audited by independent experts, depending on the type of service you provide

1.3
ACCOUNTABILITY – STAFF

When parts of a pharmacy service take place at different locations (such as in a 'hub and spoke' or 'click and collect' service) you must be clear about which pharmacist is accountable and responsible for each part of the service, and which pharmacy technician and other staff are involved.

When medicines are not given to the patient in the registered pharmacy but are delivered by a member of staff or an agent to the patient's home or workplace, there may be more risk of medicines being lost or delivered to the wrong person. You must make sure there are clear lines of accountability and responsibility in these circumstances.

If you contract out any part of your pharmacy service to a third party you are still responsible for providing it safely and effectively. You must carry out due diligence in selecting any contractors.

1.4
RECORD KEEPING
You must keep and maintain the necessary records depending on the nature of the pharmacy services you provide. This includes maintaining a daily log of the responsible pharmacist.

When a patient has direct face-to-face contact with pharmacy staff in a pharmacy no records of the sale of P medicines are usually made. And when a product is unsafe or unsuitable and no supply is made, staff tell the patient, but no records are usually kept.

When there is no face-to-face contact, you should consider what information you and your staff record and keep to show that the pharmacy service you provide is safe. The records you keep are important evidence for the judgements you and your staff make, and can be a powerful tool for service improvement and quality management.

Although medicines law says how long you should keep certain records, you should keep other records for as long as you consider, and can show, to be appropriate.

To meet the standards under Principle 1 we expect you as the pharmacy owner to make sure:

1 your records include:

- details of the staff who are accountable and responsible for providing each part of your pharmacy service

- the information and advice on using medicines safely that you give people who use pharmacy services

- the key points on which you made the decision to sell or not to sell a particular medicine

- consent to use a particular delivery method, and the date of dispatch of the medicine

- information on complaints or concerns from patients or people who use pharmacy services and what you have done to deal with these; and

- IT records (see principle 5).

PRINCIPLE 2

Staff are empowered and competent to safeguard the health, safety and wellbeing of patients and the public.

2.1
TRAINED AND COMPETENT STAFF
The staff you employ, and the people you work with, are key to the safe and effective practice of pharmacy.

You are responsible for creating a culture of patient-centred professionalism within your pharmacies. Incentives or targets must not compromise the health, safety and wellbeing of patients and the public, or the professional judgement of staff. Staff should be empowered to use their professional judgement so that they can act in the best interests of the person receiving your services.

You must make sure that all staff are properly trained and competent to provide medicines and other professional pharmacy services safely. The GPhC has produced guidance to ensure a safe and effective team. The guidance explains what you should do to make sure you are meeting the standards under Principle 2 of the standards for registered pharmacies.

To meet the standards under Principle 2 we expect you as the pharmacy owner to make sure:

1 you provide, where appropriate extra training in the following areas:

- information security management – how data is protected; and cyber security

PRINCIPLE 3

The environment and condition of the premises from which pharmacy services are provided, and any associated premises, safeguard the health, safety and wellbeing of patients and the public.

3.1

YOUR PREMISES

You must make sure your pharmacy and the premises you use for any part of your pharmacy services meet the standards for registered pharmacies.

Your registered pharmacy must be fit for purpose to reflect the scale of the work you do. If you automate certain activities, there must be enough space to use automated dispensing systems safely. You should make sure that you have suitable areas in your registered pharmacy to send medicines to patients safely.

3.2

YOUR WEBSITE

If you sell and supply P medicines on the internet, you must make sure that these are only displayed for sale on a website that is associated with a registered pharmacy. This could be under a service level agreement or some other arrangement.

The public may be able to access the site directly or through a third-party site.

Your website should be secure and follow information security management guidelines and the law on data protection. This is particularly important when you ask people using pharmacy services for personal details. You should make sure that your website has secure facilities for collecting, using and storing patient details and a secure link for processing card payments, for example, a secure link that meets the Payment Card Industry Data Security Standard (PCI DSS). For more information on the use and storage of data, see the ICO website (https://ico.org.uk/for-organisations/in-your-sector/health/).

To meet the standards under Principle 3, as the pharmacy owner:

1   We expect you to make sure your website is clear, accurate and updated regularly, and it should not be misleading in any way. Your site may include information about medicines, health advice and links to other information sources such as relevant healthcare services

and other regulators. However, your site should be clear and not mislead pharmacy service users about the identity or location of the pharmacies involved in providing your pharmacy services. This includes the identity and location of any online prescribing service

2   We expect you to make sure that any business that is either hosted on your website, or reached by an external link, is legitimate. This includes any online prescribing service. Businesses you link to must be registered with the appropriate regulator such as the Care Quality Commission (CQC), Healthcare Improvement Scotland (HIS) or the Health Inspectorate Wales (HIW) and meet the relevant national regulatory standards and requirements.

3   We expect you to be able to show how you are assured that all prescribers, whether medical or non-medical, follow the relevant remote consultation, assessment and prescribing guidance. (for more information on prescribing, please see the 'Other useful sources of information' at the end of this document)

4   Under the good practice guidance, prescribers must prescribe drugs only when they:

·   have adequate knowledge of the person's health, and

·   are satisfied that the drugs serve the person's need

5   We expect you to make sure that your website and the websites of companies you work with are arranged so that a person cannot choose a POM and its quantity before there has been an appropriate consultation with a prescriber. It should be made clear that the decisions about treatment are for both the prescriber and the person to jointly consider during the consultation. However, the final decision will always be the prescriber's.

6   We expect you to make sure your website prominently displays:

·   the pharmacy's GPhC registration number

·   your name as the owner of the registered pharmacy

·   the name of the superintendent pharmacist, if there is one

- the name and physical address of the registered pharmacy or pharmacies that supply the medicines

- the email address and phone number of the pharmacy

- details of the registered pharmacy where medicines are prepared, assembled, dispensed and labelled for individual patients against prescriptions (if any of these happen at a pharmacy different from that supplying the medicines)

- information about how to check the registration status of the pharmacy – and the superintendent pharmacist, if there is one

- details of how users of pharmacy services can give feedback and raise concerns

If the person is prescribed medicines following an online consultation, your website should also prominently display:

- the name of the prescriber and the address of the prescribing service

- the prescriber's registration number and the country they are registered in

- whether the prescriber is a doctor or a non-medical independent prescriber – for example a pharmacist, nurse or physiotherapist

- information about how to check the registration status of the prescriber

7   We expect you to make sure you consider the design and layout of your website and make sure that it works effectively and looks professional.

THE DISTANCE SELLING LOGO AND GPHC INTERNET LOGO

In July 2015, the MHRA launched the compulsory EU common logo, now known as the 'Distance Selling Logo'. If you intend to sell or supply any General Sales List (GSL), POM or P medicines on the internet you must apply to the MHRA for this logo (https://www.gov.uk/guidance/register-for-the-distance-selling-logo) and display it on every page of your website. You will need to meet all the conditions set out in the law before the MHRA will register you in their list of UK-registered online retail sellers and give you the Distance Selling Logo for display. (The Distance Selling Logo must also be displayed on the websites of nonpharmacy retailers of GSL medicines.)

You may also apply to use the voluntary GPhC internet logo on your website (https://www.pharmacyregulation.org/registration/internet-pharmacy). The logo links directly to the GPhC register entry for your pharmacy. You can have the voluntary GPhC internet logo only once you have applied for, and been given, the MHRA Distance Selling Logo. The GPhC internet logo can be displayed only on your own website.

You must not allow it to be used by a third party, prescribing or other website.

PRINCIPLE 4

The way in which pharmacy services, including the management of medicines and medical devices, are delivered safeguards the health, safety and wellbeing of patients and the public.

4.1

TRANSPARENCY AND PATIENT CHOICE

People receiving care have the right to make decisions about their care and medicines, and the services they want to receive, including being able to choose where they want their medicines supplied from. Pharmacy professionals must give the patient the information they need so they can make an informed decision about their medicines and the pharmacy services they use.

Your pharmacy service can be associated with a medical or non-medical prescribing service. The prescribing service may be:

- One where you order and collect prescriptions on behalf of people from the doctor's surgery, or

- One where you receive prescriptions by post or electronically, or

- An online service that patients can access on your pharmacy website or by a link from your pharmacy website.

If parts of your pharmacy services are provided at different locations you should explain clearly to people who use pharmacy services where each part of the service is based. You should avoid any information that could mislead the user of the pharmacy service about the identity or location of the pharmacy or of any online prescribing service.

In all cases, you and your staff must make sure people receiving care explicitly consent to any pharmacy service you provide using these prescribing services as set out in the ICO's guidance on consent. This includes services lawfully provided by a prescriber not regulated by a UK health professional regulator.

To meet the standards under Principle 4 we expect you as the pharmacy owner to make sure:

1   you provide transparency to the people using your pharmacy services, so that they:

- know who the responsible pharmacist is when their medicines or medical devices are supplied

- have enough information about the service to make an informed decision, and

- can raise concerns about the quality of the service, if they need to

2   you are able to show that your arrangements with medical or nonmedical prescribers are transparent, and do not:

- cause conflicts of interest, or

- restrict a person's choice of pharmacy, or

- unduly influence or mislead people needing services, deliberately or by mistake

3   you provide information about the indemnity and regulatory arrangements for those prescribers who are not based in the UK, especially if they are not regulated by a UK health professional regulator

4.2

MANAGING MEDICINES SAFELY

Selling and supplying medicines at a distance, including on the internet, brings different risks than those of a 'traditional' pharmacy service. You should consider these as part of your initial risk assessment. (See also principle 1.1).

To meet the standards under Principle 4 we expect you as the pharmacy owner to make sure:

1   you show the steps you have taken to minimise the risks you identify. This should include how you:

- Decide which medicines are appropriate for supplying at a distance, including on the internet

- Make sure your pharmacy staff can:

  - check that the person receiving pharmacy services is who they claim to be, by carrying out an appropriate identity check (for example by keeping to the Identity Verification and Authentication Standard for Digital Health and Care Services (https://digital.nhs.uk/data-and-information/information-standards/information-standards-and-data-collections-including-extractions/publications-and-notifications/standards-and-collections/dcb3051-identity-verification-and-authentication-standard-for-digital-health-and-care-services), which provides a consistent approach to identity checking across online digital health and care services)

  - Get all the information they need from people receiving pharmacy services to check that the supply is safe and appropriate, taking into account for example their age, gender, other medicines and other relevant issues

- Make sure people receiving pharmacy services can ask questions about their medicines

- Make sure people receiving pharmacy services know who to contact if they have any questions or want to discuss something with the pharmacy staff

- Identify requests for medicines that are inappropriate, by being able to identify multiple orders to the same address or orders using the same payment details – this includes inappropriate combinations of medicines and requests that are too large or too frequent

2   that an online prescribing service, or a prescriber, that you choose to work with is aware that some categories of medicines are not suitable to be supplied online unless further safeguards (see below for more details) have been put in place to make sure that they are clinically appropriate.

The categories include:

- Antimicrobials (antibiotics), when it is important to effectively manage their use to help slow the emergence of antimicrobial resistance and make sure that antimicrobials remain an effective treatment for infection. These should be supplied only in line with good practice guidance, taking into account antimicrobial stewardship guidelines relevant for the person and their location

- Medicines liable to abuse, overuse or misuse, or when there is a risk of addiction and ongoing monitoring is important. For example opiates, sedatives, laxatives, pregabalin, gabapentin

- Medicines that require ongoing monitoring or management. For example medicines with a narrow therapeutic index[6], such as lithium and warfarin, as well as medicines used to treat diabetes, asthma, epilepsy and mental health conditions. A particular example of a medicine that requires ongoing monitoring and management is sodium valproate, which is used for the treatment of epilepsy and bipolar disorder but which puts babies in the womb at a high risk of malformations and developmental problems

- Non-surgical cosmetic medicinal products (such as Botox, Dysport or Vistabel). In line with good practice guidelines, these should be prescribed and supplied only after a physical examination of the person

Safeguards to put in place if the above categories of medicines are to be supplied online

1   If you decide to work with an online prescribing service or prescriber, the above categories of medicines should not be prescribed unless the safeguards below have been put in place:

- you have assured yourself that the prescriber has robust processes to check the identity of the person to make sure the medicines prescribed go to the right person – for example, by keeping to the Identity Verification and Authentication Standard for Digital Health and Care Services, which provides a consistent approach to identity checking across online digital health and care services

- the person has been asked for the contact details of their regular prescriber, such as their GP, and for their consent to contact them about the prescription

- you have assured yourself that the prescriber will proactively share all relevant information about the prescription with other health professionals involved in the care of the person (for example their GP)

- for medicines which are liable to abuse overuse or misuse, or when there is a risk of addiction and ongoing monitoring is important, you have assured yourself that the prescriber has contacted the GP in advance of issuing a prescription, and that the GP has confirmed to the prescriber that the prescription is appropriate for the patient and that appropriate monitoring is in place

- if there are circumstances where the person does not have a regular prescriber such as a GP, or if there is no consent to share information, and the prescriber has decided to still issue a prescription, you should assure yourself that the prescriber has made a clear record setting out their justification for prescribing

- the prescriber is working within national prescribing guidelines for the UK and good practice guidance. This would include following relevant guidance on prescribing a licensed medicine for an unlicensed purpose known as "off-label" use. For more information please see the 'Other useful sources of information' at the end of this document

4.3
SUPPLYING MEDICINES SAFELY
You must make sure the medicines are delivered safely and effectively. You should consider how to do this as part of the initial risk assessment (see section 1.1).

To meet the standards under Principle 4 we expect you as the pharmacy owner to make sure:

1   you show the steps you have taken to manage the risks you identify. This should include how you:

- Assess the suitability and timescale of the

6 Drugs with a narrow therapeutic index are drugs with small differences between therapeutic and toxic doses.

method of supply, dispatch, and delivery[7] (for example, for refrigerated medicines and controlled drugs)

- Assess the suitability of packaging (for example, packaging that is tamper proof or temperature controlled)

- Track and monitor the package to make sure that it reaches the right person, and to monitor any unexpected interruptions in delivery

- Check the terms, conditions and restrictions of the carrier

- Check the laws covering the export or import of medicines if the intended recipient is outside the UK

- Train your staff

- Monitor third-party providers

4.4

INFORMATION FOR PHARMACY USERS

When pharmacy staff do not see the person receiving care face to face you should consider how staff can communicate any important information to patients clearly and effectively.

You must give clear information to people who use pharmacy services on how they can contact your pharmacy staff if they have any problems or need more advice. This should also include advice on when they should go back to their GP or local pharmacist.

PRINCIPLE 5

The equipment and facilities used in the provision of pharmacy services safeguard the health, safety and wellbeing of patients and the public.

5.1

SPECIALIST EQUIPMENT AND FACILITIES

You must make sure that your pharmacy has the equipment and facilities needed to provide pharmacy services, and that they are fit for purpose. Examples of specialist equipment include automated dispensing systems, labelling equipment and mobile devices used for remote access.

To meet the standards under Principle 5 we expect you as the pharmacy owner to make sure:

1 your equipment is:

- of high specification, accuracy and security. Your IT equipment should meet the latest security specifications and the security of data

should be protected when it is in transit, by either wired or wireless networks, inside your business and outside it. You should also control access to records and how you store, keep and remove records

- calibrated, maintained and serviced regularly in line with the manufacturer's specifications

2 your software and operating systems:

- are robust enough to handle the volume of work

- have control systems built in to help manage the risk

3 you understand your software and the operating systems you use – for example, how the software and operating systems work, what control systems are built in and whether there are any vulnerabilities

4 you keep maintenance logs for as long as you consider, and can show, to be appropriate

5 your business continuity plans include how you manage the risk of equipment failure, including disruptions in IT, and how you ensure patients and members of the public are made aware of any potential delay or disruption to the supply of medicines or medical devices

---

7 For more information about supplying medicines, see the Royal Pharmaceutical Society's Delivery and posting of medicines to patients (including abroad); Medicines, Ethics and Practice –

The professional guide for pharmacists, Edition 42, July 2018; or seek advice from the National Pharmacy Association (NPA) or your professional indemnity provider.

OTHER USEFUL SOURCES OF INFORMATION

Alliance for Safe Online Pharmacies (ASOP Global)
http://buysaferx.pharmacy/

Care Quality Commission
https://www.cqc.org.uk/guidanceproviders/online-primary-care
Online primary care: Information for providers:
https://www.cqc.org.uk/guidanceproviders/online-primary-care#carestandards

Centre For Postgraduate Pharmacy Education (CPPE)
Confidence in consultation skills
www.cppe.ac.uk/learning/Details.asp?TemplateID=Consult-W-02&Format=W&ID=115&EventID=-

Community Pharmacy (Scotland)
www.communitypharmacyscotland.org.uk

Community Pharmacy (Wales)
www.cpwales.org.uk/Home.aspx

Department For Business, Innovation and Industrial Strategy
www.getsafeonline.org/shopping-banking/buyingmedicines-online1/www.cyberstreetwise.com/#!/protect-business/what-youneed-to-know

General Medical Council
Ethical guidance for doctors
https://www.gmc-uk.org/ethicalguidance/ethical-guidance-fordoctors#prescribing

Sharing information with colleagues
https://www.gmc-uk.org/ethicalguidance/ethical-guidance-fordoctors/prescribing-and-managingmedicines-and-devices/sharinginformation-with-colleagues

Government.UK
Consumer protection
https://www.gov.uk/government/policies/providing-better-information-andprotection-for-consumers

Information Commissioner's Office (ICO)
Health and Social Care
http://ico.org.uk/for_organisations/sector_guides/health

Medicines And Healthcare Products Regulatory Agency
https://www.gov.uk/government/organisations/medicines-and-healthcare-productsregulatory-agency

Advertise your medicines
https://www.gov.uk/advertise-yourmedicines

Blue guide: Advertising and promoting medicines
https://www.gov.uk/government/publications/blue-guide-advertising-andpromoting-medicines

Register for the Distance Selling Logo
https://www.gov.uk/guidance/registerfor-the-eu-common-logo

Falsified medicines directive: Sales of medicines at a distance to the public
http://ec.europa.eu/health/humanuse/eu-logo/index_en.htm

Risks of buying medicines over the internet
https://www.nidirect.gov.uk/articles/risks-buying-medicines-over-internet

Valproate banned without the pregnancy prevention programme
https://www.gov.uk/government/news/valproate-banned-without-the-pregnancyprevention-programme

National Institute for health and care excellence (NICE)
NICE Guidance
www.nice.org.uk/guidance

National Pharmacy Association (NPA)
www.npa.co.uk

NHS Digital (formerly Health and Social Care Information Centre)
https://digital.nhs.uk/

NHS (England)
www.england.nhs.uk

Pharmaceutical Services Negotiating Committee
www.psnc.org.uk
Distance selling pharmacies
www.psnc.org.uk/contract-it/market-entry-regulations/distance-selling-pharmacies/
Electronic prescription service
www.psnc.org.uk/dispensing-supply/eps

Royal Pharmaceutical Society

www.rpharms.com

Prescribing competency framework

https://www.rpharms.com/resources/frameworks/
prescribers-competencyframework

Veterinary Medicines Directorate

Retailers of veterinary medicines

www.vmd.defra.gov.uk/pharm/internetretailers.aspx

Appendix 11:
Guidance to ensure a safe and effective pharmacy team

JUNE 2018

ABOUT THIS GUIDANCE

This guidance explains what the pharmacy owner[1] should do to ensure a safe and effective pharmacy team and meet the standards set out under Principle 2 of the standards for registered pharmacies.

The guidance is for pharmacy owners, who are responsible for making sure the whole pharmacy team – both registered pharmacy professionals and all unregistered staff – provide safe and effective care and pharmacy services.

We also believe this guidance will be helpful for other organisations who employ pharmacy professionals or provide pharmacy services across a range of settings – although we do not regulate all these settings.

You should read this guidance alongside our standards for registered pharmacies, which pharmacy owners must meet, and our inspection decision-making framework. The standards for registered pharmacies are about creating and maintaining the right environment, both organisational and physical, for the safe and effective practice of pharmacy

Our standards for pharmacy professionals describe how safe and effective care is delivered through 'person-centred' professionalism. Therefore, you must also be familiar with our standards for pharmacy professionals and the guidance we have published on our website to help pharmacy professionals apply our standards and meet their professional obligations.

As the pharmacy owner, you should be aware of this guidance as you are responsible for making sure it is followed. Everyone in the pharmacy team should be familiar with the guidance, including managers with delegated responsibility. If the registered pharmacy is owned by a 'body corporate' (for example a company or an NHS organisation) you should make the superintendent pharmacist aware of this guidance.

INTRODUCTION

Every member of the pharmacy team provides a vital service to patients and the public. Although registered pharmacies may have different ownership structures, it is important that the culture and processes within the pharmacy deliver safe and effective care to patients and the public.

A pharmacy owner's first responsibility is to ensure patient safety. In practice, this includes making sure:

- each pharmacy has enough skilled and qualified staff to provide safe and effective pharmacy services

- staff can meet their professional obligations and can raise concerns in an environment which encourages openness, honesty and continuing development

The needs of people who receive care from registered pharmacies, and the way pharmacy services are provided, continue to evolve and change. As such, the roles needed to deliver pharmacy services are developing to reflect these changes. Training and development for pharmacy teams should be flexible in responding to these changes, to give staff in the team the knowledge and skills to meet the new challenges and opportunities they face. Owners need

---

1   A pharmacy owner may be a registered pharmacy professional; a pharmacist as a sole trader, partner or director, or a pharmacy technician as a partner or director in Scotland; or may be unregistered as a partner or a director in Scotland; or a 'body corporate'.

also to continually assess staffing levels and the appropriateness of the skills mix within the pharmacy to ensure patient safety.

Effective team working is an essential part of providing good-quality, person-centred care. Pharmacy owners and pharmacy professionals are best placed to identify the needs of patients and the public, and the training and development their teams need to deliver person-centred care and remain competent in the interests of their patients. They also have a shared responsibility to make sure that any member of staff involved in the sale and supply of medicines has the knowledge and skills to carry out their tasks safely and effectively. This includes unregistered staff, who are often the first point of contact with patients and the public.

ACCOUNTABILITY

PHARMACY OWNERS
Pharmacy owners are responsible for ensuring the safe and effective provision of pharmacy services from a registered pharmacy. They are accountable for making sure that the standards for registered pharmacies are met, and for creating and supporting an environment in which pharmacy professionals can demonstrate their professionalism and deliver person-centred care. They are also responsible for setting the management framework within which pharmacy professionals can carry out their professional responsibilities and people in leadership and management roles can operate.
If the pharmacy is owned by a body corporate, the directors must assure themselves that the standards for registered pharmacies are being met.

As a pharmacy owner you should consider the context of each individual pharmacy. This includes:

- the range of services provided

- the skill mix and number of staff in the pharmacy team

- most importantly, the needs of patients and people who use pharmacy services. You should use the resources you have (which includes staff and their skill mix) to ensure safe and effective outcomes for patients.

You must also make sure your staff have the necessary training appropriate to their roles.

Your own accountability does not affect the important responsibility of individual pharmacy professionals to contribute to the education, training and development of the team or of others, and to promote and encourage a culture of learning and development.

LEADERSHIP AND MANAGEMENT ROLES
We realise that for anyone operating a registered pharmacy there will always be competing demands. These may be professional, managerial, legal or commercial. However, medicines are not ordinary items of commerce. Along with pharmacy services, the supply of medicines is a fundamental healthcare service.

In a limited, or public limited, company the board of directors has a significant role in and ongoing responsibility for making sure people receive safe and effective care from registered pharmacies. The Companies Act, and other relevant legislation, sets out the legal responsibilities for directors. In a pharmacy where healthcare is being delivered to the public, there is further guidance for directors about their extra responsibilities in delivering a public service. This applies whether they are in a private or a voluntary organisation.

Staff in leadership or managerial roles, such as branch or area positions, may be pharmacy professionals or unregistered, and are involved in how pharmacy services are developed and delivered. This guidance will help all those who work in leadership and management roles to know what we expect them to do.

PHARMACY PROFESSIONALS
Pharmacists and pharmacy technicians are regulated professionals and must meet the standards for pharmacy professionals. This includes demonstrating leadership when providing safe and effective care. Pharmacy professionals should contribute to the education, training and development of the team, or of others, and must delegate tasks only to people who are competent and appropriately trained or in training. They must also exercise proper oversight.

Pharmacy professionals should have open and honest conversations with the pharmacy owner about anything which could affect their ability to provide the full range of services that the pharmacy provides.

UNREGISTERED STAFF

Unregistered pharmacy staff do not have the same responsibilities, as they are not regulated by the GPhC. But we expect them to meet our training requirements according to their role, to make sure they provide safe and effective care.

Unregistered pharmacy staff work in a variety of roles including as dispensers, medicines counter assistants, delivery drivers and pharmacy managers. They may work full time, part time or occasionally, and their responsibilities may include:

- providing information and advice on symptoms and products

- selling and supplying medicines

- receiving and collecting prescriptions, including assembling and dispensing prescribed items

- delivering medicines

- ordering, receiving and storing medicines and pharmacy stock

- leading and managing teams

Unregistered pharmacy staff are accountable firstly to their employer, who will generally be the pharmacy owner or an NHS trust or health board.

Unregistered staff should, within the resources provided, keep their knowledge and skills up-to-date. They should only carry out roles for which they have the necessary skills and competency, or, if they are in training for that role, with appropriate oversight from a qualified member of the pharmacy team.

GUIDANCE TO ENSURE A SAFE AND EFFECTIVE PHARMACY TEAM

This guidance is set out under Principle 2 of the standards for registered pharmacies.

PRINCIPLE 2:
STAFF ARE EMPOWERED AND COMPETENT TO SAFEGUARD THE HEALTH, SAFETY AND WELLBEING OF PATIENTS AND THE PUBLIC

The staff you employ and the people you work with are key to the safe and effective practice of pharmacy. Staff members, and anyone involved in providing pharmacy services, must be competent and empowered to safeguard the health, safety and wellbeing of patients and the public in all that they do.

STANDARDS

2.1 There are enough staff, suitably qualified and skilled, for the safe and effective provision of the pharmacy services provided

2.2 Staff have the appropriate skills, qualifications and competence for their role and the tasks they carry out, or are working under the supervision of another person while they are in training

2.3 Staff can comply with their own professional and legal obligations and are empowered to exercise their professional judgement in the interests of patients and the public

2.4 There is a culture of openness, honesty and learning

2.5 Staff are empowered to provide feedback and raise concerns about meeting these standards and other aspects of pharmacy services

2.6 Incentives or targets do not compromise the health, safety or wellbeing of patients and the public, or the professional judgement of staff

1

SETTING STAFFING LEVELS AND RESPONDING TO CONCERNS ABOUT PATIENT SAFETY

The number of staff and the skill mix needed to provide safe and effective pharmacy services will vary significantly between pharmacies, depending on the context in which each pharmacy is operating. As the pharmacy owner you should consider the individual context of each pharmacy, including:

- the volumes of dispensing

- the sale or supply of medicines over the counter

- how and where medicines are supplied to patients (for example 'hub and spoke' or internet pharmacies)

- the changing demands throughout the day

- the population served by the pharmacy, including vulnerable patients

- changes in the number of patients and their individual needs

- the use of technology, including robotics

- the range of different services provided

- the different sets of skills, knowledge and experience within the team

- the ongoing learning and development of the pharmacy team

- previous incidents and errors, and the reasons for them

- feedback from patients and members of the public

This means you have to take a tailored approach to staffing levels; one that is flexible and makes sure people receive safe and effective care from every registered pharmacy.

To meet the standards under Principle 2 we expect you as the pharmacy owner to make sure:

1   you carry out risk assessments that are specific to the pharmacy and the team working there

2   the way you manage risks includes procedures to make judgements about the appropriate number of staff and the skill mix

3   you develop, working with the responsible pharmacist, a staffing plan which takes account of how you manage risks and the individual context of the pharmacy

4   the responsible pharmacist and all members of the pharmacy team are aware of the staffing plan for their individual pharmacy

5   each registered pharmacy has a contingency plan for short- and long-term staff absence, whether planned or unplanned

6   you actively review the actual number of staff in the pharmacy who are competent and trained to deliver the pharmacy services provided, against the staffing plan – in line with changing services, workload, feedback and concerns

7   all members of the pharmacy team know who they should contact within their individual pharmacy or wider organisation to raise concerns, without fear. This includes when staffing plans are not effective, and staffing levels and the skill mix may no longer be appropriate

8   everyone in the pharmacy team has the knowledge and confidence to raise concerns about the quality of pharmacy services and, in particular, concerns about patient safety

9   there are systems, evidence and records to show the steps taken to deal with any concerns raised, so patient safety is not compromised. This includes recording occasions when the pharmacy is closed during normal hours of operation

10   feedback is provided to the pharmacy team about concerns raised and how the concerns have been dealt with

11   the reasons for any dispensing errors are assessed and appropriate remedial action taken to learn from these. This includes action to change the number or skill mix of the pharmacy team when necessary

12   the pharmacy team record, review and learn from near misses, mistakes or incidents

2

LEADERSHIP AND MANAGEMENT ROLES

Pharmacy owners must make sure that pharmacy professionals who work for them can meet their own professional and legal obligations and are able to exercise their professional judgement in the interests of patients and the public.

Managers who have responsibility for leading and managing teams, and for co-ordinating many aspects of the day-to-day pharmacy operations, have an important role to play. Members of the board, people in leadership roles and managers have significant responsibilities, and influence over the culture, practices and environment of the pharmacy, and how the safe and effective delivery of pharmacy services is maintained.

To meet the standards under Principle 2, we expect you as the pharmacy owner to make sure those in leadership and management roles:

1   understand the legal and regulatory framework they are working in and the responsibilities of the pharmacy owner

2   are familiar with the standards for registered pharmacies and with this guidance

3   are familiar with the standards for pharmacy professionals, and the supporting guidance that we publish

4   understand that pharmacists and pharmacy technicians, as regulated pharmacy professionals, have professional responsibilities. These include making patient safety a priority and taking action to protect the wellbeing of patients and the public

5   understand that pharmacy professionals are accountable to the GPhC for meeting the standards for pharmacy professionals

6   make sure everyone in the pharmacy team knows and understands the procedures in place in the pharmacy, as well as their own duties and responsibilities and those of other members of the team

7   make sure pharmacy professionals and unregistered members of staff are supported and empowered to handle challenging situations confidently and professionally, whether that means having the right conversations with managers or knowing when and how to raise a concern with the pharmacy owner

8   understand how to manage appropriately any personal or organisational goals, incentives or targets without compromising the professional judgement of staff to deliver safe and effective care

9   make sure people who use pharmacy services can easily see who staff are and the role they are carrying out

3

MAINTAINING A PERSON-CENTRED ENVIRONMENT

Having staff with the right knowledge and skills is one part of being able to provide safe and effective care. It is equally important for the pharmacy team to demonstrate the attitudes and behaviours that people who use pharmacy services expect to see. Behaviours and interpersonal skills – such as effective communication and professionalism – can put patients at ease and make a difference to the care they receive.

To meet the standards under Principle 2, we expect you as the pharmacy owner to make sure everyone in the pharmacy team:

1   provides compassionate care which is adapted to meet the needs of each person

2   can adjust their style of communication, and recognise and reduce barriers to effective communication

3   is aware of safeguarding procedures and can identify people who may be vulnerable.

4   helps individuals to make informed choices about their health and wellbeing

5   works with other healthcare providers to provide 'joined-up' care and demonstrate effective team working

6   is encouraged to ask patients appropriate questions to make sure they are giving suitable advice

7   recognises and values diversity, and respects cultural differences – making sure that every person is treated fairly whatever their values and beliefs

8 understands the principles of privacy and confidentiality[2] and puts these into practice

9 takes steps to maintain privacy and confidentiality and to ensure discussions are not overheard by people not involved in the person's care

10 understands their responsibilities for keeping records up to date, complete and accurate, and for storing information in line with established procedures

4
KNOWLEDGE, SKILLS AND COMPETENCE

The GPhC sets the minimum training requirements for pharmacy staff. However, we also know that education and training does not stand still, and must reflect developments in medicines and technology and the diverse nature of pharmacy services. Pharmacy owners must make sure staff have the appropriate knowledge, skills and competence for their role and the tasks they carry out, or that they are working under the supervision of an appropriately trained person while they are in training.

Education and training requirements for such a diverse workforce should be flexible and proportionate to allow the pharmacy team to respond to changes in pharmacy practice.

4.1
INITIAL EDUCATION AND TRAINING REQUIREMENTS

To meet the standards under Principle 2, we expect you as the pharmacy owner to make sure:

1 you understand the options for relevant training provision, so you can make decisions on what courses are appropriate for your staff. This may include speaking directly to course providers and pharmacy professionals about training needs

2 a role-specific induction is carried out as soon as possible for all new members of the pharmacy team

3 you recognise and address differences in competency requirements for specific practice settings and for the types of services being delivered in that setting

4 you assess the competence of staff when they start in their role, and work in partnership with a pharmacy professional to make an informed decision about what further knowledge or training staff may need. This should include considering the staff member's previous education and training, their qualifications and their work experience

5 initial training covers a common set of skills and abilities including professionalism, good communication skills, and effective working in multiprofessional teams

6 unregistered pharmacy staff who need education and training to meet the required competency level for their role are enrolled on an appropriate training programme within three months of starting in their role

7 unregistered pharmacy staff who are involved in dispensing and supplying medicines are:

- competent to a level equivalent to the elements of the relevant knowledge and skills of a nationally recognised Level 2 qualification in England and Wales, or a Level 5 qualification in Scotland, or

- training towards this and working under the supervision of a qualified member of staff

8 you keep complete and accurate records of training for all staff, which are accessible to those who need them

4.2
LEARNING AND DEVELOPMENT

To maintain a competent and empowered pharmacy team, it is vital that learning and development continues beyond initial education and training. Pharmacy owners, working with pharmacy professionals, should:

- encourage and enable all staff – particularly those still in training – to reflect on their performance, knowledge and skills, and to identify learning and development needs, and

- support them in meeting those needs, to enable them to carry out their role

---

2 Overview of the General Data Protection Regulation (GDPR): https://ico.org.uk/for-organisations/guide-to-data-protection/guide-to-the-general-data-protection-regulation-gdpr/

Staff should be empowered to use their judgement, make decisions where appropriate and be proactive in the interests of patients and the public.

To meet the standards under Principle 2, we expect you as the pharmacy owner to make sure:

1   you understand the learning and development needs of your team and take appropriate steps to meet those needs, having decided whether you can make protected time available for learning and development

2   pharmacy staff work within the limits of their competence and refer to other, more appropriate, staff when they need to

3   everyone in the pharmacy team, with the help of other members of the team, within the resources provided, keeps their knowledge and skills up to date

4   managers have the competence, skills and experience needed to carry out their role

5   essential elements of training are identified for each role within the team, and these are actively reviewed and reassessed in response to changing needs and circumstances, and any changes are made in a timely manner

6   you can demonstrate that learning and development is taking place

7   individual and team development plans are in place to make sure pharmacy staff are not carrying out roles they have not been trained for

8   you take a tailored approach to learning and development which is continued throughout individuals' employment to make sure the knowledge and skills of pharmacy staff remain up to date

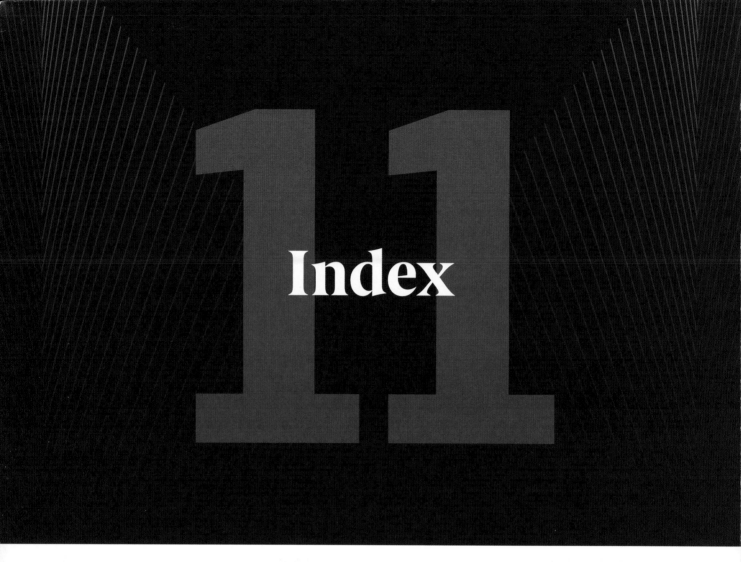

Index

A

D

R

Notes

ACKNOWLEDGEMENTS

Acknowledgements

We would like to thank the GPhC for permission to reproduce their regulatory standards and guidance within the MEP appendices. The most current versions of these documents will be on the GPhC website www.pharmacyregulation.org

We are also grateful to the following persons who have provided expert advice and information during the preparation of MEP 43 as part of the MEP advisory panel.

The RPS welcomes members from all sectors and all stages of practices to volunteer their time to contribute to improving future editions of MEP. To volunteer to join the advisory panel please contact support@rpharms.com

ADVISORY PANEL
Catherine Baldridge
Chris Bell
Stephen Bennett
Francesca Brownless
Carol Candlish
Sarah Cockbill
Cathy Cooke
Aimi Dickinson
Steve Eggleston
Judith Gajree
Amira Guirguis
Karen Harrowing
Carole Hunter
Sarah Karthauser
David Keith
Dilesh Khandhia
Sally Lau
Jayne Lawrence
Baguiasri Mandane
Paul Mooney
Katie Perkins
Karan Rana
Lara Seymour
Jennifer Smith
Paul Summerfield
Mary Tully
David Tyas

RPS STAFF
Editorial team
Rakhee Amin
Sonia Garner
Wing Tang

Marketing and design
Maeve O'Leary

Production and Distribution
Laura Bushell
Nick Judd
Mary Simpson
Calvin Smith
The Pharmaceutical Journal Team

Contributors
Regina Ahmed
Yogeeta Bhupal
Rebecca Braybrooks
Aileen Bryson
Rakesh Bhundia
Helen Chang
Ivana Kynght
Annamarie McGregor
Rachel Quinlan
Helena Rosado
Jordan Stroulger
Sabes Thurairasa
Yen Truong

DESIGN
planningunit.co.uk